FAITHFUL ENCOUNTERS

MCGILL-QUEEN'S STUDIES IN THE HISTORY OF RELIGION
Volumes in this series have been supported by the Jackman Foundation of Toronto.

SERIES ONE: G.A. RAWLYK, EDITOR

1 Small Differences
Irish Catholics and Irish Protestants, 1815–1922
An International Perspective
Donald Harman Akenson

2 Two Worlds
The Protestant Culture of Nineteenth-Century Ontario
William Westfall

3 An Evangelical Mind
Nathanael Burwash and the Methodist Tradition in Canada, 1839–1918
Marguerite Van Die

4 The Dévotes
Women and Church in Seventeenth-Century France
Elizabeth Rapley

5 The Evangelical Century
College and Creed in English Canada from the Great Revival to the Great Depression
Michael Gauvreau

6 The German Peasants' War and Anabaptist Community of Goods
James M. Stayer

7 A World Mission
Canadian Protestantism and the Quest for a New International Order, 1918–1939
Robert Wright

8 Serving the Present Age
Revivalism, Progressivism, and the Methodist Tradition in Canada
Phyllis D. Airhart

9 A Sensitive Independence
Canadian Methodist Women Missionaries in Canada and the Orient, 1881–1925
Rosemary R. Gagan

10 God's Peoples
Covenant and Land in South Africa, Israel, and Ulster
Donald Harman Akenson

11 Creed and Culture
The Place of English-Speaking Catholics in Canadian Society, 1750–1930
Edited by Terrence Murphy and Gerald Stortz

12 Piety and Nationalism
Lay Voluntary Associations and the Creation of an Irish-Catholic Community in Toronto, 1850–1895
Brian P. Clarke

13 Amazing Grace
Studies in Evangelicalism in Australia, Britain, Canada, and the United States
Edited by George Rawlyk and Mark A. Noll

14 Children of Peace
W. John McIntyre

15 A Solitary Pillar
Montreal's Anglican Church and the Quiet Revolution
Joan Marshall

16 Padres in No Man's Land
Canadian Chaplains and the Great War
Duff Crerar

17 Christian Ethics and Political Economy in North America
A Critical Analysis
P. Travis Kroeker

18 Pilgrims in Lotus Land
Conservative Protestantism in British Columbia, 1917–1981
Robert K. Burkinshaw

19 Through Sunshine and Shadow
The Woman's Christian Temperance Union, Evangelicalism, and Reform in Ontario, 1874–1930
Sharon Cook

20 Church, College, and Clergy
A History of Theological Education at Knox College, Toronto, 1844–1994
Brian J. Fraser

21 The Lord's Dominion
The History of Canadian Methodism
Neil Semple

22 A Full-Orbed Christianity
The Protestant Churches and Social Welfare in Canada, 1900–1940
Nancy Christie and Michael Gauvreau

23 Evangelism and Apostasy
The Evolution and Impact of Evangelicals in Modern Mexico
Kurt Bowen

24 The Chignecto Covenanters
A Regional History of Reformed Presbyterianism in New Brunswick and Nova Scotia, 1827–1905
Eldon Hay

25 Methodists and Women's Education in Ontario, 1836–1925
Johanne Selles

26 Puritanism and Historical Controversy
William Lamont

SERIES TWO: IN MEMORY OF GEORGE RAWLYK
DONALD HARMAN AKENSON, EDITOR

1 Marguerite Bourgeoys and Montreal, 1640–1665
Patricia Simpson

2 Aspects of the Canadian Evangelical Experience
Edited by G.A. Rawlyk

3 Infinity, Faith, and Time
Christian Humanism and Renaissance Literature
John Spencer Hill

4 The Contribution of Presbyterianism to the Maritime Provinces of Canada
Edited by Charles H.H. Scobie and G.A. Rawlyk

5 Labour, Love, and Prayer
Female Piety in Ulster Religious Literature, 1850–1914
Andrea Ebel Brozyna

6 The Waning of the Green
Catholics, the Irish, and Identity in Toronto, 1887–1922
Mark G. McGowan

7 Religion and Nationality in Western Ukraine
The Greek Catholic Church and the Ruthenian National Movement in Galicia, 1867–1900
John-Paul Himka

8 Good Citizens
British Missionaries and Imperial States, 1870–1918
James G. Greenlee and Charles M. Johnston

9 The Theology of the Oral Torah
Revealing the Justice of God
Jacob Neusner

10 Gentle Eminence
A Life of Cardinal Flahiff
P. Wallace Platt

11 Culture, Religion, and Demographic Behaviour Catholics and Lutherans in Alsace, 1750–1870
Kevin McQuillan

12 Between Damnation and Starvation
Priests and Merchants in Newfoundland Politics, 1745–1855
John P. Greene

13 Martin Luther, German Saviour
German Evangelical Theological Factions and the Interpretation of Luther, 1917–1933
James M. Stayer

14 Modernity and the Dilemma of North American Anglican Identities, 1880–1950
William H. Katerberg

15 The Methodist Church on the Prairies, 1896–1914
George Emery

16 Christian Attitudes towards the State of Israel
Paul Charles Merkley

17 A Social History of the Cloister
Daily Life in the Teaching Monasteries of the Old Regime
Elizabeth Rapley

18 Households of Faith
Family, Gender, and Community in Canada, 1760–1969
Edited by Nancy Christie

19 Blood Ground
Colonialism, Missions, and the Contest for Christianity in the Cape Colony and Britain, 1799–1853
Elizabeth Elbourne

20 A History of Canadian Catholics
Gallicanism, Romanism, and Canadianism
Terence J. Fay

21 The View from Rome
Archbishop Stagni's 1915 Reports on the Ontario Bilingual Schools Question
Edited and translated by John Zucchi

22 The Founding Moment
Church, Society, and the Construction of Trinity College
William Westfall

23 The Holocaust, Israel, and Canadian Protestant Churches
Haim Genizi

24 Governing Charities
Church and State in Toronto's Catholic Archdiocese, 1850–1950
Paula Maurutto

25 Anglicans and the Atlantic World
High Churchmen, Evangelicals, and the Quebec Connection
Richard W. Vaudry

26 Evangelicals and the Continental Divide
The Conservative Protestant Subculture in Canada and the United States
Sam Reimer

27 Christians in a Secular World
The Canadian Experience
Kurt Bowen

28 Anatomy of a Seance
A History of Spirit Communication in Central Canada
Stan McMullin

29 With Skilful Hand
The Story of King David
David T. Barnard

30 Faithful Intellect
Samuel S. Nelles and Victoria University
Neil Semple

31 W. Stanford Reid
An Evangelical Calvinist in the Academy
Donald MacLeod

32 A Long Eclipse
The Liberal Protestant Establishment and the Canadian University, 1920–1970
Catherine Gidney

33 Forkhill Protestants and Forkhill Catholics, 1787–1858
Kyla Madden

34 For Canada's Sake
Public Religion, Centennial Celebrations, and the Re-making of Canada in the 1960s
Gary R. Miedema

35 Revival in the City
The Impact of American Evangelists in Canada, 1884–1914
Eric R. Crouse

36 The Lord for the Body
Religion, Medicine, and Protestant Faith Healing in Canada, 1880–1930
James Opp

37 Six Hundred Years of Reform
Bishops and the French Church, 1190–1789
J. Michael Hayden and Malcolm R. Greenshields

38 The Missionary Oblate Sisters
Vision and Mission
Rosa Bruno-Jofré

39 Religion, Family, and Community in Victorian Canada
The Colbys of Carrollcroft
Marguerite Van Die

40 Michael Power
The Struggle to Build the Catholic Church on the Canadian Frontier
Mark G. McGowan

41 The Catholic Origins of Quebec's Quiet Revolution, 1931–1970
Michael Gauvreau

42 Marguerite Bourgeoys and the Congregation of Notre Dame, 1665–1700
Patricia Simpson

43 To Heal a Fractured World
The Ethics of Responsibility
Jonathan Sacks

44 Revivalists
Marketing the Gospel in English Canada, 1884–1957
Kevin Kee

45 The Churches and Social Order in Nineteenth- and Twentieth-Century Canada
Edited by Michael Gauvreau and Ollivier Hubert

46 Political Ecumenism
Catholics, Jews, and Protestants in De Gaulle's Free France, 1940–1945
Geoffrey Adams

47 From Quaker to Upper Canadian
Faith and Community among Yonge Street Friends, 1801–1850
Robynne Rogers Healey

48 The Congrégation de Notre-Dame, Superiors, and the Paradox of Power, 1693–1796
Colleen Gray

49 Canadian Pentecostalism
Transition and Transformation
Edited by Michael Wilkinson

50 A War with a Silver Lining
Canadian Protestant Churches and the South African War, 1899–1902
Gordon L. Heath

51 In the Aftermath of Catastrophe
Founding Judaism, 70 to 640
Jacob Neusner

52 Imagining Holiness
Classic Hasidic Tales in Modern Times
Justin Jaron Lewis

53 Shouting, Embracing, and Dancing with Ecstasy
The Growth of Methodism in Newfoundland, 1774–1874
Calvin Hollett

54 Into Deep Waters
Evangelical Spirituality and Maritime Calvinist Baptist Ministers, 1790–1855
Daniel C. Goodwin

55 Vanguard of the New Age
The Toronto Theosophical Society, 1891–1945
Gillian McCann

56 A Commerce of Taste
Church Architecture in Canada, 1867–1914
Barry Magrill

57 The Big Picture
The Antigonish Movement of Eastern Nova Scotia
Santo Dodaro and Leonard Pluta

58 My Heart's Best Wishes for You
A Biography of Archbishop John Walsh
John P. Comiskey

59 The Covenanters in Canada
Reformed Presbyterianism from 1820 to 2012
Eldon Hay

60 The Guardianship of Best Interests
Institutional Care for the Children of the Poor in Halifax, 1850–1960
Renée N. Lafferty

61 In Defence of the Faith
Joaquim Marques de Araújo, a Brazilian Comissário in the Age of Inquisitional Decline
James E. Wadsworth

62 Contesting the Moral High Ground
Popular Moralists in Mid-Twentieth-Century Britain
Paul T. Phillips

63 The Catholicisms of Coutances
Varieties of Religion in Early Modern France, 1350–1789
J. Michael Hayden

64 After Evangelicalism
The Sixties and the United Church of Canada
Kevin N. Flatt

65 The Return of Ancestral Gods
Modern Ukrainian Paganism as an Alternative Vision for a Nation
Mariya Lesiv

66 Transatlantic Methodists
British Wesleyanism and the Formation of an Evangelical Culture in Nineteenth-Century Ontario and Quebec
Todd Webb

67 A Church with the Soul of a Nation
Making and Remaking the United Church of Canada
Phyllis D. Airhart

68 Fighting over God
A Legal and Political History of Religious Freedom in Canada
Janet Epp Buckingham

69 From India to Israel
Identity, Immigration, and the Struggle for Religious Equality
Joseph Hodes

70 Becoming Holy in Early Canada
Timothy G. Pearson

71 The Cistercian Arts
From the 12th to the 21st Century
Edited by Terryl N. Kinder and Roberto Cassanelli

72 The Canny Scot
Archbishop James Morrison of Antigonish
Peter Ludlow

73 Religion and Greater Ireland
Christianity and Irish Global Networks, 1750–1950
Edited by Colin Barr and Hilary M. Carey

74 The Invisible Irish
Finding Protestants in the Nineteenth-Century Migrations to America
Rankin Sherling

75 Beating against the Wind
Popular Opposition to Bishop Feild and Tractarianism in Newfoundland and Labrador, 1844–1876
Calvin Hollett

76 The Body or the Soul?
Religion and Culture in a Quebec Parish, 1736–1901
Frank A. Abbott

77 Saving Germany
North American Protestants and Christian Mission to West Germany, 1945–1974
James C. Enns

78 The Imperial Irish
Canada's Irish Catholics Fight the Great War, 1914–1918
Mark G. McGowan

79 Into Silence and Servitude
How American Girls Became Nuns, 1945–1965
Brian Titley

80 Boundless Dominion
Providence, Politics, and the Early Canadian Presbyterian Worldview
Denis McKim

81 Faithful Encounters
Authorities and American Missionaries in the Ottoman Empire
Emrah Şahin

FAITHFUL ENCOUNTERS

Authorities and American Missionaries in the Ottoman Empire

EMRAH ŞAHİN

McGill-Queen's University Press
Montreal & Kingston • London • Chicago

ISBN 978-0-7735-5461-0 (cloth)
ISBN 978-0-7735-5462-7 (paper)
ISBN 978-0-7735-5549-5 (ePDF)
ISBN 978-0-7735-5550-1 (ePUB)

Legal deposit third quarter 2018
Bibliothèque nationale du Québec

Printed in Canada on acid-free paper that is 100% ancient forest free (100% post-consumer recycled), processed chlorine free

This book has been published with the help of a grant from the Canadian Federation for the Humanities and Social Sciences, through the Awards to Scholarly Publications Program, using funds provided by the Social Sciences and Humanities Research Council of Canada.

Funded by the Government of Canada | Financé par le gouvernement du Canada | Canada

Canada Council for the Arts | Conseil des arts du Canada

We acknowledge the support of the Canada Council for the Arts, which last year invested $153 million to bring the arts to Canadians throughout the country.

Nous remercions le Conseil des arts du Canada de son soutien. L'an dernier, le Conseil a investi 153 millions de dollars pour mettre de l'art dans la vie des Canadiennes et des Canadiens de tout le pays.

Library and Archives Canada Cataloguing in Publication

Şahin, Emrah, 1980–, author
Faithful encounters: authorities and American missionaries in the Ottoman Empire/Emrah Şahin.

(McGill-Queen's studies in the history of religion. Series two; 81)
Includes bibliographical references and index.
Issued in print and electronic formats.
ISBN 978-0-7735-5461-0 (cloth). – ISBN 978-0-7735-5462-7 (paper). – ISBN 978-0-7735-5549-5 (ePDF). – ISBN 978-0-7735-5550-1 (ePUB)

1. American Board of Commissioners for Foreign Missions. 2. Missions, American – Turkey – History – 19th century. 3. Missions, American – Turkey – History – 20th century. 4. Turkey – Church history – 19th century. 5. Turkey – Church history – 20th century. I. Title. II. Series: McGill-Queen's studies in the history of religion. Series two; 81

BV3170.S24 2018 266.009561 C2018-903203-0
C2018-903204-9

This book was typeset by Marquis Interscript in 10.5/13 Sabon.

Contents

Illustrations

Acknowledgments

I felt dismayed. In April 2001 I visited the chair of the History Department at Middle East Technical University. Nearing graduation, I decided to enter graduate school to study Muslim and Christian relations. When I solicited advice, the chair pointed to the cheval glass by the door. "Look in the mirror," he said, "and then tell me if you see a man who can juggle that huge ball of research." I did look but did not understand what my intellectual prowess had to do with my physical preparedness. The chair was telling me that I did not fit advanced research because I was a nobody, a peasant kid educated in a low-profile religious high school. The message was to give it up.

Those who inspire. I decided to see for myself, and the most creative minds became my inspiration. Stanford Shaw, Halil İnalcık, and Kemal Karpat put their faith in me. Gonda Van Steen, Üner Turgay, Jason Opal, Timothy Roberts, and Edward Kohn encouraged my intellectual pursuits. I also learned from them a valuable lesson, namely that true scholarship is the sum of three assets: a pure interest in knowledge, a critical mind, and a procedural system. Without their knowledge, friendship, and advice, I could have given up writing this book.

Those who give. Many good people lent me their support without expecting anything in return. Laila Parsons and my dissertation committee, comprised of Ariel Salzmann, Malek Abisaab, Rex Brynen, Jason Opal, and Üner Turgay, gave me thought-provoking ideas. Michelle Campos, Kemal Karpat, and Benjamin Soares oversaw my drafts. Selçuk Esenbel and Suraiya Faroqhi listened to me. I received insightful comments and constructive criticisms from many colleagues, including Deanna Womack, Owen Miller, Christine Lindner, and Ellinor Morack. During the 2016 Florida panel "Turkish-American

Encounters," Justin McCarthy and Ross Wilson reviewed my views of Ottoman statecraft. İhsan Sezal and Haldun Yalçınkaya hosted me as a writing scholar in Turkey, and while in the United States, I received welcome distractions from my colleagues Alice Freifeld, Edit Nagy, Matthew Jacobs, Tamir Sorek, Terje Østebø, and Tom Kostopoulos. Rachel Geshay drew the exact same map as the one I had in mind. My reading friends, Maithili Jais, Greg Mason, and Hasher Majoka, helped me to clarify my thoughts. At McGill-Queen's University Press, senior editor Kyla Madden bestowed all of the patience and expertise I could hope for as an author. Thanks to her, I looked for the truth of what had happened rather than building a case to support my narratives. The press's anonymous readers paved the way for a historico-critical approach, and assiduous experts, like copy editor Robert Lewis, helped with the wording. Despite the prospect of working with other university presses in Utah and Massachusetts, publishing with McGill-Queen's became the more exciting reality because it bestowed upon me, a proud Canadian, the honour of launching my first book at home.

I received acknowledgment. Supporters and shortcomings notwithstanding, I selfishly took much credit for a work in progress. Bilkent University, Harvard University, McGill University, the Turkish-American Association and the US Embassy in Ankara, the National Library of Turkey, and the Ottoman Archives accommodated and funded my research agenda at critical moments. Gleaned from my research findings, my presentations also received memorable awards, including a Turkish Cultural Foundation Fellowship and a Sakıp Sabancı International Research Award.

Those who exist. I owe dearest thanks to my family, friends, and students. My students motivated me with their genuine comments in class and outside. Çağlar Doğuer, Gonda Van Steen, Hakan Gelgeç, Haluk Gelgeç, Haluk Karadağ, Sean Swanick, Özlem Ayar, and many more friends made my tasks bearable, which included writing this manuscript, teaching ten courses a year, serving on departmental committees, and organizing public events. My beautiful wife, Sema, my mother, Ayşe, and my daughters, Elif Neva and Zeynep Sena, made the journey delightful and meaningful.

I wish to dedicate this book to *those who exist, inspire, and give*. I believe that my book is a statement of how far my research has come since I saw the department chair in April 2001 – and looked "in the mirror" in his office.

Note on Translation

The naming of the lands and peoples of the Ottoman Empire is complicated. In Turkey, southeast Europe, and the Middle East, American missionaries and modern authorities have used the same, similar, and different names for them. For the purposes of coherency, consistency, and relevance, this book prefers anglophone names or original names in the absence of anglophone names. In the terms transcribed from Ottoman Turkish to modern Turkish, *c* is pronounced like *j*, *ç* is *ch*, and *ş* is *sh*. The silent *ğ* lengthens the preceding vowel. The letter *ı* is pronounced like *io* in "motion," *ö* is like the French *eu* in "peu," and *ü* is like the French *u* in "lune." The bibliography includes translations of non-English sources used in the manuscript. I have made all of the translations by respecting the original text and applying English expressions if necessary to render the contextual meaning.

Prologue

FAITH AND THE FAITHFUL

This book may well change the way you think about the Ottomans. The context is the late Ottoman world stretching from eastern Europe to the Middle East. The characters are the sultans and bureaucrats who managed this vast region from the capital city of Istanbul, the local agents who executed the capital's orders, and the Protestant missionaries who engaged with them in dialogue and deed. The matter is how Muslim authorities treated Christian missionaries.

Christian missionaries belonged to the American Board of Commissioners for Foreign Missions. New England evangelicals founded this organization in 1810 with an ambitious mandate to civilize the world. They invested the largest amounts of assets in their missions to Ottoman communities. Figures for 1909 indicate the breadth and wealth of these missions, recording 169 American missionaries, 65,240 native workers and adherents, 57 schools, 20 hospitals, and 125 churches – along with $99,111.07 in locally collected donations. This enterprise, seconded by missions to Imperial China, merits study in its own right. This book explores especially how the Ottoman authorities noticed, assessed, and handled the evangelical news. Evangelical missionaries raised the stakes precisely because their ideals and outreach collided with imperial faith and order.[1]

Faith mattered in the Ottoman Empire. It forged the imperial self-concept and public order. A confluence of classic, Islamic, and pragmatic models transformed the state edifice over the long term. But faith, in and of itself, netted greater than the sum of applied models. Its presence transcended time and space. Imperial authorities saw the wider world figuratively on a map of green, red, and white – three shades of faith depicting the abodes of Islam, war, and peace. Foreign nations thus had to decide whether to become Turks by joining the eternal state, to fight the Turks to the end, or to ally with them in trade and times of war. Salient examples that illustrate these scenarios are, respectively, the conquest of Bosnia in 1463, protracted wars with the Habsburgs, and the well-honoured Franco-Turkish alliance.[2]

Called millets, local communities coexisted as discrete faith units. These people made similar choices about submission, resistance, or exchanging favours. In the vision of the avant-garde modernizer Sultan Mahmud II, the central state "shall only differentiate" the "Muslim subjects at the mosque," "Christian subjects at the church," and "Jewish subjects at the synagogue." A step outside God's house, Mahmud called them all "my sons and daughters." In fact, however, faith meant more than ritual visibility. The matters of faith subsumed and disrupted realities even in the speech of a fatherly sultan. The imperial state strayed further away from the Mahmudian ethics as its bureaucrats began to ascribe to a new type of unconditional political trust, aiming to restore the faith of local subjects in the imperial order.[3]

The bureaucrats called the sultan's house to order in post-Mahmudian decades. This period marked some serious trouble exacerbated by internal traumas such as bankruptcy, disorder, and massacres – along with external pressures regarding European political and religious claims, as in France's occupation of Egypt and later interference in the Catholic millet's affairs. Then American missionaries came aboard, showing a real potential to breach the empire's faith defences, which were virtually crumbling from the inside out. Dramatically, Mahmud's vision was transformed into an illusion of faithful order and then collapsed as an obsolete resolution.[4]

Historians have not overlooked American missionaries in the Middle East. Yet practically every scholar examines missionary accounts to discuss modernity and the American involvement in the region. They reference the missionaries while debating the issues of ethnicity, education, gender, religion, and society. The extant studies tend to repeat a binary pattern, portraying evangelical missionaries as "liberal thinkers" or "warm and smiley faces" who concealed the "cold face" of American imperialism. These versions likewise describe Ottoman authorities as "autocratic" or "double-faced," largely due to the actions of Abdulhamid II, the despotic sultan from 1876 to

1909. In his classic book *Protestant Diplomacy and the Near East*, for instance, Joseph Grabill claims that Ottoman imperial authorities did not appreciate the "considerable benevolence and aid" shown by American missionaries. Such narratives teach us about the missionaries' accomplishments, but they impart little about imperial perspectives and nearly nothing about the chemistry of state policies and local realities. In my version, I illustrate how imperial authorities made sense of missionary exchanges and formulated certain responses to them.[5]

The assertive turn in later policies reflected prevalent views in the state centre. Strikingly, state bureaucrats imagined local subjects as "ignorant masses." In their elite minds, the rural people were reminiscent of the people in Plato's cave, who were chained in a dark place and thus unqualified to know the truth from its mere reflection on the cave wall. They seemed naturally vulnerable and notoriously prone to manipulation in troubled times. This mentality invented a moral pretext for powerful statesmen to mould their superior body into a purported common good. European and homegrown literature often streamlined this *govern-mental* transition. The ideas of prolific intellectuals, especially Montesquieu, Jean-Jacques Rousseau, Victor Hugo, Émile Durkheim, Şemsettin Sami, and Ahmet Mithat, placed the establishment bureaucrats virtually at a crossroads between the world of passion and intrigue and the world of tradition and reality. The vogue also initiated some unpredictable reactions in downtown Istanbul in April 1873 when performances of Namık Kemal's play *Fatherland or Silistria* electrified huge crowds. Its patriotic and irredentist message goaded the crowds into protesting about the regime. Sultan Abdülaziz eventually pushed Kemal and his colleagues into exile. By agitating the public purposely or not, homegrown authors walked a fine line between law and chaos. In this case, Kemal suffered punishment for his alleged trespass into the latter.[6]

The life of Mehmet Faik Memduh encapsulates the careers and minds of establishment bureaucrats. He was born in 1839 into a prominent family. His grandfather Ömer Lütfi led the Izmir Tax and Customs Office, and his father, Mustafa Fehmi, administered the sultan's private treasury. Memduh studied sciences and French before interning in the Communications Department of the Ministry of Foreign Affairs. He then became the chief correspondent in the Ministries of Education and Finance, served on the Financial Affairs and State Councils, and governed the provinces of Konya, Sivas, and

Ankara. Meanwhile, he standardized the state recruitment protocol and regulated the main tasks assigned to public security officers. While at his later post as the interior minister (1895–1908), Memduh worked with the purpose of centralizing the imperial state. His political and social platform issued from his field experience. He had governed in Konya during the great famine of 1887–88 and in Sivas during the ethnic clash of 1889–92.[7]

Memduh envisioned the Ottoman world as a garden and its subjects as delicate flowers desiring affection and upkeep. In his book *The Mirror of Affairs*, he described his species as the educated, loyal, and Muslim "cream of the crop." He suggested that only they could grasp "realities" and correct "ignorant masses." Memduh accordingly ordered the Ministry of the Interior to teach loyalties and preach to locals. He calculated they would halt colonial and local chaos this way. Under the watch of foreign and public powers, such strategic views turned into a litmus test when put into effect.[8]

Above all, bureaucrats and missionaries claimed the fate of locals in this world and thereafter. To evaluate the intensity and quality of their outlook, it is necessary to turn to their contacts and conflicts. In doing so, I proceed from the late nineteenth to the early twentieth century, revealing how ideas, conditions, agents, and groups interacted; in other words, I aim your attention at the discursive, imaginative, institutional, and social realms. This book may well change the way you think about the Ottoman Empire as it weaves Ottoman property into the evangelical narrative. Religious interactions are fascinating as well. Given that past Muslim-Christian interactions have stunning relevance to the present, it is even more significant to read the clamouring Turkish and Muslim voices that have echoed across time. When listened to closely, these voices allow us to retrieve from the past some familiar rhythms of how politics and religions generate difficult situations – and all the while the instrumental characters counteract and interact with each other through a vocabulary commonly shared by faith and the faithful.

ENCOUNTERS IN CONTEXT

Recent hate crimes have revived an old debate in Turkey. Several attackers have hit local minorities on recent occasions, including the firebombing of the International Protestant Church in the capital city of Ankara and the torture of an American missionary in the Syrian border town of Antep. Although these assaults yielded no casualties, they heralded the fiercest of their kind. It happened on 18 April 2007 at the Zirve Publishing House, a Protestant publisher of Bibles located in the eastern city of Malatya. Five young Muslim nationalists patiently waited for the converted pastor Necati Aydın to start his sermon. Once the sermon began, they unleashed carnage on the unsuspecting congregation. They tied the pastor and his parishioners, Tilman Geske and Uğur Yüksel, to chairs and then tortured and massacred them.[9]

Police officers hotly pursued and apprehended the subjects. As interrogations proceeded, the focus of the case shifted from the cold-blooded act itself to a discussion about the Ergenekon – an alleged ultra-nationalist, secularist, and secret organization aiming to oust Prime Minister Recep Tayyip Erdoğan's party from government. The perpetrators had visited the crime scene several times and had reportedly met the victims before the day of the incident. During the trial, the chief perpetrator, Yunus Günaydın, mentioned that Varol Aral, an Ergenekon member who was a journalist, had urged somebody to "step up and do something about the missionary activity." He sought "state support" and asked whether Günaydın would volunteer. Aral also prodded him to hit the Zirve Publishing House by persuading him that its staff operated as an enemy of the state – namely as a tentacle of the Partiya Karkeren Kurdistane (Kurdish Workers Party), whose terrorists have been fighting for three decades to liberate eastern Turkey in order to benefit the Kurdish people. When the judge called for a merger of the Zirve case with the Ergenekon trial, nobody predicted that the case would drag on for nine years and more than a hundred sessions.[10]

The Zirve massacre sparked immediate reaction in Turkey and abroad. Hamza Özant, the director of the Zirve Publishing House, regretted not summoning police for protection after receiving threatening calls. Local supporters of the Malatya Soccer Club denounced the massacre in a game against the Gençlerbirliği Soccer Club, shouting, "We Condemn Terror!" Meanwhile, thousands paraded through Taksim, Istanbul's central square, to demand human rights modelled after the European Convention on Human Rights. The Christian Concern and other organizations expressed condolences about the "satanic" act, demanding in the same breath that the killers be prosecuted. Turkish authorities also denounced the "savagery," vowing to punish the "slayers." Their raging and mourning aside, the authorities were put in the spotlight by international media already suspicious about their sincerity.[11]

Turkey's report card showed repeated failure to protect civil liberties and legal practices. From an outside perspective, the resurgence of religious violence seemed to unmask the ethos of the Turkish administration. Critics became deeply skeptical of the government's action plan on the Zirve incident – even though the prime minister declared that "we, the people of responsibility," would be "willing and able to catch the perpetrators." Given the glaring failure of the Turkish state to deliver criminal justice, official statements sounded rather hypocritical when state authorities announced that the judicial process was already "well underway" and that they would remain "supportive of it."[12]

Prominent linguist and activist Noam Chomsky reflected on the chronic violence in the region and endorsed the January 2016 Academics for Peace petition. He dubbed the petition an intellectual call for "the state to punish those who are responsible for human rights violations" and "compensate those citizens who have experienced material and psychological damage." The collective effort registered 2,218 scholarly signatures against forced migrations, civilian deaths, state-sanctioned curfews, and entrenchment campaigns ongoing in southeastern towns. Somewhat indignant, Chomsky also rejected Erdoğan's invitation to visit Turkey and "see with his own eyes what is really going on." He certainly would "not visit the site" when government authorities were perpetrating "a deliberate massacre of Kurdish and other peoples in the region," as well as not pushing through any reforms at all. Then, once again, violence flared up when Turkish officials undercut their legitimacy by not practising what they were preaching. Inconsistent political discourse undermined the nation's prestige at home and abroad as well.[13]

Where hate crimes evoked the pathos of past tragedies, news outlets chimed in and opined that ethno-religious terror had struck root in the Islamic world. Figuratively, the Zirve assailants seemed to be some kind of shamans who had resurrected the barbaric and bestial spirits of the Muslim Turk, once destroyed with the dismantling of the Ottoman Empire. While *Der Spiegel* portrayed them as part of the larger organized "attack on Christians," other papers blamed the Turkish state for "fanning the growing hostility against non-Muslims." In the partisan view of the bulletin the *Florida Baptist Witness*, state officials were traditionally malevolent. "The prosecutors and police authorities" remained generally "reluctant to pursue reported incidents of vandalism or threats against church buildings or personnel."[14]

Protestant missionaries imbued the media coverage with historical drama. Thomas Schirrmacher, the director of the International Institute for Religious Freedom, construed the situation of Christians in Muslim lands against the backdrop of the latest massacre. He portrayed the members of "the tiny Protestant or Evangelical minority" as the victims of "uninterrupted and unrestrained slander," as they were still suffering from unfair treatment by "the highest levels in the government." For nationalists and Islamists, "their dislike of Turkish Christians" is the "one thing on which they strongly agree." They talk "about overly aggressive missions" even when they see a Muslim purchasing the Bible from a local store. This sort of incident might happen "only in Turkey." Given the anti-Christian consensus, the Zirve massacre "almost had to happen."[15]

The Middle East may strike some evangelical eyes as a region that has succumbed to the Islamic-Turkish yoke over the centuries. In Schirrmacher's view, for instance, the Ottoman Turks granted local churches little to no "freedom of religion." The First World War halted their reign and at long last ended "the time of the Sultans." The region's upward march regressed to anguish, however, as ethno-religious fanaticism returned with poignant force. Historical memory and personal calamity likewise harboured much pessimism about local minorities. As social chaos resumed, Schirrmacher martyred his own student, Necati Aydın, in the Zirve massacre.[16]

It is true that the time of the sultans is over and that the local people are permitted to practise the ways of their races and creeds in complete freedom. But ethnic hostility and religious terror continue and thus compel our attention to their historical context. If we can retrieve from social memory the relevant cases of savagery, violence, and massacres, it is also timely and critical for us to evaluate the ways that Muslim authorities treated Christian missionaries and local minorities. Consequently, this examination will revolve around Istanbul for understanding the heart of the Ottoman administration, all the while explaining the inner dynamics of the Ottoman world by conveying the variety of local narratives.[17]

The tragic progress of the Zirve case presents more lessons harking back to Ottoman history. After numerous sessions, the Penal Court decided to free the suspects while monitoring their movements through the use of trackable bracelets in March 2014. Although the court's decision satisfied the statute regarding case-time limitations, it ignored substantial evidence against the suspects. It also exposed the nation's precarious legal standards and shook the public's fragile trust in state authority. The court's verdict certainly embittered the plaintiff's grieving family. Even Tilman Geske's kind and mild-mannered widow made a statement of reproach, saying, "Of course, this is injustice."[18]

Two years after the Zirve gang was freed, the court conducted a retrospective study. The judge found the pre-existing risk of an attack to be a cause of the incident and declared the official ranks guilty of "defective service" for not preventing it. He ordered that the Ministry of the Interior and the City Governor's Office pay the plaintiff Geske family damages of $138,616. His ruling referenced the European Convention's legal standards as stipulated in article 9, which states, "Everyone has the right to freedom of thought, conscience and religion," including "freedom to change his religion or belief" and "freedom, either alone or in community with others and in public or private, to manifest his religion or belief, in worship, teaching, practice and observance." Although this landmark order signified progress toward religious freedoms and healed sentimental wounds, the plaintiff's family would rather not have seen "the murderers walk free" than be awarded the money.[19]

The trial's concluding verdict came on 28 September 2016 – after 115 sessions, eight years, eleven months, and fourteen days. In the last session, the Ergenekon journalist Varol Aral claimed the Zirve massacre to be "a crime of national consensus." The perpetrators also did "not wish to be sentenced" for a state-planned crime and sought "refuge in the justice and conscience" of the state court. The verdict sentenced the murderers to "aggravated life in prison" and released the journalist. The court closed the case with specific evidence still unexamined. As much as the Geske family wished the massacre had not occurred, their victimhood supported the legal maxim that justice belated is justice denied.[20]

What follows is the Ottoman context in which religious encounters took place.

THE OTTOMAN WORLD

The Ottoman Empire symbolized exchanges between Europe and the Orient. It had become a world power by the sixteenth century, stretching from southeast Europe to southwest Asia. A range of cultural and political dynamics created the Ottoman world. These dynamics offer the key to understanding missionary activities and modern nations in the region.[21]

The Ottomans began in a favourable location. Unlike the peoples of other Turkic principalities huddled within Anatolia, they were nestled on the Byzantine Empire's wavering eastern frontier and courted Turcoman-Muslim tribes migrating westward. Although the incoming tribes fought to conquer the Christian lands, imperial state leadership and local Christians were both entwined in the social fabric. The conflux of positive developments expanded the frontier, and all the while the expanding frontier bolstered the accommodating authority, military ascension, and economic vitality. With the conquest of Constantinople in 1453, the Ottoman state emerged as a European Muslim great power. As Constantinople became Istanbul, imperial authorities set the essentials of their ruling standards. Professional bureaucrats steered administration under the sultan's authority in compliance with state laws that combined Turkish mores, Islamic laws, and local circumstances. They likewise categorized local subjects into confessional communities and made them the foundation of social order.[22]

A concerted force of opponents contested the aggressive expansion of the Ottoman Empire. As the Ottoman realm had reached its limits bordering the Habsburg Empire and Persia by the sixteenth century, the imperial army started waging protracted battles on both sides and the Mediterranean. Meanwhile, the Ottoman monopoly on global trade networks faded with competition and the invention of alternative trade routes. State bureaucrats in Istanbul launched a series of massive reforms in November 1839 to restore the health of the empire – an empire then called the "sick man of Europe" by foreign diplomats and intellectuals. Their agenda focused on revising laws, finances, and liberties, but their success eventually depended on a fine compromise between state sensibilities and novel ideologies, such as nationalism and positivism. The bureaucratic soul-searching crossed three ideological currents – Ottomanism, Islamism, and Turkism – and converged over negative developments. In fact, the imperial state was lacking consensus, its army was losing battles, and Europe-based colonial aggression was undermining the state's integrity. After all, local subjects rejected the ideologies ascribed from the centre. Christian minorities were demanding independence, or at least autonomy.[23]

State Formation

Ottoman sultans originated among the Oghuz Turks, a group of central Asian nomads who migrated to western Eurasia in the ninth century. From the founder, Osman, to Mehmet II (1299–1481), the first seven generations of them pursued a hyperactive protocol of engagement and settlement, transforming an insignificant chiefdom into a veritable empire. Places, people, and faith cooperated along the way.[24]

Osman's principality had stepped into an unguarded space in western Anatolia. His army – positioned between vulnerable yet rich Byzantine townships on the western flank and quarrelling Turkish principalities on the eastern flank – attacked the Christian west while waiting out the Muslim east. The Turcoman-Muslim converts, then fleeing from the marauding Mongol Empire, supplied the Ottoman forces with soldiers and labourers. The sultans granted pasturelands for the converts' herds and parlayed their fighting talents into further expansion. Indeed, all ambitions led to the west. The holy-war ideal precipitated spatial advance toward Europe and political ambivalence toward the Turkic-sibling rivalries on the eastern flank.[25]

Diverse communities and a nuanced brand of nonegalitarian tolerance emerged in the post-expansion era. Strikingly, imperial authorities sanctioned Muslim dervishes to settle and proselytize in new lands but prohibited any possibilities of conversion from Islam. American missionaries contacted non-Muslim minorities partly because the Ottoman state set punitive barriers to Muslim missions and partly because the Muslims disdained them.[26]

Historical Condition

The conquest of Istanbul fashioned economic dynamism and political consolidation in the late fifteenth century. As the empire's eastern and western domains merged, Ottoman merchants prevailed in the Mediterranean trade. In the south, the locals annexed in Mecca, Medina, and Cairo lauded the Ottoman sultans as leaders of the Muslims. Indeed, for five centuries following the conquest of Egypt in August 1516, the Ottoman state had wielded political and spiritual leadership in the Islamic world. During this time, decisive victories delivered vast territories from Algeria to Belgrade and secure access to the Persian Gulf. The diplomatic overtures bore alliances with the

Dutch Republic, England, and France, together aspiring to envelop their common enemies, Austria, Spain, and Italy.[27]

New shipping technologies, trade routes, and industrialized competition challenged the Ottoman monopoly on the Mediterranean trade. When coupled with catastrophic defeats after the failed siege of Vienna in September 1683, such developments induced the Ottoman authorities to find ways to restore the central state and its revenues. However, the mounting crisis did not correlate with European progress because internal problems were exacerbated in parallel with external failures. Although authorities, merchants, and intellectuals knew what was going on in Europe, they worried more about what was going wrong within the Ottoman Empire. Their inward-looking approach emphasized collective alienation from traditional and Islamic roots, widespread official corruption, inadequate military performance, and several individual insurgents who were provoking local subjects to nonconformity. The imperial authorities adopted a mix of progressive reforms and coercive measures in response.[28]

The Ottoman Empire tottered from crisis to crisis and then dissolved. Following a humiliating defeat against Russia in 1774, the imperial delegation signed the Küçük Kaynarca Treaty, admitting that their non-Muslim subjects could be a topic of diplomatic discussion. They also declared bankruptcy upon the failure to repay emergency loans taken out later during the Crimean War (1853–56). Two decades later, the Public Debt Administration overtook imperial revenue streams under the pretext of collecting the payments owed to European banks and companies.[29]

The ambitious reform agenda coped with local nationalist movements and with arrangements of the United States. As a political and social force, nationalism penetrated the Ottoman world from western provinces and galvanized the Balkan peoples. The first revolution, staged by the Serbian subjects and suppressed by Janissary rulers, opened the pathway to disintegration. The second revolution created modern Serbia a decade later in 1814, thus offering an aspiring path for the Greek, Moldavian, and Bulgarian communities. The Arab, Armenian, and Kurdish peoples also followed suit, albeit with little or no success. Besides the rampant public disorder, successive military defeats and weakening diplomatic clout persuaded imperial authorities to launch a process of reformation. Called Tanzimat (1839–76), the reform project made three key adjustments by centralizing the state, modernizing the military, and bestowing civil liberties. Further regulations emulated European practices, developed a modern financial and educational system, and granted liberties to the minorities.[30]

As progressive reforms failed to stem the civil crisis, Ottoman authorities sought to bond their diverse subjects by ascribing them an adjoined Ottoman, Islamic, and Turkish collective identity. Some limited impact aside, these invented ideologies did not inspire fondness for the state. Identity politics did not strike a chord with the public even after the pro-reformer, extroverted, elite bureaucrats integrated French institutions and liberties into the imperial system. From 1876 onward, the new Constitutional Parliament continued to discuss the limits of amendments, freedoms, and rights.[31]

In Istanbul intellectuals and officers drew up separate agendas for reconstruction, but they all found a common enemy in the person of Sultan Abdulhamid II. In fact, the proactive members of the Young Turk movement organized secret committees and defamation campaigns as part of a widespread effort to outmanoeuvre him. Although the powerhouse Union and Progress Committee splintered on the course of action, the movement's inner caucuses agreed on radical modernization. In particular, Turkish nationalist members agreed to topple the regime. Union and Progress members coalesced with a secret association of Turkish officials and officers in Thessaloniki. They staged the July 1908 revolution and proclaimed the Constitutional Era. Strikingly, the Young Turks founded an air force, sanctioned the first women's organization, and screened the first Turkish movie with an anti-Russian storyline. They also launched soccer teams in Istanbul and funded two Ottoman athletes to compete in the 1912 Olympic Games in Stockholm. Put together, such ambitious projects attempted to advertise the Young Turk regime by modernizing the military, empowering women, and importing competitive sports.[32]

The post-revolution government nevertheless staggered under weighty matters. The committee-controlled armed forces fought in North Africa, the Balkans, and then the First World War as a German ally, but wartime measures and mobilization would prove disastrous for local communities. Internecine strife surged, forced deportations became commonplace, and ethnic massacres took place. Eventually, in August 1920, the Sèvres Treaty recognized Armenia and the Kingdom of Hejaz as new countries, while authorizing the victorious powers to create regional spheres of influence. It also subdued the Ottoman imperial state. Specific treaty articles required downsizing the imperial army, sequestering the state treasury, and neutralizing Bosphorus and Dardanelles, the strategically important straits between the Black Sea and the Mediterranean. In a remarkable struggle, Mustafa Kemal Atatürk and other Turkish officers rejected these terms, united the Kurds and Turks, and declared a war of independence. In July 1923 the Treaty of Lausanne superseded the previous settlements. Three months later, the Republic of Turkey emerged as a new nation-state from the Ottoman remnants in Anatolia.[33]

Administrative Philosophy

The Ottoman state formed around a governmental philosophy called the circle of justice, which dated back to ancient Aristotelian logic. The concept premised justice to be the reason for being. It described the nature of authority and responsibility with a circular metaphor. The world was a vineyard walled by the state, the law governed the people, the sultan safeguarded the law, the army defended the sultan, wealth assembled the army, people accumulated wealth, and justice protected the people in the vineyard. Times and conditions changed what the world, law, and justice meant in the administrative mentality. Imperial authorities and local subjects nonetheless orbited the allegorical circle until the 1890s, when the government authorities became more authoritarian, less humane, and too big.[34]

The centralized decision-making process involved numerous state agents, especially the grand vizier, supreme judge, treasurer, foreign and internal affairs officials, governors-general, chief military judge, and the *nişancı* (sealer), a senior officer who certified the edicts. The sultan legitimized state laws, and provincial governors executed these laws. Besides the governors, local notables and spiritual leaders administered community affairs in line with the directives transmitted from the centre. Additionally, the authorities in Istanbul supervised a network of judges and guards. Locally headquartered, the judges resolved specific disputes, and the guards enforced imperial laws. Ideally, the circular order of governance anticipated effective collaboration in keeping peace and order.

Political decisions considered the changing contexts along with Turkish and Islamic practices. In the nineteenth century, however, new sensibilities and challenges made the code of laws problematic and oppressive as it increased constraints on the upward and lateral mobility of local subjects. Virtually always, the legislative pragmatism remained in effect and benefited the Ottoman state even though it contradicted the Islamic tenets. In an early striking example, the code advised that the sultan "kill his brothers to secure the universal order." Indeed, the fratricide law became a common practice, as "the majority of scholars consented" in favour of overruling the Islamic penal code.[35]

In the long term, Ottoman state philosophy developed three economic principles: provisionism, fiscalism, and traditionalism. These principles aimed to provide basic needs like food and shelter, disregarded the supply-demand balance, maximized income with taxes and war prizes, minimized expenditures with thrift and budget cuts, and resisted change unless warranted by subsistence and fiscal policies. War prizes generated significant assets, but merchants and peasants generated the main source of revenue for the essentially agrarian economy. In earlier times, the lucrative Ottoman routes linked Eastern goods and European markets, and the arable Mediterranean basin facilitated multicultural farming. Until the late nineteenth century, the consumer class – bureaucrats, officers, and scholars – received salaries in kind. The sultan typically awarded a tract of newly conquered lands to courageous soldiers with the proviso that they raise and ready conscripts from the tenured land for future battles. Additionally, strategic investments manifested the government's desire to create regional economic hubs. Industrial and commercial subsidies benefited the coastal, fertile, and resourceful cities. Aleppo, Bursa, Istanbul, Izmir, Kayseri, Sofia, Trabzon, and several other cities served as centres of agricultural exchange, banking, carpentry, furniture, fur processing, jewelry, and textiles. The bread makers, carpenters, cloth makers, porters, fur processors, and other exclusive guilds orchestrated artisan societies in the urban centres. They also trained apprentices, standardized prices, and monopolized the sector.[36]

The Ottoman Empire advanced militarily, stagnated militarily, and collapsed militarily. But Ottoman scholars and patrons, aware of their own temporal presence, made substantial contributions to architecture, ethics, music, physics, and politics, especially a comparative analysis of Christian progress and Muslim decline. In the later stage of the crisis, cultural productions also thrived, creating new forms of poetry, hymns, legends, and morality. In the early twentieth century, indeed, Ottoman arts and sciences demonstrated a strikingly rich synthesis of cultural elements across Eastern and Western civilizations. However, the circle of justice had collapsed from within. It did not matter that imperial authorities emulated European ideals, hoping to restore peace and order, because local minorities distrusted their judgment and had lost faith in the eternal state.[37]

Imperial Regime

The late Ottoman government was characterized by a loyal, elitist bureaucracy in the capital. During the Hamidian Era (1876–1909), the government withstood strong foreign pressure and heated internal disputes, all the while standing against reconciliation and being "freed of outside control." To understand the remarkable changes, it is worth looking at different governments. In the government led by Sultan Abdulaziz from 1864 to 1876, central bureaucrats handled state affairs through the agency of the grand vizier, the Ministries of Foreign Affairs and Internal Affairs, and several councils, such as the Ministers Council and the Judicial Ordinances Council. These high-level government branches worked in cooperation with the ranks of education, finance, land registry, pious foundations, public works, customs, trade, and agriculture.[38]

The 1908 Parliament retired and exiled the Hamidian bureaucrats. It nevertheless left the nature of the government branches largely intact, aside from establishing the new Ministry of Justice and the Bureau of the Posts, Telephone, and Telegraph. Likewise, the inner workings of the bureaucratic machine underwent no major changes until the end of the empire. The Ministry of Foreign Affairs is a case in point. In 1873 the Ministers Council established the Consular Affairs Office to offer "political information services" by coordinating the consular corps, receiving their reports, and compiling statistical reports. In the 1900s the office was still employing rank-and-file officials "led by supervisory officials of long-familiar kinds." Indeed, the consecutive terms of Ministers of Foreign Affairs Kürt Said and Ahmet Tevfik between 1895 and 1909 indicate that the state bureaucracy continued in a steady fashion.[39]

Local Communities

The millet system divided and ruled local subjects as confessional communities. It defined legal and societal organization throughout the nineteenth century. The 1897 imperial census recorded Muslims as one-third of the total population, whereas Armenian, Orthodox, Jewish, and other peoples made up the remainder. Non-Muslim peoples held some degree of autonomy. Grand rabbis and patriarchs administered the affairs of the Jewish, Armenian, and Orthodox millets. They exercised free reign to make civil laws and collect local taxes, provided that their followers remained loyal subjects to the Ottoman state. According to premodern standards, this contract guaranteed the rights and responsibilities of authorities and subjects. It also led to the co-option of diverse communities into the imperial mainstream. Early spiritual leaders accepted the task of political leadership in alignment with the imperial centre.[40]

The millet structure was not an Islamic innovation. Whereas the citizens of Rome lived under law and state-sanctioned authority, the Christians coexisted with the Zoroastrian majority in the fifth-century Sassanid Empire. Later Muslim empires also categorized Christian and Jewish minorities as millets, granting them freedom of communal worship in return for civil obedience. In the Ottoman case, the Edict of 1453 designated the ecumenical patriarch of Istanbul as the leader of the Greeks, Orthodox Albanians, Arabs, Bulgarians, Romanians, and Serbs. The Jewish community gained recognition around the same time. Eight years later, an additional edict recognized a third community by appointing the archbishop of Bursa as the patriarch of the Armenians, Syriac Orthodox, and Copts. In an innately nonegalitarian and nonterritorial fashion, these millets elected only leaders who were self-committed to acting as steadfast state agents and accepting Muslim superiority. In return, the millet leaders exercised autonomy in commercial activity, educational planning, legal arbitration, property management, and tax regulation. In court, Islamic law overrode other laws in specific cases that involved Muslim subjects. As the official and military ranks preferred to employ people with Turkish and Islamic roots, upward mobility remained unlikely for ambitious non-Muslim locals. Local communities also retained distinct dress codes and lived in separate quarters.[41]

The Armenian community splintered into Catholic and Protestant millets in the nineteenth century. The Tanzimat reforms further regulated social conduct by declaring new millets and by branching older millets into ethnicities such as those of the adherents of the Bulgarian and Greek Churches. Indeed, the 1897 census registered fifteen separate millets, whose citizens were 75 per cent Muslim, 14 per cent Orthodox, 6 per cent Armenian, 4 per cent Protestant and other, and 1 per cent Jewish. The existing literature tends to disagree on the attributes of the millet system, interpreting it as a facade of Ottoman pluralism or as another dimension of Islamic oppression. As central authorities failed to localize egalitarian policies, then, the non-Muslim communities rebelled against the state.[42]

The modern Balkan and Middle East nation-states originated from the millet matrix. In Kemal Karpat's analysis, these nations discredited their roots "regardless of their historical experience and political culture." As the social order collapsed in the face of civil inequalities and public disorder, younger Ottoman generations sought inspiration in revolutionary ideals and in idealistic missionaries from Britain, France, Russia, and the United States. They challenged the imperial integrity and claimed national sovereignty. Today, the millet system continues to evoke animosity and irredentism in heated debates over the Armenian genocide, Cyprus, the Kurdish question, Islamist politics, ethnic conflicts, and religious hostilities.[43]

FAITHFUL ENCOUNTERS

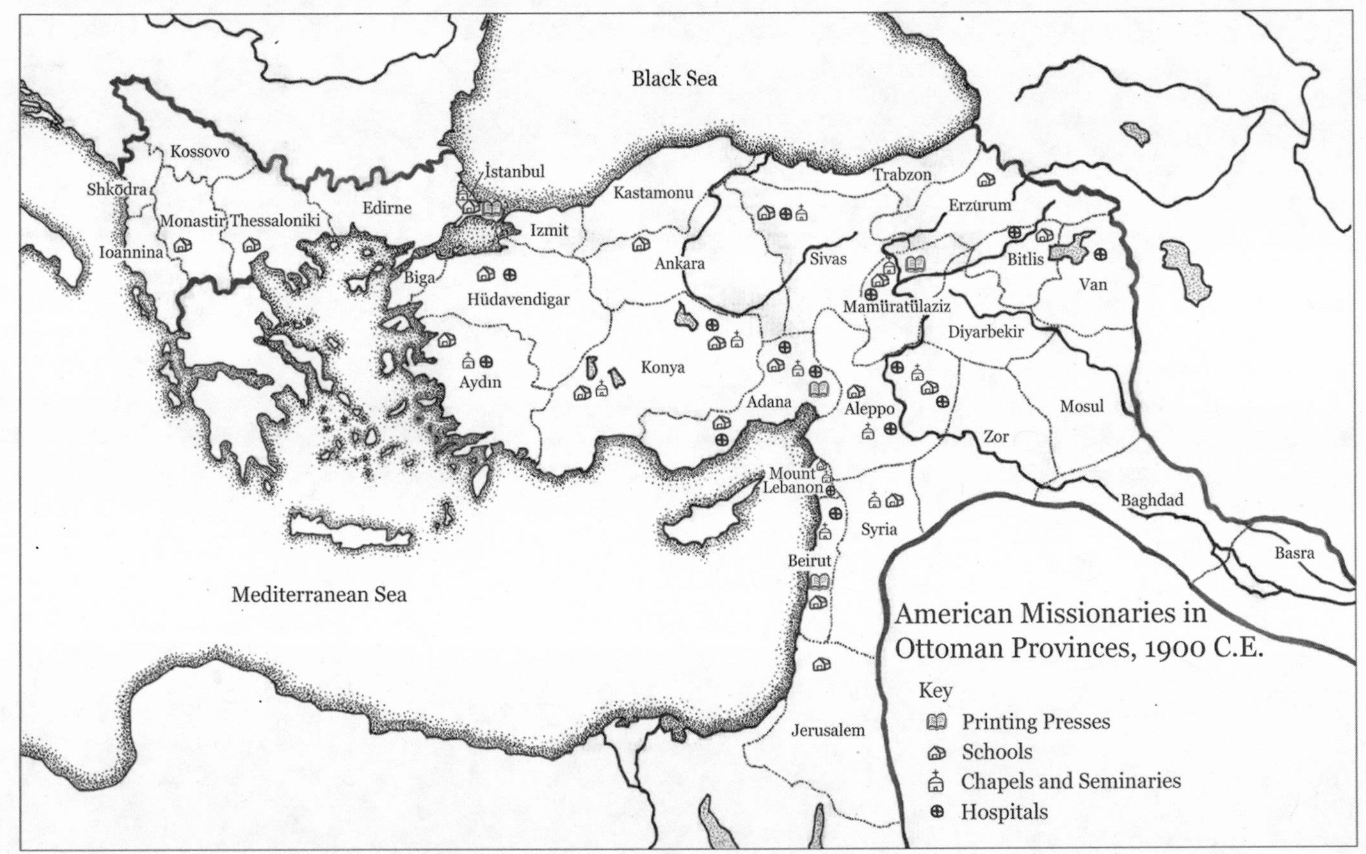

1.1 Map showing American missionaries in Ottoman provinces, 1900.

1

Introduction

The American Board of Commissioners for Foreign Missions embodies the thickest description of US involvement in the Old World. Several idealistic graduates of New England seminaries founded the board in Boston in 1810. They ventured out to civilize and evangelize the nations of the world. Their favourite destination was the Middle East. In his 1913 pamphlet *What Next in Turkey*, David Eddy stressed the strategic importance of this region since the beginning. With degrees from Yale, Auburn, and Hartford, he was ordained in 1904 and then went into the field as a missionary. He predicted that "if the Gospel life can make a strong impression" in the Ottoman Empire, "the dynamic of it will be carried into every hamlet of Kurdistan," thereby opening the door to the Orient.[1]

Substantial investment went into Ottoman missions. By the early twentieth century, 179 missionaries were operating 450 educational institutions and 19 health centres. Remarkably ambitious, this enterprise served as an opportune space for women and locals, with the 1914 figures indicating that there were 123 women versus 58 men, 1,299 native labourers, including 210 preachers, 897 teachers, and 90 Bible women, as well as 55,240 adherents and 25,911 students. The longevity of these missions likewise immersed the second and third generations of missionaries in closer contacts with the people and facilitated chain migrations from Ottoman provinces to New England.[2]

This book tells about American missionaries, yet it is a tale that revolves around the imperial state in Istanbul. State authorities defined them as strangers and countered their operations by empowering imperial institutions and employing new tactics. To locate these developments, I trace intelligence gathering, decision making, and legal regulations in the areas of construction, education, healthcare, publication, and security. This focus addresses the steps taken by authorities to restrain the missionaries in an already restless situation. An in-depth look from this perspective also helps to chart the features of imperial rhetoric and to measure the progress of policies regarding missionary activities.

By the late nineteenth century, some bureaucratic initiatives had revamped the Ottoman regime, which had embraced the tenets of centralism, conservatism, and favouritism. Where central authorities espoused these tenets, however, the regime's exclusionary proclivities became palpable. The state payroll listed 40,000 employees in 1908, yet the leaders of this robust staff still consisted of Istanbulites – those well-born, educated, and well-connected elites who occupied key roles in administration and virtually all tenured positions in colleges and courts.[3]

One of those bureaucrats who followed a typical career track was Mehmet Sait, who was born in 1830 into a distinguished scholarly family and educated at the Hagia Sofia College in Istanbul. This diligent, courtly, and loyal twenty-year-old had proven to be a good prospect during his internship at the imperial assembly. He quickly rose to the top. He served as the sultan's first secretary, minister of justice, grand vizier, and president of the imperial assembly. Between 1876 and 1912, the committed, seasoned, and faithful Sait revised the ordinances of the Justice and Security Administration, founded modern secular schools and the Attorney General's Office in the Imperial Chamber of Commerce, and balanced the imperial budget by slashing state expenditures and raising direct taxation. Given that upward mobility depended on loyalty, the highest career paths were contingent on fidelity, besides other qualifications. The regime enabled and shaped Sait by promoting or demoting him during ideological changes in 1876, 1896, 1908, 1911, and 1913. Likewise, the tens of thousands of lower-ranked officials remained vulnerable to political transitions.[4]

The imperial edifice not only made such bureaucrats in Istanbul but also structured the larger society according to a primordial formula. A compound of moral and national traits articulated the status of a given agent. If a non-Muslim community emphasized its distinctive qualities, for instance, the state authorities regarded it as a social behaviour inimical to its interests and considered an entire populace to be legally suspicious. This equation was faulty, as it regarded certain communities as guilty until proven innocent. It nevertheless proved potent in the 1890s when the Armenian minority contacted American missionaries and challenged the status quo.[5]

Several important questions remain unexamined to this day. Particularly, how did Ottoman authorities interpret messages of an ethno-religious nature, and how did their views impact local contexts? Why did they approach the missionaries the way that they did? Broadly, how did missionary activities map onto the competing notions of religious conservatism and state freedoms, as well as onto the underlying conditions of the centralizing state and a decentralized society? As Ottoman-missionary encounters connected these themes across time and place, I aim to explore these themes, as well.

CHAPTER SUMMARY

Chapter 2, "Strangers in the Land," deals with the early expansion of American missions. Local leaders accused the missionaries of preaching sedition and disrupting order. In Beirut, Harput, Urfa, and other cities, the governors, notables, and priests petitioned the central state to punish or deport them. However, the bulk of their complaints failed to convince the authorities, further signalling a breach of the fragile trust between the centre and the provinces. Mehmet Faik Memduh and Mehmet Sait, who respectively headed the Ministries of the Interior and Foreign Affairs, reckoned that local requests conveyed biased views and lacked detail. In December 1883 the Ministries of Education and Finance conducted a survey and counted foreign and native residents. Then the cautious Ministers Council deliberated on these findings and estimated the actual capacity of missionary activities. Based on the survey, intelligence reports, and petitions, they adjusted the existing laws to control the missionaries effectively. Although instructions ensured that the missionary propaganda would not address the Muslims, further regulations complicated the vetting process for missionary entrepreneurs by demanding official authorization as an imperative to conduct any public activity. Through instructions and regulations, imperial authorities highlighted their superiority in local and religious matters.

Chapter 3, "Crime and Order," illustrates the missionaries' diplomatic rights and security concerns. In various cases, local vigilante groups attacked them and destroyed their property. One such example was the notorious Miss Stone Affair. A group of bandits kidnapped the American Board's missionary Ellen Stone in September 1901, precipitating the first modern hostage crisis in the United States. The shocked American diplomats complained that the Ottoman government was repeatedly failing to protect their people in the region. Whereas American authorities intervened on behalf of their suffering citizen-missionaries, Ottoman authorities labelled missionary-bound cases as internal affairs and sought to resolve them by stemming diplomatic interference. This approach delegated the greatest share of responsibility to provincial governors, leaving them to restore public order and to cope with specific incidents. Although the governors executed interrogations and operations, imperial bureaucrats doubted their competence and thus charged the Ministry of Public Security with the duty of screening the missionaries and handling security matters. Indeed, an 1899 memorandum indicated that public security authorities had blamed and punished several of their subordinates for gross misconduct in resolving cases such as the Miss Stone Affair. Broadly, the later penal policies reflected a new justice concept by which the imperial state made American missionaries the subject of special surveillance and protection at the same time.

Chapter 4, "Institutional Regulations," elucidates the vision and path of missionary institutions. On many occasions, American missionaries converted houses into hospitals, presses, schools, and orphanages. In central Anatolia, for instance, William Dodd turned his residence into a fifteen-bed hospital. Maria Gerber housed eleven orphans in her residence as boarded students. The authorities called these cases "sinister practices" and argued that Dodd and Gerber had ignored the existing property laws, which prohibited the public use of private property. Given the extent of such violations, general vigilance by the state became paramount. Regulations facilitated the vetting process by ordering the institutions to register with the American Board rather than under their individual names. The Ministers Council designed this decision with reliance on common cooperation, but despite expecting the missionaries to act more responsibly, it ordered local state agents to screen the entire process. Nonetheless, these hopeful expectations were not fulfilled, and many missionaries did not cooperate. The ministers then responded by developing another strategy: they permitted renovations in the existing institutions but forbade extensions beyond the original locations. This strategy of containment legitimized the closure and removal of missionary institutions near strategic areas such as military barracks.

Chapter 5, "Ink Saw the Daylight," discusses the course of publishing activities. Against the growing literature of American missionaries, Ottoman authorities insisted on assessing its content and potential impact on general readers. Having sifted through inspection results in April 1898, Minister of the Interior Mehmet Faik Memduh argued that missionary publications contained largely "controversial ideas" that would "foment sedition" if preached in the countryside. His views expressed a targeted policy of prohibiting foreign literature for rural folks – those subjects deemed by the authorities to be susceptible to imported ideologies. By adding a qualitative distinction, the policy allowed and welcomed educational texts but censored and banned religious pamphlets.

State departments collaborated on carrying out a Herculean task. The Press Services, Communications and Telegram Centre, Ottoman Embassy in Washington, provincial administrations, and customs offices transmitted the American Board's publications to the Inspection and Examination Committee. The committee's rank-and-file officials then inspected and reported on them. The committee director also consulted other departments before advising on whether to release certain publications in the provinces. Despite all of these efforts, missionary authors printed materials faster than state agents could handle them. The book inspectors could not really match the tenacity of the authors. The Ministers Council addressed the problem at its roots by ordering the inspection of printing machines as well as the literature in circulation. This policy change turned out to be less than a solution, as missionary presses eventually printed millions of pages and delivered them to Ottoman readers.

MISSIONARY HISTORIOGRAPHY

Early studies stressed how the missionaries had impacted local peoples. Travellers and missionary-turned authors extolled evangelical enthusiasm for enlightening the world, indicating that the missionaries coveted a dual objective of invigorating evangelical zeal and salvaging even the wicked from hellfire. American Board missionaries sanctified the Ottoman Empire as an area where the Holy Lands stood and future Christians lived. Some authors sought divine symbols in support of a US presence in the region, but they did so by stereotyping the Oriental norms and realities. Because cultural conversion was the main concern, the scholarship generally reflected a distorted Turkish-Islamic image.[6]

Perspectives shifted toward the revisionist spirit of the 1960s. John Fairbank, the president of the American Historical Association, called evangelical Christian missionaries "the invisible men of American history." In his 1968 annual address, he laid out recent studies, noting that historians had become interested in saving the missionary history from missionary authors themselves. In the Cold War context, indeed, historians reconsidered Protestant missions in the Third World. Turkish scholars likewise reoriented their position in a globalizing milieu. They championed the national will, refused to become the United States' petty satellite, and published in tune with the domestic public mindset. Some historians told the capitalist, missionary-minded Yankees to "go back home." The prism of familiar binary positions thus contributed various dimensions to the field.[7]

A priori assumptions nevertheless demarcate the field's boundaries to this day. Whereas Michael Oren and Ussama Makdisi emphasize American productivity in the Middle East, Çağrı Erhan and Uygur Kocabaşoğlu criticize American imperialism in the Ottoman Empire. Given that nation and narration are intertwined and that national identity is a salient feature of intellectual pursuit, the extant studies have not yet exposed the multiplicity of contextual realities surrounding Ottoman-missionary encounters.[8]

This lacuna is twofold. The dominant narratives overlook alternative connotations of the US presence and instead address the degrees to which American missionaries enlightened the local people. Although this pursuit prompts some analysis and stimulates debate over specific encounters, it largely disguises coproductivity and some internal dynamics. The point here is to explore the less-travelled archival trails in order to explain Ottoman views and compare alternative stories with missionary stories.[9]

HISTORICAL APPROACH

In Montreal, Canada, a Cree hunter once testified about the fate of his hunting lands. In the 1970s a new hydroelectric scheme jeopardized the resources of his people, who hunted to survive. While in court, he hesitated to narrate his story after being asked to tell nothing but the truth. "I am not sure I can tell the truth," he said. "I can only tell what I know." Consistent with that statement, I regard historical truths as interpretive and their meanings as relative to the lifeworld of individuals. To evaluate what people knew they knew, it is essential to appreciate the variety of truths and to avoid the simplicity of telling a story as the true story.[10]

A particularly useful tool in approaching history is the multifaceted method – developed by Peter Katzenstein as a systematic study of "multiple, simultaneous, and often contradictory knowledge claims" asserted by different parties in context. This method seeks to identify empirical anomalies and to strip "notions of what is 'natural' of their intuitive plausibility." In the history of religious encounters, although it may sound novel, it is more useful than a "specific analytical perspective." The extant literature tends to obscure intricate relationships and to privilege the "parsimony" that has become "the hallmark of paradigmatic debates." Where scholarly positions represent an internal-external dichotomy – in this case, a portrayal of American missionaries as "hegemonic" or "benevolent" and Ottoman authorities as "despotic" or "tolerant" – the dominant views tend to depict the Ottoman missions as a quintessential example of Christian and Muslim clashes. In fact, the literatures substantiate the debate over American diplomatic and religious designs in the Muslim world at the risk of reducing the agents to obsolete and unreasoning parties. They rob the subject of alternative stories – even though Ottoman-missionary encounters "defy any analytical capture by any one paradigm."[11]

Faith and politics were complex matters in the Ottoman Empire. Evangelical missions intersected with Ottoman centralism and US expansionism. As well, authorities and missionaries modified their views over time, not always acting upon religious motives. The imperial government's agenda proved conducive to change even when central authorities wished to oversee regional circumstances. State sensibilities, then, allowed for a dynamic matrix composed of competitive stakeholders, including missionaries and communities.

Viewed from the state centre in Istanbul, American missionary encounters took place in two episodes. The authorities advocated a peaceful coexistence until 1883. They did not distinguish these missionaries from their British, French, German, or Russian colleagues, and they handled most incidents on a local case-by-case basis. Whereas provincial governors and notables accused the missionaries of being troublemakers who were menacing public order, central authorities listened to the other side and made decisions based on state interests.[12]

Worthy of particular attention is the post-1883 period, during which public tensions and missionary activities spread on an unprecedented scale. The Istanbul authorities singled out American missionaries and conducted proactive manoeuvres to handle them and local matters. Factual and partial, field reports warranted new policies, at times claiming the missionaries were showing disdain for the state authority and testing its legitimacy. The cumulative effect of these reports amounted to general vigilance, which further diminished tolerance and freedom of operation. This period offers a gateway through which it is possible to take a holistic, critical look at faithful encounters between authorities and missionaries all the way from the imperial headquarters in Istanbul to the remotest villages in Van. It also enables us to review the dominant scholarly views on the subject. In his pioneering study *The Well-Protected Domains*, Selim Deringil finds that Ottoman authorities defined American missionaries as "a danger for the future." If we take a broader and deeper view of Ottoman-missionary relations, however, we find that the danger did not hinge only on spiritual prospects. For imperial authorities, the missionaries' rapid expansion and direct engagement in the conflict-ridden countryside made the danger rather imminent and thus more relevant to the here and now.[13]

New rules came with harsh standards. In its instructions to provinces and foreign governments, the Ottoman government delivered an identical message: glorify the state, identify critical aspects of the issue at hand, and mandate the kind of resolutions preferred by government authorities. The typical preamble claimed state legitimacy, and the main text presented the issue with multiple layers of meaning. On missionary matters, an edict's subliminal message reiterated the "eternal" and "well-protected" status of the imperial state, as well as the "divine" and "just" qualities of the sultan-caliph. The body of its text noted the occurrence of incidents that "sowed the seeds" of "distrust," "hatred," and "sedition" among the already "ignorant" and "malleable" subjects. Such demeaning language provoked the minds and hearts of local subjects "against the state and its norms." Its rhetoric imagined the subjects to be inert and passive recipients of imported ideologies and the officials to be morally responsible and capable of executing "what is deemed necessary."[14]

If the regime shaped the public mindset with both legible and hidden messages, the coded nature of its messages widened the centre's radius of action and expedited its reactions to local incidents. In this respect, an empire-wide vigilance besieged evangelical publications when a May 1898 memorandum predicted that the missionaries would "nurture sedition" in the "ignorance-plagued" countryside. Ottoman authorities thus incriminated third parties and eliminated their reaction against the burden of bureaucratic incompetence and diplomatic hindrance. In efforts to stymie specific crimes, the public security officials took the more demanding duty of field operations and ultimately served as a conduit for carrying out whatever was deemed necessary from the viewpoint of the capital. In tandem, the crafted rhetoric and stretched duties enabled the capital to cast a long, visible shadow in the provinces.[15]

The concerted efforts to regulate institutions merit substantial focus. The institutions owned by the American Board mushroomed in Ottoman lands when missionary homes were turned into hospitals, orphanages, and schools. Imperial authorities devised a strategy of containment to counter the proliferation in the 1880s. New directives demanded that illegal expansion cease, and all foreign institutions had to register under the board's auspices. Regulations allowed for renovations but forbade any growth of the existing institutions. Based on the centre's practical yet inaccurate calculation, shrinking and containing the physical space was expected to result in the shrinking and eventual cessation of missionary institutions.

Writing and publishing activities constituted a vehement arena of conflict between authorities and missionaries. On this front, the authorities showed signs of exceptional care rather than an "attitude of negligence." They assessed the reputation of missionary authors, the substance of their publications, and the potential impact of these publications on local readers. Assessment-based decisions allowed or forbade the board's "propaganda." In a striking principle, religious and educational books belonged to two discrete classes, and so did their elite and general audiences.[16]

A multifaceted and eclectic analysis helps to explore these topics. In this book, I reconsider how to make sense of ethnicity, power, order, and religion in the Ottoman world and beyond. After all, Ottoman authorities and American missionaries were both the subject and the object of history throughout the course of East and West relations – and they remained so under circumstances not always of their choosing. One way to understand their stance is through the archives, what is left to us from the past.

MANUSCRIPT SOURCES

Turkish archival sources are at the core of this book. The previously untapped documents contain substantial data on various practices that converged over the issues of missionary activity and public order.

They enable us to reconstruct the steps taken by Ottoman authorities to collect and assess the intelligence, opinions, and reports that the local officials transmitted to the central state in Istanbul. These documents also depict American missionaries as viewed from the state centre as well as from the provinces.

Held in the Ottoman Archives Division of the Prime Minister's Office in Istanbul, the historical documents are written in the Ottoman Turkish language – an urban elitist language that combined Arabic, Persian, and Turkish vocabulary in the Arabic script. They comprise a vast array of state laws and regulations, sultanate and ministerial records, judicial reports, and local correspondence. These records are divided into dossiers placed in collections such as administrative orders, capitulations and contracts, economic affairs, education and cultural affairs, excise and special taxes, finance, foreign affairs, imperial decrees, internal affairs, judicial affairs, military affairs, municipal affairs, organizational ordinances and regulations, public security, public works, and telegraph and post office.[17]

Ottoman records present prospects and challenges. Dossier summaries are not instructive of what the enclosed documents may reveal. For instance, a summary notes that the dossier dated 8 November 1895 contains the "vizierate, incoming, urgent-affairs documents" of the internal affairs collection. It states, "We completed the required investigations of what the Harput and Maraş incidents cost in American missionary property," and "we attached the letters of the suffering party who petitioned against the Adana incidents." The summary cues regarding the dossier's content do not describe what the documents, fifty-nine sheets in total, tell us about the missionaries, incidents, and locations in question. These general summaries do not facilitate research on specific subjects. However, the more substantial dossiers contain plentiful material for researchers who are flexible with their time and focus.[18]

My research draws its core material from the collections of various documents on educational and cultural affairs, internal affairs, foreign affairs, public security, and the telegraph and post office. I cross-checked numerous summaries with several themes of interest and located 6,540 dossiers referencing American missionaries. After briefly assessing the documents, I obtained and studied 42 dossiers from each collection, narrowed the focus to 2,225 dossiers, and transcribed the most relevant data in Turkish using the Latin script. Logical and practical reasons prompted this process. Three collections – excise and special taxes, judicial affairs, and military affairs – proved to be remotely related to the research topic. The less irrelevant sections of sultanate and ministerial records from the Hamidian Era (1876–1909) did not merit further scrutiny. I also assessed portions of debates, memorandums, and motions in the collection of imperial decrees generated by the Ministers Council.

Some other sources await future study. For instance, I obtained 152 documents from the collections related to foreign affairs and to capitulations and contracts. These documents expose substantial cases of the locals who migrated to the United States and became American citizens with the support of American missionaries back in their homeland. For the particular topic of this book, I sourced and corroborated 2,225 dossiers and 6,154 documents from the collections related to educational, cultural, internal, and foreign affairs, public security, and the telegraph and post office.

2

Strangers in the Land

Americans heard terrible things about the Ottomans. In April 1892 the *New York Times* devoted a lengthy editorial to the draconian measures that Ottoman authorities were imposing on American missionaries. The editorial allegorized the authorities as "double-faced" Turks and accordingly outlined their legal violations. It advocated the missionaries' right to life, trade, travel, worship, and the pursuit of happiness, as well as their right to "claim redress" if "any of these rights have been unjustly infringed upon." These rights, already stipulated in the Commerce and Navigation Treaty, failed to catch on. The authorities in Istanbul were withholding them, supposing that American missionaries had undertaken work meant to "inevitably end in the overthrow of the Moslem Government." They thus subjected the missionaries to "nonsensical formalities" and arrested several of them.[1]

Other US newspapers addressed similar concerns, one portraying the missionaries "under the patronage of the Sultan" and another castigating the "Turks as Violators." In most accounts, oppression had become the norm in that part of the world. Observed in the continuing Armenian massacres, Turkish atrocities became so ubiquitously notorious that James Ross, a reader from Boston, readily placed the "whole world" and its common "judgment" against the *Washington Post* and the claim of its deceptive editorial that "the Moslems do not indulge in religious persecutions." He argued that this editorial was dogmatic – "ipse dixit" – and had to be recanted. The presentation of "missionaries" as allies of local rebels had to be "recalled," as well. At local levels, anti-Turkish public sentiments survived over decades. Later, in 1911, the coastal Mainers encountered Ahmet Yalman, a

Turkish doctoral student in Columbia University's School of Journalism, when he came to visit their town on a holiday trip. Sometime before his arrival, they changed the door locks – "even that of the jail" – because the "Turks were coming."[2]

Whereas the double-faced authorities occupied the headlines, Turkish wrestlers fighting in American rings captured the back pages. The *Hartford Courant* announced that the wrestling champion Ernest Roeber had beaten Yusuf "the Terrible Turk" at the 1899 World Wrestling Championship (except Yusuf was disqualified, not defeated). Ten years later, the *Chicago Tribune* gladly reported that the giant-killer Frank Gotch had retained his title by "easily downing" Yusuf Mahmud, the Terrible Turk's student and namesake. The reporter quipped that the Turk had finally lost the title of being terrible, his "mere pseudonym." With the historic defeat that day, the Turk had become "terrified." Figuratively, such reports on Ottoman bureacrats and athletes offered their readers an exotic body fit to provoke scorn for the Ottoman Empire. The glad tiding was that imperial potency, which had long oppressed hapless locals, would eventually succumb to American muscle. From the front pages to the back, the print media in New England, home of the evangelical missionaries, judged the host government's behaviour from this perspective.[3]

This should not come as a historical surprise. As Patrick Hogan observes, emotionally engaged public minds "pluck out causal sequences from the complex of events," "bound those sequences," and "bring them into comprehensible relations with one another." In short, we select, segment, and structure the stories unfolding around us. In portrayals of Ottoman authorities, the grand idea of Orientals oppressing Christians proved particularly sensational. It nevertheless seemed realistic, perhaps more real than reality. Additionally, a comparison of the declining Muslim Ottoman Empire and the rising Christian American Republic well nurtured the spirit of "manifest destiny" – that century's journalist-made ideal that divine providence destined the rising republic to civilize the declining empire.[4]

The field's scholars equate the Ottoman imperial regime with some insular and distinct qualities. Roderick Davison notes that Muslim authorities downgraded Christian subjects to "second-class citizens" and subjected them to "unequal treatment." He argues that the non-Muslim subjects lost more of their rights in the nineteenth century, even though an 1856 edict granted them equal rights. Ussama Makdisi also engages with this discussion by linking it to Orientalism – Edward

Said's thesis depicting the egotistic West's sense of an exotic East. In Makdisi's curious discovery, the Turkish Muslim elite bludgeoned into submission the Arab Muslims in addition to the Balkan Christians. Likewise, several others indicate that the *fin de siècle* sultan, Abdulhamid II, ruled in a "reactionary" manner and that his "absolutism" signified the apex of a collapsing-empire syndrome. Ultimately, the Turkish Sunni yoke failed all its subjects. In this respect, the extant literature overlooks the issues of government sensibilities shaped by the various views *of* bureacrats themselves. It is equally worth looking beyond the sultan's persona to understand how state sensibilities developed in the imperial centre and affected local circumstances.[5]

To assess Ottoman conscience and evangelical presence, it is necessary to perceive missionary activities from the imperial perspective and explore how central authorities learned about the missionaries. In fact, the facade of the Ottoman government was a dynamic matrix composed of multiple stakeholders. Whereas missionaries and minorities pressured the central state to deliver rights, local officials and notables petitioned it to rid them of the missionary problem. This dialectical process involved traditional and novel tactics, and it steered state conscience to the relative strengths of competing factions. Throughout the process, government policies created pragmatic and partly biased mechanisms, thus virtually turning the central state into a police state that was intolerant of and extremely aggressive toward troublemakers. As missionaries became common suspects later in the 1880s, the state urged that their activities be vigilantly monitored and restricted using a wide range of legal and preventive measures.

IMPERIAL REACTION TO MISSIONARY EXPANSION

The number of Protestant missions peaked in the nineteenth century. Whereas before 1860 there were 376 missionaries, 787 local affiliates, and 80 institutions, by 1885 these missions had grown exponentially, boasting 422 missionaries, 2,183 local employees, and over 400 institutions around the world. One-quarter of the missionaries operated in Ottoman lands. In New England, evangelical congregations cheerfully endorsed them because 18 million "souls" had suffered so long and thus deserved their spiritual and financial support. At an 1867 Boston meeting, leaders of the American Board of Commissioners for Foreign Missions boldly claimed that the missionaries were even "settling the Eastern question," namely the political and social anarchy in the region, which invited international concern and intervention. It was therefore just a matter of time before "the evangelization of the Turkish Empire" was assured. But how did the Ottoman government – not represented at that meeting – view the ever-growing Protestant missions?[6]

The factors of the missionary problem required knowing the coordinates of the actors. Ottoman authorities thus began by collecting intelligence. However, despite locating the problem, they realized that the missionary presence eluded the cartography. Additionally, consistent with Selim Deringil's findings on the legitimation of power, Ottoman bureaucrats considered local communities to be "good" and "always capable of loyalty." Later, in the 1880s, this naive imagery contradicted the rise of a new elite sensibility. The subjects seemed to be "silly" and incapable of "telling good from evil," thus becoming highly prone to "fooling" and "provoking" by third parties such as American missionaries. Provincial administrations rated the missionaries as *personae non gratae* and associated their operations with public disorder in their regions. Even though local governors and the American Board's leaders exaggerated specific impacts of the missionaries, the anti-Ottoman position of the missionaries was seriously evident to imperial bureaucrats. Indeed, the bureaucrats in Istanbul agreed that the evangelical message might well "confuse the minds" of people and "sow the seeds of discord" among the public.[7]

The existing ruling mechanisms already featured some pivotal tools, from data collecting to lawmaking, and all the while the missionary expansion whetted the bureaucratic appetite for documentation. In her socio-legal study of Antep, an old Anatolian town, Leslie Peirce describes the imperial obsession with documentation as a result of the conviction that documentation was the "handmaiden of control." Regarding the missionaries, numerous records of investigations, surveys, court rulings, and petitions streamed into the central state for complex processing that involved the top-level bureaucrats in education, finance, foreign and internal affairs, public works, the Ministers Council, Customs Receivership, land registry, and the Sublime Porte. Within a nested structure, they shared and evaluated the incoming data. In earlier centuries, Cambridge geologist Warrington Smyth and other travellers had acclaimed the Ottoman state for its "justice," "inexpensiveness," and "simplicity." But in the nineteenth century, Ottoman authorities prioritized intelligence affairs and bureaucratized the centre's modes of operation. New procedures, virtually

2.1 Drawing of first Parliament meeting at the Çırağan Palace, 1877.

"non-sensical" from an outsider's perspective, became partial, expensive, and increasingly "complex."[8]

The Ottoman world had intrigued voyagers, pilgrims, and writers since the fifteenth century. Numerous travel narratives, such as Henry Barkley's accounts of his time in Anatolia and Bulgaria, told Western readers about local architecture, landscapes, Muslims, and Christians. In her classic *The Ottoman Empire and the World Around It*, Suraiya Faroqhi finds that most visitors and merchants gained "easy access" to the region. Surprisingly, some foreigners even defied the imperial laws that forbade non-Muslim males to "marry local women or acquire real estate." The regulations likewise did not institute "stringent controls at entry points" for sojourners. However, American missionaries posed a different case. Imperial authorities saw them coming in large numbers, staying for the long haul, and engaging with the communities. State agents thus intercepted them frequently and warned them to report to the authorities when landing and moving in the country.[9]

In June 1890, when several missionaries reached the province of Damascus to settle in Beirut, Minister of the Interior Ahmet Münir reprimanded them for defying the laws and exhorted local agents to "investigate this case." Then the agents detained, interrogated, and released the group on the condition that its members report every step of their movements to the state. The minister also used the occasion to call for "constant vigilance." Cases of this sort did not reflect an overall propensity to neglect the laws, yet the related verdicts captured the imperial quest to locate and monitor the missionaries anytime and everywhere. This quest manifested itself in warnings and instructions to the missionaries about reporting the purpose and destination of their trips.[10]

Numerous surveys sketched the visibility and mobility of foreigners, indicating that American missionaries were operating virtually everywhere. They were in Anatolian, Arab, and Balkan provinces and cities, including Adana, Beirut, Ioannina, Kayseri, and Yemen. Indeed, Seçil Akgün has found that 427 of 540 missionaries had settled in Anatolia by 1895. At a time of local revolts and massacres, their presence implies that the missionaries became involved in some incidents both physically and emotionally. At the same time, provincial reports asked for full-scale resistance to missionary mobility. The reports also emphasized that anti-missionary incidents escalated commensurate with the missionary expansion, noting that the missionaries encouraged local Christians to obtain US citizenship and benefit from "capitulations" – diplomatic and commercial privileges granted by the Ottoman government to foreign nationals.[11]

A holistic interpretation of the links between American missionaries and local incidents induced and sustained a rather assertive reaction from the state centre. In an extreme late case, Mehmet Talat, the fanatically ambitious official who functioned as interior minister for seven years in two separate terms between 1909 and 1918, ordered a duplication of missionary-related reports. He discredited any assistance to the Armenian minority during massacres and blamed the missionaries for sheltering in east Anatolia several "rebels" who had operated in service of the Armenian Revolutionary Federation. Talat finally ordered that American missionaries quit supporting the terrorists and leave the land.[12]

In Ottoman lands, demographic surveys fulfilled financial and military functions and indicated biological and physical information of the subjects (i.e., name, gender, birthdate and place, residential address, and travel history). Several specific surveys also identified the existing foreign population. In this sense, the December 1883

L'Univers illustré

JOURNAL HEBDOMADAIRE

RÉDACTION & ADMINISTRATION
Vente au Numéro et Abonnements
Rue Auber, n° 3 — Paris
40 CENTIMES LE NUMÉRO

N° 2121
38e Année — 16 Novembre 1895.
LE JOURNAL PARAIT TOUS LES SAMEDIS

PRIX DE L'ABONNEMENT :
PARIS : Un an, 24 francs, Six mois, 12 francs, Trois mois 6 francs.
DÉPARTEMENTS : Un an 24 fr. : avec la prime franco, 26 francs.
UNION POSTALE : Un an 25 fr. ; avec la prime franco, 27 francs

NAZIM PACHA
Ministre de la police.

REDVAN PACHA
Préfet de Stamboul.

LE SULTAN ABDUL HAMID II

LA POLICE TURQUE ATTAQUÉE PAR LES ARMÉNIENS DANS LES RUES DE STAMBOUL

LES ÉVÉNEMENTS DE TURQUIE ET D'ARMÉNIE. — Voir page 759.

2.2 Newspaper cover depicting the affairs of Turkey and Armenia.

survey proved resourceful, as it counted locals and foreigners at the same time. The seasoned foreign affairs minister, Ahmet Arifi, took the idea to do so from Asım Efendi, the general director of the Citizenship Bureau, and brought it to the attention of his colleagues in the Ministers Council. Then the Ministries of the Interior and Public Works demanded "citizen-identification reports" from the American, British, and French Consulates – the agents of those states that sent the largest numbers of merchants and missionaries to the region. The consuls would prepare "registries" by listing the location, profession, and legal status of their citizens and submit their reports to the imperial state in a "prompt and adequate" fashion. This initiative particularly targeted the American missionaries and the Ottoman subjects they had converted. For the first time, a consular-level intelligence request stretched beyond Istanbul and Izmir, where foreign diplomats and merchants were concentrated. It absorbed Anatolian and Arab provinces, where American missionaries made up the largest nonlocal demographics.[13]

Rather than "providing a registry book" as per instructions, the consuls questioned the legitimacy of the request. The US Consulate certainly did not submit a registry book, wondering why the Ottoman government required access to "classified information" regarding US citizens. Arifi replied with a one-word answer, "efficiency." He further claimed that the information would help them to provide foreigners with "better and faster service." In reality, however, the diplomatic exchange camouflaged an unspoken motive. The registry would pinpoint the missionaries and allow the government to profile them.[14]

Given the consular noncooperation, Ottoman ministers bypassed bilateral calculations and advocated internal agency as an alternative source for the task. They instructed provincial officials to count foreigners along with the locals. However, this plan overlooked another setback. The foreigners, no less skeptical than their consuls, rejected the call. They would "not disclose their identity to the officials unless their government so willed."[15]

Some legal sanctions might have reversed this objection. Arifi and the internal affairs minister, İbrahim Ethem, proclaimed that "any person domiciled in the Ottoman domains shall be treated as Ottoman subjects." In cases where "one claims to be alien, this claim must be authenticated. Otherwise, the [alien] status will not be granted." Further instructions urged foreigners to obtain an "imperial certificate," a document to be issued by the officials in order to verify foreigners' legal status. The ministers warned the noncompliant parties that they would forfeit rights to property and service. These sanctions aimed to deter two large groups: American missionaries purchasing lands to build stations and the US-turned converts among the locals who were benefiting from tax incentives offered to the "most-favored nation," as stated in article 3 of the 1862 US-Ottoman treaty. Other foreign-Ottoman subjects also bore the brunt of new sanctions because the rules applied to any foreigners. Additionally, the regulations adjured the foreigners to inform officials of their itinerary. The Ministry of the Interior even created a special committee to process travel permits and trace the status of their holders. The committee assigned the applicants one of two positions: "alien-status accepted" or "alien-status rejected."[16]

Besides new data, the local censuses, surveys, and reports formed the main arteries of imperial databases. They repositioned the Ottoman state as an interventionist power in part because the content of inbound data caused state authorities to regard the ideas associated with public tensions as synonymous with American missionaries. The authorities thus determined to control local circumstances by coercing people into compliance with imperial regulations. Viewed from Istanbul, the missionary enterprise had grown to such a degree that some "incompetent officials" were failing to grapple with the problem.[17]

US diplomats had qualms about the long-range tactics of the Istanbul authorities and pressured Ottoman diplomats to abate hostile reactions to American citizens. Indeed, Leo Bergholz, the American consul in Erzurum (1896–1903), frequented Istanbul with such concerns. Minister of Foreign Affairs Ahmet Tevfik recounted his meeting with the consul in May 1898. When the minister said that the missionaries "went about activities in violation of laws and order," the consul assured him that he would "defend no person or case against imperial state laws." The US government likewise could not reprimand the Ottoman government for "deporting missionaries and banning illegal action."[18]

Illegal action this time implicated the missionaries in the crime of fuelling civil unrest, especially agitating the Armenian Christian youth against the Kurdish Muslims in Anatolia. When the Ottoman minister reminded the American consul of Istanbul's right to act if "concrete evidence" revealed foreign "citizens' affront to the Ottoman state," the consul understood the gravity of the situation. He nevertheless doubted the wrongdoings of US citizen-missionaries, noting that "the

Armenian Patriarch and local authorities made up and attributed those crimes" to the missionaries. Governors and patriarchs blamed others for their own failures, arguing that the missionaries had "converted and provoked the Armenian children" against the imperial state. They made this claim because the missionaries deprived local authorities of "material benefits" that they otherwise would have sustained through a larger submissive populace. All of this scapegoating was "arbitrary" and "unfair," only "benefiting those who trumped up the charges." The consul concluded that the US government would understand Istanbul's anti-sedition stance but also asked if recent events had justified it. The Ottoman minister replied that they indeed had. It is hard to discern whether the minister narrated the meeting as it had happened or how he remembered it had happened. His account nevertheless reveals the imperial perspective on the complex impact of the missionaries on the local situation.[19]

Imperial authorities continued to collect information in an effort to answer the disquieted American officials. For instance, Minister of Education Ahmet Zühdü consolidated the available statistics in an inventory in March 1900. His inventory recorded the capacity, situation, and management of registered missionary institutions. Related to the key state norms on legality, the penal code, and faith, the inventory described whether the missionaries renewed operation permits, cooperated with local officials, and taught Muslim students. Zühdü's successor, Mustafa Haşim, later updated the inventory by also addressing unregistered institutions. He indicated that the recorded figures had not reflected the actual numbers. The missionaries were operating twice as many institutions as previously estimated. The unrecorded half of their institutions were "hiding in odd corners and thus escaping detection." This "illegal practice" spurred "extreme caution."[20]

In the Anatolia section of the inventory, the governor of the province of Harput, Halit Efendi, reported "463 male and 434 female students" at American Board schools. All students were "Armenians except 12 Assyrians," and 201 of them were "boarded." The governor stated that "just as is the case with the licensed French school and unlicensed German school, these schools have enrolled no child of Islam." For the missionaries, this was an important note because such statements saved their institutions from suffering fines or closures, as well as from losing their constituents in less serious cases.[21]

Local inventories revealed significant realities. Strikingly, the farther missionary establishments were from Istanbul, the more nebulous their official status. In detail, Western Anatolia's reports identified sixteen legally operated institutions. But in the eastern provinces, where the imperial state was less powerful and local minorities were more prominent, a far greater number of foundations lacked imperial authorization. Some distant neighbourhoods hosted thirty-five non-licensed schools. Furthermore, the authorized investments were concentrated in the central, northern, and western provinces, accounting for three colleges in Istanbul, nine schools in Izmir, one college and one orphanage in Izmit, two schools in Bursa, seven schools and two orphanages in Sivas, and one school each in Ankara, Bitola, and Trabzon. Other "inconspicuous" foundations were clustered around the east. In Harput the seminary and three schools held licences, but one orphanage did not. In Adana and Jerusalem, nine of thirteen institutions had not been registered. Farther south in Mount Lebanon and Beirut, thirty-seven of fifty-one foundations remained "unlicensed." The only authorized missionary institution in Beirut was Syrian Protestant College, still operating today as the American University of Beirut.[22]

For authorities and missionaries, Beirut was an exceptional region. Minister of the Interior Ahmet Münir declared it a province in 1888 by virtue of its exponential population and revenue growth. The new province included the city of Beirut and the adjacent towns of Latakia, Tripoli, Acre, and Nablus. It had already become a focal point of religious activity by then, hosting a sizable group of American, British, French, German, and Russian missionaries. More than others, American missionary investments in the region were off the imperial state's radar. In his February 1903 letter to Minister of Foreign Affairs Ahmet Tevfik, US diplomat John Leishman demanded that the American Medical College's degrees be examined and certified by officials in Beirut, not by central authorities in Istanbul. This request also revealed that American missionaries outnumbered other missionaries in the region and thus were expecting to receive the same treatment given to their French counterparts. Seeing it as an opportunity to negotiate, the Ottoman minister asked for a complete list of American institutions in the provinces, as many of the American Board's establishments were unregistered. Although it remains a mystery whether the graduate diplomas continued to make roundtrips to Istanbul, central authorities received only a partial list of the board's institutions.[23]

Halil Efendi, the governor of the province of Beirut, investigated the later capacity of American institutions. In a March 1907 report, he recorded that "27 daytime and boarding schools are offering arts, business, and science education without an imperial permit." These schools "enrolled 100 Muslims and 650 Christians from Egypt and Beirut." He located no Muslim students in the "mission houses" in Latakia, Tripoli, and other towns but identified "41 nonlocals, 11 Christians, and 3 Muslims" in Safed, the southern district of Beirut.[24]

Viewed from the state centre, then, the expansion of American missionary institutions was conducted legally around the radius of Istanbul and less legally in the peripheral areas, where distance dimmed imperial control. In the late nineteenth century, when Ottoman authorities attributed local tensions partly to missionary activities, it became all the more critical to locate and monitor American missionaries. The ensuing efforts reshaped the authorities and etched a belligerent perception of missionary motives in their minds. The entire process, which unfolded alongside the imagined ideal of an abiding faith in authority and order, convinced them to devise policies in order to immunize the susceptible public, contain local missionary mobility, and punish local official misconduct. Strikingly, as well, central authorities sought to counter the missionary impact by establishing missionary-like imperial colleges.[25]

OTTOMAN AUTHORITY AND MISSIONARY ACTIVITY

In the early nineteenth century, Ottoman officers interrogated several American missionaries to mitigate an alleged "public nuisance," having been petitioned by local parties who were against missionary contact with Armenian youngsters in Istanbul's downtown district of Beyoğlu. Albeit trivial at first glance, this case marked the attitude of imperial authorities and nonstate actors toward the missionaries. In coming decades, the missionaries encountered a wider range of hostile attitudes. Local officials and notables who considered them a threat to public order highlighted the matter of "conversion," a ubiquitous feature of religious encounters, and assumed that since the missionaries were potential suspects of proselytization, imperial authorities would turn against their activities.[26]

Peaceful coexistence became a vain hope later in the century as state authorities resorted to aggressive policies such as coercion, relocation, and punishment, with a view to stopping religious interactions. One of the latest laws, a 1916 executive order against the American Board's local presence, reflected state choices in times of war. It came at the end of a long process that not only exacerbated the authorities' frustrations with the American Board but also signified the collapse of their tactics to keep missionaries and minorities under control.[27]

Conversion was a public matter. In the faith-driven Ottoman world, it was a buzzword, indeed. By default, the central government rewarded Islamic conversion but restricted apostasy, or conversion from Islam to other faiths. As the patriarchies administered their communal affairs in line with imperial laws, several patriarchs disdained the missionaries, fearing that missionary activity would "poison" their flock and breach their rules of conduct. Their petitions demanded that these foreigners be silenced or made to depart from their regions. In some cases, the patriarchs inflated the occurrence of real conversions. In response, central authorities did not issue general directives on this matter and left it outside their agenda. This early position isolated conversion cases from the American Board's general operations regarding teaching, nursing, and preaching in the countryside. However, the authorities legitimized some complaints with their verdicts. In May 1849, for instance, the Catholic patriarch Maximos III proposed "revoking the appointment of Michael Mishaqqa," his congregant and a recent Protestant convert, as a regent of the Damascus Consulate. He claimed that the conversion had "uprooted" the prospect, thus "leading him astray." An official edict confirmed this view by denying the convert the consulate job.[28]

In later decades, even the potential for conversion worried central authorities. Strikingly, because non-Ottoman spouses risked diminishing the loyalty of officials, it was urged that these officials be fired from the office. In March 1898, for instance, the authorities demoted Muzaffer Reşit, the Ottoman Embassy's chief physician in Rome, because he had "married an American woman" and thus had become overly exposed to foreign customs.[29]

Real conversions, however, always remained limited. In 1898 Henry Jessup, the missionary pioneer in Beirut, wrote a biography of Kamil Abdul Messiah, one of the few Arab Muslim converts, and proudly counted him among those "first-fruits of a mighty harvest to be gathered for Christ." In his monograph *Artillery of Heaven*, Ussama Makdisi likewise narrates the story of Butrus al-Bustani, another one of the few Arab converts. Bustani accepted the evangelical call despite being faced with political and local reactions to his decision. Within official ranks, Captain Mehmet received a sharper reaction to his conversion than Kamil and Bustani. Like other loyal and skilled officers, Mehmet made his way up in the imperial armed forces in early 1900. Yet during his service in the Baghdad Reserve Corps as a sergeant-major, he received a governor's note saying that his missionary "friends" and manifest "apostasy" were unacceptable. Minister of the Interior Mehmet Faik Memduh first discharged him and then ordered his relocation to his hometown of Malatya, where he later lost his mental health as well as his professional career.[30]

Authorities and local families believed that the missionaries might secretly compel their students to stop practising Islam and to eat pork – a Middle Eastern, Islamic, cultural, and ecological taboo. In fact, the president of Merzifon Anatolia College, George White, mentioned that his administration had even "assigned our Moslem students a room where they could repeat their prayers" and "made it easy for them to go to the mosque on Friday." As well, "in deference to the ruling sentiment in the country," pork "was never served on our College tables." The "government officials" and "Turkish friends" continued to fear that the college would "forbid their Mohammedan prayers" and "give their sons pork to eat, without letting them know." Although far from reality, such emotional judgments prevailed over time and affected official state views of local missionary objectives.[31]

Occasionally, spiritual matters continued to be interlinked with financial matters. In his June 1896 petition, Stephanos Azarian repeated that the missionaries were stealing members from his congregation. As the Armenian patriarch of Cilicia, he also criticized their double standards in helping the poor and needy, saying that American missionaries were "handing out American and British money *only* to Protestant Armenians." Following a discussion on this issue, the Ministers Council concluded that nonstate agents might arbitrarily "favour a group against another" and ordered state officials to take over local aid distribution.[32]

The missionaries antagonized Istanbul-based patriarchs the most. Joachim III, the ecumenical patriarch of Istanbul (1878–84 and 1901–12), observed the insistence of his non-Greek congregants on using native languages in church rites and ceremonies. This threatened the integrity of the Orthodox Church. Joachim worried that the missionaries would further fragment the church by "provoking" his young followers. Later in a 1902 petition, he claimed that American missionaries never showed respect for local traditions. He condemned the missionary colleges and printing presses in Malta and Syria. Likewise, Malachia Ormanian, the Armenian patriarch of Istanbul (1896–1908), denounced the missionary intrusion in his community. With the help of authorities, he wanted to stop American missionaries and unite the Armenian nation. Three of his loyal supporters – Zalimian, Gaspar, and Kigork – submitted a follow-up petition to the central state asking for removal of the missionaries from their neighbourhood.[33]

The Greek Istanbulites contested missionaries in the spatial and spiritual realms. In a collective 1913 petition, they complained that the Arnavutköy American College for Girls had taken over portions of the land owned by their church. Teodorakis Kalpakçıoğlu, one of the petitioners, contacted the Imperial Order and Justice Court and sued the college. On the American Board's behalf, James Barton contended that they had purchased the disputed land, not seized it. The case dragged on while the court called in several interviewees and transcripts of land surveys. Central authorities meanwhile removed themselves from the case altogether, focusing instead on other issues virtually more urgent than this municipal case.[34]

More than central authorities, provincial governors had high stakes in local matters and thus deeply committed themselves to reporting all types of cases to the centre. In a salient example, the governors of Diyarbakır and Mersin revealed that the professors of the American Protestant Girls' College, including US citizens and a local faculty member named Metini, had "brainwashed" and "converted" some Muslim and Nestorian students. They had even "compelled" several Nestorians to migrate to the United States. The situation seemed comparable to the situation in other provinces. In his later report of sedition, the governor of Bursa recorded an incident that took place in the American Girls' College in northwest Anatolia. One day when Muslim students were reciting the Quran, the principal came in, "snatched" their holy book, and "forced" them to read the Bible instead. Although lacking evidence, such cases sent ripples of shock through the central state and caused the authorities to grow increasingly sensitive to the potential dangers of anti-Islamic propaganda.[35]

IMPERIAL PERSPECTIVES AND LOCAL STORIES

The late Ottoman context offers a lens through which to look at changes in the inner dynamics of the government and how these changes affected authorities at the central and local levels. In the decades before 1880, a two-tiered administrative system ran the imperial government. The primary tier administered standard matters, such as conscription and taxation, and imposed strict adhesion to the laws and edicts transmitted from the capital to the provinces. The secondary tier oversaw nonstandard affairs, like construction and jurisdiction, and delegated responsibilities to provincial officials. Most incidents thus reflected the mentality and conduct of these officials. Eastern Anatolia's governors suppressed the missionaries as troublemakers, and the patriarchs considered them to be a public threat.[36]

After 1880 the missionary problem was expelled from the secondary tier. Against the rise of public disorder, the bureaucrats in Istanbul recognized the gravity of the concerns about American missionaries and moved them into the primary tier, wherein their operations became a stock subject. Meanwhile, the bureaucrats also stripped local officials of discretionary power. This structural shift of the centre's position from passive to proactive reflected and shaped imperial missionary policies in the coming decades.[37]

As a critical state matter, the missionary threat synchronized imperial interests with local concerns. Linking public disorder with missionary work, provincial authorities expected state support for their anti-missionary cause. But until the late nineteenth century, their pleas failed to sway imperial decisions in their favour. Central authorities in Istanbul tended to uphold an intermediary role, wishfully hoping that social cohabitation would withstand religious hostilities. They avoided interference in December 1849 when angry mobs burned the American Board's Ahur Seminary in north-central Anatolia and blamed local officials for allowing it to happen. Allegedly, they could have averted it but did not. Minister of Foreign Affairs Mehmet Emin Ali also recognized the suffering missionaries as a legal party – with "rights to life and security" – and suggested that the Ottoman government compensate them and admonish the agents who had failed to execute vigilance.[38]

The imperial call for general order reverberated in the provinces. An 1854 directive instructed local officials to temper civil tensions and protect the missionaries "by any means necessary" – even though these same officials had previously reported that the missionaries had "provoked" the people "in the first place," who had "then retaliated" by harassing the "instigators." Clearly, central authorities had prioritized the safety of missionaries across the board.[39]

Where local agents maintained belligerence toward the missionaries, their parochial prism of anathema served their sense of exoneration, a sort of self-acquittal that caused them to incriminate foreigners in local disorder. In one database regarding local tensions, for instance, fifty-two anti-missionary reports were submitted by prominent agents such as Aleppo's chief of police and the governors of Aydın, Bursa, Edirne, Salonika, Syria, and Trabzon. These reports, while informing the socio-legal status of American missionaries, included personal commentaries on the missionaries' objectives – their "hidden agenda" that aggravated public disorder.[40]

Besides channelling a hefty dose of anxiety, local reports generated their own momentum. Some officials defended the anti-missionary backlash even in violent incidents where the missionaries had faced lynching. They implied the missionaries had deserved this punishment, further speculating that their activities had instigated these incidents. Although the rationale behind such convictions remains unclear, the agents evidently elicited imperial sympathy by ducking their share of responsibility and blaming the missionaries for local tensions. Whereas American newspapers blamed the double-faced Ottoman authorities, provincial officials blamed American missionaries for exciting anarchy under the pretense of philanthropy. By inciting reactionary sentiments, then, both claimants sought to convert their respective governments into a corrective political weapon.[41]

Where the existing laws were failing to obviate the complex situation, imperial ministers superseded their intermediary role by taking a more proactive position. They combined attention to the public order and devotion to justice standards by generating rigid instructions. However, these instructions did not satisfy the governors, missionaries, or any other parties concerned. In October 1890, when American Board students scheduled an epic drama in the Selamsız neighbourhood of Istanbul, the municipal administration urged that the performance be banned. In response, however, Minister of the Interior Ahmet Münir studied the script of the play and declined the request. He authorized the event because it fostered educational awareness, not seditious sentiments. His successor, Halil Rıfat, also discredited the local caveat filed against several missionary preachers, such as Kazaros and Parsih, who were "scouting" for followers in east Anatolia. On various other occasions, the incoming petitions presented "no evidence" with which to substantiate the missionaries' "malicious intentions." Given that theatre plays and itinerant preaching did not satisfy Istanbul's demand for hard evidence, imperial authorities continued to refute specific claims and to defend the missionaries' endeavours.[42]

In principle, individuals remained "innocent until proven otherwise." Münir thought so in December 1890 when the governor of Sivas, Giritli Sırrı, called several Armenians "agents provocateurs." At that time, his province had 1 million residents, including visible Greek and Armenian minorities who made up 12 per cent of the population. The governor worried that revolutionary ideas would exacerbate ethnoreligious tensions, but he still needed proof if the persons he had blacklisted were to be punished. Indeed, he presented no evidence against many of these individuals except for Abkarian, who was an Armenian physician and US-turned convert to Protestantism. When "exhorting" the Armenian nation to liberate themselves one day, Abkarian saw the spying officers and rushed to the US Consulate for refuge. In response, Münir expatriated him from Sivas and rejected the consul's objection. He also warned the consul not to interfere in such "domestic affairs."[43]

Local qualms and partial reports reached the central state, but they hardly solicited the centre's sympathy. A case in point was the story of the Şişmanyan house. As a US-turned convert to Protestantism and Armenian resident of Istanbul, Gabriel Gregory Şişmanyan had rented the missionaries his home in the Kumkapı quarter. Municipal officials suspected that his property would not remain residential. In January 1891 they claimed that the rental agreement served a "clandestine proselytization agenda" and argued that the missionaries would use the property to "convert" neighbourhood children. This sinister act of converting juveniles drew attention from imperial authorities. Staff of the Ministry of the Interior discussed the possibility of punishing the landlord and the tenants. Based on the underdocumented report, Münir ordered that the case be furnished with evidence.[44]

Further correspondence shows no reaction other than a sound instruction "not to shut down" Şişmanyan's house and to have "the US Embassy register it" as a school. Local officials continued to monitor such in-house missions, and imperial authorities put them on the state's radar while maintaining their legal status. In the case of Şişmanyan's house, the month-long inspections did not find "any provocative elements" in the books found in the house and the Ministers Council recognized it as a nonprofit institution in 1891.

The authorities thus modulated municipal injunctions brought against missionaries by issuing an executive order.[45]

Similar cases required different methods in the countryside. As far as rural subjects were concerned, Ottoman ministers showed little or no tolerance of missionary activities and public disorder. For instance, they accepted the claims made by the governor of Mosul in his 1896 petition, which noted that the new "unlicensed" college "inculcates heresy, treason, and sedition" in the nearby villages. The authorities ordered the deportation of the missionary faculty, who had been found guilty on these grounds. The Ministers Council also expedited an edict to restore order as deemed necessary when local turmoil erupted in several towns of Aleppo. The central state rapidly interfered in this state of emergency for the sake of restoring law and order, but the ensuing legal procedures dragged on for several years.[46]

Where interfaith relations deteriorated after the 1880s, peaceful interactions between officials and missionaries became tentative. Backed by civilian petitions, some officials scapegoated American missionaries as the first cause behind what was going wrong, and all the while the missionaries were suffering both personally and financially. Istanbul was swarmed with alarming reports around this time. The Greek residents in Izmir stoned American Board institutions, bandits robbed two of the board's students near Adana, angry mobs burned the missionary school in Elazığ, and gangs attacked missionaries during public anarchy in Malatya. In the Malatya incident, local gangs publicly assaulted the missionaries and burned down a house with one missionary occupant inside. Essentially, these incidents were related to local massacres and inflicted substantial damage on the missionaries as well as the minorities. Amid the Adana massacre in May 1908, for instance, five preachers were murdered – all of whom had been American Board "college and seminary graduates."[47]

Kabadaian, a local faculty member at the Collegiate Institute in Izmir, mentioned various incidents to show that the Ottoman government was turning against the Armenians. To halt organized oppression at their hands, he told his Armenian students to unite and fight. International agents were expected to support such a noble cause given that Western newspapers were already predicting that the frustrated US government would soon dispatch battleships to the Mediterranean. On the contrary, however, imperial authorities linked the collapsing order with two paradoxical realities. While the anti-missionary hatred was fuelling violent reactions to the missionaries, the anti-Ottoman insurrection was fuelling violent rebellions against the authorities.[48]

The loyalist Armenian patriarch Matheus feared that local conflicts would agitate and splinter his younger followers. He hoped that the central state could abate missionary involvement in public upheavals. In response, the Ministers Council exerted vigilant control over religious interactions as well as urging local agents to protect the missionaries against hate crimes. In Adana, Harput, Sivas, and other troubled areas, the ministers also charged some agents with the task of "relocating" foreigners from the countryside to town centres for safety purposes.[49]

In urgent cases, however, imperial policies still respected regional practices. In Kayseri in May 1907, the chief of police, Mahmut Ali, stormed into a female missionary residence and grabbed six girls attending the sermon in session. Despite resistance, his men hauled the girls back to their families. Governor Sabvar Bey said that, "albeit unnecessary," the officers "expropriated the house, which had served as a mission school preaching to the children." He added that the missionaries were constantly fanning "the flames of turbulence," already evident between the Armenian, Greek, and Muslim communities. The governor thus warranted the officers' arbitrary action. Strikingly, provincial officials had violated the legal procedures by not reporting an illicit activity and by conducting a security operation without prior notice. Mustafa Haşim and Mehmet Faik Memduh, the education and interior ministers, approved of their misconduct and did not reverse the expropriation. They also agreed that this was a case of an emergency – noting that the in-house presence had threatened the life of children. The imperial centre thus tacitly approved of a specific operation because the officials had risked overstepping their authority for the sake of protecting the state's interests.[50]

Unlike the hyper-vigilant officials in Kayseri, passive officials drew critical attention from the central state. Central authorities took it seriously when public petitions denounced local agents as "unqualified" and demanded that they be dismissed. They certainly found Haydar Efendi to be incompetent in governing the ethnically diverse city of Harput in east Anatolia. The Muslim residents accused Governor Haydar of failing to monitor the Armenian insurgents and the American Board's Palu district school. In April 1899 the Ministers Council replaced him with Mazhar Efendi, a former Court of Appeals bureaucrat who had special experience with missionary institutions.

The council fired the governor of Haçin for similar reasons. To the public's dismay, he had betrayed the state by "conspiring" with and allegedly accepting "bribes" from the missionaries who had paid him to establish a neighbourhood school. These cases obscured potential scores that the petitioners had to settle with their governors, yet public complaints help to explain why the authorities in Istanbul hired specific officials to get the job done while firing others who failed to do so.[51]

Hate crimes did not spare missionaries in western provinces. In Tirana, Albania, in April 1899, the residents attacked Charles Erickson and burned his property upon learning his plans to build a missionary college in the neighbourhood. In response, the authorities in Istanbul ordered the relocation of the missionary family from Tirana to Durres in the south. The Ericksons were kept there even though they wished to return to Tirana due to the poor health of family members. Although imperial authorities aimed to avert further tension in this case, they repeated to US diplomats the local narrative that implicated Erickson in the agitation of conservative Muslims.[52]

Local surveys and petitions generally described missionaries through a reflexive prism and exaggerated their impact on the minorities. They nevertheless fed the imperial database with regular updates coming in from all directions, especially from Aleppo, Beirut, Harput, Ioannina, and Kayseri. These updates suggested that the missionaries were turning the youth against the state. The anticipated state responses were deportment, punishment, and admonishment of the missionaries. Instead, imperial authorities viewed this slough of information from their own perspective and produced mixed reactions that at times conflicted with provincial hyperbolism.[53]

The ambivalent authorities remained alert and proactive in cases that aligned evangelical propaganda with slander and conversion. In Bitola, Macedonia, the missionaries told the residents that the "Rumelian Reforms," which were libertarian laws proclaimed in June 1896, would not "come to their town." Regarding this quasi-slanderous argument, the Ministers Council reminded local agents of their task to ward off such propaganda because it would confuse people and plunge them into chaos.[54]

The governor of Bitola, Hafızi Efendi, examined the situation and noted that American missionaries had recently founded a school "with legal authorization" and started offering an "elementary and college-level education." They accepted "no Muslim students" but enrolled

Bulgarians, Greeks, and Gypsies. There was an issue, however, with the older Protestant college. Reportedly, its faculty members were openly criticizing the Ottoman government in their "lectures." The professors also had designated a boarding house despite a legal warning against it. The governor thus "notified the consulate officials," requesting that they "enjoin missionaries to observe the laws of the land." Although US diplomats had "not yet acted on that matter," the case revealed that central authorities were still failing to forestall illegal and radical acts in western and eastern provinces.[55]

Missionaries inspired the inhabitants of Ioannina, Greece, in some indirect ways. In a March 1907 report, Governor Seyfullah Efendi stated that his coast was clear; American missionaries did not own "unlicensed" institutions and the Italian-operated "primary school enrolled only Italian-speaking children," "not a single Muslim student." Yet the winds of change swept his province three years later when the "attitudes and actions" of Turkish and Greek residents shifted to open hostility. Although the American Board still ran no schools and posed no imminent danger, some local "people started to commit *pious fraud*," with the board's "students" helping them "poison the public mind." Additionally, missionary "books and pamphlets exposed residents to revolutionary ideas" at a time when the Greeks, who "had escaped from Ioannina to foreign countries," promoted separatist ideas in the region. The governor reported that the Greeks had "changed [their] loyalty from the eternal state to the Megali Idea," rallying behind irredentist nationalism for a Greater Greece. The police had already identified "houses in possession of anti-state literature," and the court had "sentenced the owners of [those] homes to two or three years in prison." They also "located and interrogated" the people "who gave provocative speeches" in public areas such as "coffeehouses and meeting places" with a view to removing general "interest in the books and documents of a 'seditious' nature."[56]

As a corollary to the public security debate between Istanbul and Ioannina, the case of Muhammad Dari demonstrated a nuanced preferential treatment of the missionary audience. In 1907 a governorate telegram surprised Istanbul with the news that Dari, a respected "teacher and imam" in Ioannina, had recently joined the "band of dissidents" after years of his service to the Muslim community. In defiance of his noble profession, he had turned into "a corrupt traitor," condemned the Ottoman state as unjust and urged the community to protest state authorities. Central authorities intended to halt the anti-state frenzy and urged the officers to interrogate all "Muslim and Christian dissidents" in a May 1907 decree. Strikingly, the decree ordered them to "take no action against Dari" with "due respect to his position." Thus cases of slander and propaganda alarmed the central state, but the public standing of individuals involved in these cases also mattered. The decree took the occasion to motivate state teachers to "raise the ethical values of their students and restore faith and loyalty to the state."[57]

In dual efforts to restore state power and public order, imperial authorities called on the missionaries and governors. Specific directives ordered American missionaries to refuse "children of the parents blacklisted by the state" and required provincial governors to "monitor public order and record the Muslim presence" in foreign schools. In a later case dated September 1915, the American University of Beirut expelled its student Dimitri because the authorities said he was a "Russian spy." Meanwhile, the governor of Izmir, Faik Efendi, reported that he had told the Muslim parents of eight students at the missionary college to "break off relations with the missionaries."[58]

From 1880 into the 1910s, numerous cases demonstrated that the Ottoman state was transitioning into a cautious reactionary mode of operation. Earlier in 1873, when the American University of Beirut solicited their support for an art exhibition on college premises, central authorities had denied the dean's request in a kind and sympathetic fashion. Reflective of later skepticism, however, their successors rejected an 1887 Mormon petition for ordinary travel permits. In a negative manner, the authorities declared that since "this congregation is unknown" to them, its "literature has to be inspected" before the arrival of its members. By then, the anti-missionary consensus already dominated the imperial centre; thus, not surprisingly, on 28 December 1916 an executive order urged American missionaries to leave the country with no intention to come back.[59]

CONCLUSION

Ottoman ministers knew that US authorities and newspapers stigmatized them as "atrocious" and "double-faced" characters. They observed that American missionaries were responsible for the imperial government's notorious image in the United States. Imperial ambassadors reported on "what manner of evil" the missionaries' "malicious work" was "capable of" in the Ottoman Empire and abroad. "No doubt," the Islamist authors likewise noted, the final objective of "the united forces of the missionary high command" was "the destruction of [Islamic] religion and morals." In agreement, early patriarchs and provincial governors described the missionaries as instigators of local tensions.[60]

Imperial authorities took a nuanced position toward the missionary problem at a time when substantial accounts manifested the rise of mixed public sentiments. They still abstained from enacting anti-missionary policies and launched a counterpropaganda campaign instead. In May 1892 Sultan Abdulhamid II discussed the socio-diplomatic implications of missionary activities. Aware of the problem, he allied with the ministers on this matter. "Firm measures" would not rid the state of American missionaries so "the only way to fight them is to increase the Islamic population and spread the belief in the Holiest of Faiths."[61]

The perspectives of Ottoman and American parties were nurtured by emotions more than by realities. They selected, segmented, and structured their respective views and thus created two competing narratives on Ottoman-missionary encounters. Even the idea of "manifest destiny," which prophesied US world supremacy, clashed with its older Ottoman cousin's enduring conviction that Islam would eventually triumph over other faiths.

While learning about unrecorded missions in the distant "odd corners" of their realm, Ottoman authorities redefined state sensibilities using old and novel tactics with a view to restoring state power. To their credit, the imperial edifice remained complex and principled in its own way. Post-1880 perspectives nevertheless registered a change in policy from limited tolerance to containment. Any variations in state rhetoric and practice owed their origins to the shared concerns of the centre and the provinces and to the relative strengths of local stakeholders; indeed, imperial-provincial dialectics affected the ways that the Ottoman government handled religious contacts and conflicts.[62]

3

Crime and Order

The story of Ellen Stone captures a momentous episode of missionary encounters. She was born into a New England elite family and educated at the Chelsea Grammar and High School. She taught in her alma mater and wrote spiritual editorials until thirty-two years of age. Then, at the First Congregational Church in 1878, she accepted a "special call" to enlighten the less fortunate people and sailed to southeast Europe for the task. Her service proved a success. She spearheaded a women's Bible group, established a Sunday school, led church prayers, and performed other duties for the children and mothers of her boarding school. But a horrible intervention brought these missions to an abrupt halt.[1]

Ellen Stone and the Bible women had just completed a three-week study at the Raslog Evangelical Church. On 3 September 1901, when returning to the central mission town of Cuma Bala, an armed gang of twenty bandits ambushed them and kidnapped Stone along with her companion Katerina Tsilka. As members of the financially strained guerilla movement of the Internal Macedonian Revolutionary Organization, which was struggling to liberate Adrianople and Macedonia from Ottoman control, the bandits demanded $110,000 for the captives' release, unknowingly sparking America's first modern hostage crisis.[2]

Ellen Stone's kidnapping appalled Christian America. Across the nation, newspapers told about her being "in the hands of lawless Turks." The headlines described "why" everybody had to worry about her. Some journalists invoked support for the blessed nation by noting that the Russians were also "co-operating" and "doing everything in their power to effect the woman's release." For doomsayers, the Miss

EXTRA
THE WORLD'S BEST SEPTEMBER
2,312¼
cols. of advertising printed in The World during September. Gain, over the same month of last year. 171½

The World. EVENING EDITION

NIGHT EDITION.
THE WORLD'S BEST SEPTEMBER
93,253
advertisements printed in The World during September. Gain, 9,336

"Circulation Books Open to All."

PRICE ONE CENT. NEW YORK, MONDAY, OCTOBER 7, 1901. PRICE ONE CENT.

ROOSEVELT HOPES TO GET RESPITE FOR MISS STONE, BRIGANDS' CAPTIVE.

MERCHANT SUSPECTED IN THE BOY MURDER CASE.

Police Say They May Have to Arrest the Reputed Father of the Dead Negro Lad.

Missing Young Colored Man Is Also Wanted —Parents and Another Prisoner Held in Court.

BOURKE COCKRAN TO SPEAK FOR GREATER N. Y. DEMOCRACY

W. Bourke Cockran will address the meeting to be held by the Greater New York Democracy at Cooper Union next Monday night.

There has been some doubt as to whether Mr. Cockran would speak during the coming campaign, but it is officially announced that he will speak at several meetings for his organization.

TWO MEN CHARGED WITH ABDUCTION.

ALLEGED SILK FRAUD CASE DISMISSED.

LATE RESULTS AT HARLEM.

AT ST. LOUIS.

President in Close Touch with State Department, Which Has Indirect Communication with Bandits and Is Working to Have Time for Payment of Ransom Extended.

FLOOD OF LETTERS SENT TO PRESIDENT ROOSEVELT.

MONEY COMING IN STEADILY TO MAKE UP THE RANSOM.

MARRIED, HE WOOED MANY

Startling Charge Made by Wife Against William Parkins of Newark.

MAD PET DOG CAUSES PANIC

Attacks Its Mistress, Then Rushes in Among Crowd of School Children.

MINISTER DROPS DEAD.

Rev. R. Arundel Simpson Succumbs in Brooklyn Street.

LIPTON WANTS ANOTHER RACE

Says Shamrock Is Better Boat and Columbia Was Lucky in Winning.

LOSES HIS FIGHT FOR $2,000,000

GIRL IN TOMBS FOR NO REASON

LONDON PRESS AIMS AT FENIANS

TEACHES BOYS TO STEAL.

FILIPINO MAJOR CAUGHT.

COMING WITH THE TREATY.

BRIDGE OFFICIALS MAY BE INDICTED.

WEATHER FORECAST.

3.1 Citizen letters imploring officials to save Ellen Stone.

Stone Affair could possibly turn "all of Uncle Sam's wrath upon Turkey." If anything happened to her, the US government would "not hesitate to bring a fleet through the Dardanelles." This was a threat based on reality. Five battleships – the USS *Albany*, *Buffalo*, *Chicago*, *Dixie*, and *Nashville* – were cruising nearby and could be "assembled at very short notice."[3]

For officials and relatives, the Miss Stone Affair demanded a temperate and realistic solution, not outright muscle flexing. President

Theodore Roosevelt had been sworn into office on 14 September 1901, about a week after the victim had fallen into the hands of terrorists. Concerned letters from the public flooded his office immediately, helping him to prioritize the national *cause célèbre* and sympathize with it. He instructed Secretary of State John Hay to "spare no efforts" on the affair and discussed the safety of the hostage with Charles Dickinson, the diplomatic agent stationed in Istanbul.[4]

Neither Ellen Stone's extended family nor her missionary organization could afford to pay the ransom that the kidnappers had demanded. To cover the exorbitant sum, they opened the national Great Ransom Fund in collaboration with New England church circles and journalists. The fund did not reach the $110,000 mark, but remarkably it raised $17,808 in the first month. President Roosevelt meanwhile urged any capable agents to bargain with the bandits. Although negotiations to bring the hostage home were started in haste, it took months of effort and rounds of discussion to reach an agreement. On 23 February 1903 the bandits accepted a bottom-line offer of $72,500 and released the fifty-six-year-old Stone. Back home, a Christian nation sighed with relief at the news of her release. The bandits also released her companion, Katerina Tsilka, who had birthed a baby while in the custody of the bandits. To the faithful nation, that little, healthy cherub personified a divine blessing, a kind of miraculous gift bestowed by God after times of great testing.[5]

The story of Ellen Stone described the state of local anarchy to the world. Leaving the Ottoman Empire exposed and vulnerable, it undermined the reputation and credibility of the imperial state. The authorities in Istanbul also found themselves embroiled in a crisis-resolution dispute with a US government that had reiterated its legal obligation to "render full justice" to US citizens. They argued that any commitments invoked by their existing treaties with the United States applied only to US diplomats and merchants, not the missionaries. For imperial ministers, the extension of legal status to American missionary citizens would have entailed repercussions and greater pressures from the US government. The ministers thus denied criticisms of how poorly they were handling hostage takings in general and claimed not to be liable for the recent Miss Stone Affair. The seasoned grand vizier Mehmet Sait likewise rejected "foreign influence" in official and personal affairs. In a January 1902 memorandum, he sifted through the existing intelligence information and declared that "our side, *viz.*, the government" maintained its position of "nonresponsibility" for "that woman."[6]

Despite the political manoeuvring, Sait had an inner sense of responsibility concerning Ellen Stone. Based on a discussion with the sultan and ministers, he dedicated state resources to saving her. The Ottoman government thus established a special committee to instruct on-site agents and to handle the situation. Through a specific decree, Sultan Abdulhamid II also planned on "evacuating nearby villages" and mobilizing "the 3rd Cavalry Regiment" to corner bandits and rescue Ellen Stone farther south in Strymoniko. But US authorities demanded that imperial forces be withdrawn, predicting that military moves would cause more harm than good by propelling the bandits into panic. Imperial authorities then cancelled the scheduled operation. So why did their actions contradict their outlook?[7]

Triumphant views of history tend to champion the winners and discredit the failing tactics. In evangelical Christian historiography, such a view remains ubiquitous. It seldom pays attention to Ottoman efforts to protect and safeguard the missionaries. In his classic *American Interests and Policies in the Middle East*, for instance, John DeNovo calls the Miss Stone Affair a "notorious outrage against the missionaries." This narrative, while presenting all American essentials, obscures the host state's reactions. A focus on the negligence of the Ottoman government is consistent with the general propensity to overlook any other narratives, thus attributing to imperial authorities less credit than they actually deserved. The literature has not addressed how these authorities perceived and affected the safety of missionaries. This is a complex question worth exploring also because it reveals much about religious crimes, public tensions, and state reactions at a critical time and place.[8]

The Ministry of Public Security was the primary department responsible for processing every type of criminal case. Indeed, the rising demand for public security endowed the ministry with provisions and new funds, such as the Military Forces Law and Reform Commission Act of 1869–79, and turned its Istanbul headquarters into an ambitious powerhouse in the mid-nineteenth century. The ministers of public security – in order of succession, Hafız Mehmet, Kamil Pasha, Hüseyin Nazım, and Şefik Pasha – were "the most trusted" veteran bureaucrats. For instance, Hafız Mehmet and Şefik Pasha assumed their posts after long-time service respectively as the aide-de-camp to the sultan and the chief magistrate to the Court of Appeals. Including police and gendarmerie forces, the ministry's provincial agents conducted strategic operations and took charge of guarding American missionaries.[9]

Regarding the imperial security establishment, Ferdan Ergut explains that the development of public order as an official concept "initiated the centralization of the police." The Ottoman Empire "subsumed" specific "crime fighting" policies "within a wide concern for administration" and for "the good order of society." Moreover, imperial authorities modified their justice politics in response to diplomatic, religious, regional, and personal sensibilities. Broadly, the late state rhetoric of crime and order reflected the sum of three vital goals: to actualize the eternal state, to restore political trust, and to foster greater public good. A salient feature of this rhetoric was the aim to exclude American missionaries from the diplomatic purview and handle them as an object of public security. Although the post-1890 public disorder invoked serious efforts to protect the missionaries and curtail their operations, the central state also sought to satisfy the United States as a strategic ally. Not coincidentally, the integration of missionary cases into the body of public crimes became consequential for all the parties involved. Imperial sensibilities, then, dictated the application of three related doctrines "by any means" necessary: upholding state laws, guarding the missionaries, and eliminating foreign influences. These tenets are key to understanding how the imperial regime confronted challengers, including its local agents who abused power or failed to execute the instructions transmitted by central authorities in Istanbul.[10]

DIPLOMATIC TREATIES AND THE RIGHTS OF MISSIONARIES

During the Miss Stone Affair, the Ottoman government refused to claim any responsibility. Minister of Foreign Affairs Ahmet Tevfik had expressed this position earlier during the "disturbances" of 1894–96. After the burning of several missionary buildings in Anatolia in February 1896, he told US diplomats that his government was working diligently "for the protection of the properties and the lives of the Americans." But the Ottomans were not "in any way bound to make good the losses suffered," and thus there shall "not be any question of the payment of an indemnity for the damage at stake." As the missions continued to suffer in such incidents, Ottoman and US authorities turned to bilateral agreements and discussed how they would move forward. Although Ottoman authorities desired to cope with missionary-related incidents in a unilateral fashion, their perspective was not isolated from their larger position in US relations. Their choices were limited and connected to social and economic circumstances.[11]

Social and economic circumstances circumscribed the relations between the Ottoman Empire and the United States. Whereas imperial officials emphasized commercial prospects, US officials addressed the status of missionaries and minorities. Strikingly, the conflicting nature of their respective positions extended bilateral interactions rather than collapsing them.[12]

Viewed from Washington, the Ottoman world presented prospects and challenges at the same time. In an early example, Henry Clay, who was the Kentucky senator and the secretary of state, worried about the Greeks fighting the War of Independence of 1821–32 against the Turks. He bemoaned how the lucrative Mediterranean markets were blinding Americans to the great tragedy happening in the region. In a January 1824 jeremiad to the House of Representatives, he labelled the "suffering" of the Greek nation as "the oppression of a people endeared to us" by the cruel Turkish rulers in "this remote quarter of the world."[13]

Henry Clay pleaded for the mercy of the American nation, including the mercy of those profit-minded businessmen from Boston. "A wretched invoice of figs and opium" was "spread before us," supposing that it would "repress our sensibilities and eradicate our humanity." "Ah! Sir," he said, "what shall it profit a man if he gain the whole world and lose his own soul?" He turned the comparison of Turkish goods and Greek freedoms into a moral question: "What shall it avail a nation to save the whole of a miserable trade, and lose its liberties?"[14]

Financial considerations postponed other concerns when US officials were demanding an Ottoman alliance to secure the transatlantic trade. Since the American Revolution of 1765–83, Muslim pirates and privateers had been attacking American ships navigating through the Mediterranean, whose south seas were under Ottoman control. Sailing from naval bases in Algeria, Morocco, and Tunisia, the corsairs captured American merchants, vessels, and cargoes. The indecisive five-year-long Barbary Wars eventually convinced US officials to settle the matter in the imperial capital.[15]

David Offley and two other functionaries came to Istanbul to cut a deal. The US government presumed that an imperial order could stop the pirate attacks on US vessels. The Commerce and Navigation Treaty, drafted by the bureaucrats and signed by Sultan Mahmud II, went into effect in May 1830. It recognized the United States as the "most-favored nation" and granted its citizens entitlement to "capitulations" – those rights and privileges "observed toward other" Europeans in the Ottoman realm.[16]

Given that the French forces invaded Algeria and ended the pirate attacks around the same time, Ottoman authorities expedited US transactions by releasing trade permits and giving direct access to warehouses in port cities such as Izmir. They also established the Tariff Commission and lowered the duties imposed on US-bound exports, imports, and inland transits. To their benefit, American architect, engineer, and shipbuilder Henry Eckford came to help rebuild the imperial fleet destroyed off the coast of the Peloponnese in the 1827 naval battle of Navarino. In company with New England businessmen, Ottoman farmers and brokers began to thrive on trading opium, figs, and raisins in exchange for American rum and colonial products. As indicated in imperial and consular reports, the two-way traffic exponentially increased until the early twentieth century and registered the only favourable trade balance of the Ottoman Empire. In detail, the 1900 statistics noted the record-high value of $16,075,756 on an export-to-import ratio of 1.07. For the financially bankrupt Ottoman government, which had accepted European control over its central treasury since the 1870s, such numbers had become remarkably significant.[17]

Article 4 of the existing treaty became an item of contention as social affairs took precedence. It stipulated that an American interpreter "be present" in case "litigations and disputes should arise." Without an interpreter, the concerned "parties shall not be heard, nor shall judgment be pronounced." But substantial cases, "in which the sum may exceed 500 piasters," would "be submitted to the Sublime Porte" and "be decided according to equity and justice." State authorities would always avoid "harassing foreign citizens" if they were "quietly pursuing their commerce" and had not been "charged or convicted of any crime." Strikingly, "when they may have committed some offence," the authorities shall "not arrest" foreigners and "not put [them] in prison." The suspects had to "be tried by their Minister of Consul and punished according to their offence." In this respect, whereas Ottoman authorities relinquished their right to detain US citizens even when they were found guilty, US authorities acquired the right to engage with the legal cases of their citizens and resolve them by applying the European codes, cited in the English Convention of 1838.[18]

Although the Commerce and Navigation Treaty stood until 1923, the involved parties adopted additional provisions. The 1862 and 1874 amendments guaranteed that US citizens could "purchase [property] at all places in the Ottoman Empire." The Ottoman government would "render full justice" to them "for all losses and injuries which they may duly prove themselves to have suffered thereby." The 1874 clauses likewise implemented preventive measures, noting that criminals – those "fugitives from justice" and others who had been "convicted" or "charged with crimes" – would be delivered to the appropriate authorities.[19]

Taken superficially, these terms and conditions may lead to an attempt to quantify the loyalty or disloyalty of Ottoman authorities to the powers engaged in treating the life and property of US citizens as "inviolable." However, the authorities reserved the right to bypass arrangements in worst-case scenarios. In cases of "murder" and "armed rebellion," they could legally break into the private property owned by US citizens. Indeed, some security operations took place on foreign property. Regardless of the nature and scene of the crime, the 1874 clauses sanctioned such operations by trivializing the questions of "whether the crime was committed by a foreigner" and "whether it took place in the residence of a foreigner." Viewed from Istanbul, the Ottoman government "exercised" security measures "freely" and "without reserve."[20]

The treaties paid lip service to US citizens by leaving them in a legally vulnerable position. In and of itself, the 1830 treaty anticipated that "differences of opinion as to the true meaning of [its] certain portions" existed and continued to be "the subject of diplomatic correspondence without reaching an accord." In fact, most legal cases ended up in Ottoman courts, not the US Consulate, because their aggregate value exceeded 500 piasters. The contrast between the rights on paper and the rights in effect, then, represented more than mere differences of opinion, amounting to a legal battle over the treaty conditions and the implications of specific terms. As Ottoman authorities defined criminal cases as domestic affairs, they denied legal liabilities that they would otherwise have to admit based on the existing agreements. The loopholes enabled them to "evade fulfillment of legitimate requirements of burden of proof." By playing on these loopholes, they resorted to a strategy of "plausible deniability," which they applied in the Miss Stone Affair and other little-known cases.[21]

American missionaries claimed that the existing treaties entitled them to certain rights and privileges. Henry Dwight, a missionary and author in Istanbul with the American Board of Commissioners for Foreign Missions, discussed the crucial times between 1876 and 1902, noting that the Ottoman government "appears to deny the existence of any such rights." In his 1893 pamphlet *Treaty Rights of the American Missionaries in Turkey*, he surveyed the past capitulations and concluded that "ancient principles of Turkish law and usage" had "authorized" the missionaries' rights, including "their privilege of worship, their schools and their publication department." He argued that "the Treaty of 1830, and that of 1862 while it was in force, merely consecrated as the treaty rights of Americans, privileges already existing everywhere in Turkey." While respecting the Ottoman authorities' "claim to regulate the use of Treaty rights," he reminded them that "the means for doing this is the same as the means of modifying … any privilege conferred by the treaties." Whereas the authorities justified their position with references to the loopholes and domestic troubles, missionaries like Dwight challenged their position by stressing that only a "mutual agreement between the Powers concerned" would legitimize the design of imperial regulations concerning American citizens.[22]

Henry Dwight wrote to US officials and asked that evangelical investments be protected "against arbitrary action designed to destroy, under guise of regulation." The Ottomans were violating the existing treaties by not recognizing their legal status and failing to safeguard the missionaries trapped in local anarchy. Several decades later, the historian Leland Gordon likewise explained that the Ottoman government had "denied that the treaty granted such privileges" to the missionaries. The denial of protection to them manifested "evidence of bad faith" on the part of Istanbul.[23]

Although Ottoman officials had purposely removed missionary-related incidents from the diplomatic agenda, their political manoeuvre did not stem from "bad faith" but hinged on the historical precedent of capitulations as a state policy. Back in 1830, Sultan Mahmud II had signed the US treaty in the unilateral fashion of capitulations, granting rights and privileges to the United States as well as France,

Britain, and other European nations. As grantor, the Ottoman government held the upper hand in modifying the existing agreements. The ongoing debates over terms and conditions – including the rights of US citizens to protection and representation as cited in article 4 – reflected essentially conflicting sensibilities in Istanbul and Washington. The Istanbul authorities called the United States a "most-favored nation" and regarded Ottoman-US rapprochement as a strategic partnership. On the other side, the Washington authorities took a more literal view and considered their agreements to be binding in all matters.[24]

Alexander Mavroyeni, the Ottoman ambassador to Washington, advised his government not to extend rights and privileges to missionaries who sought assistance from the US government. From the viewpoint of Istanbul, however, the missionary problem proved more complex than a capitulatory matter. The United States had emerged as a commercial partner and a potential ally to help offset the European colonial intrusions in North Africa and the Middle East. Therefore, imperial authorities feared that issues with American citizen-missionaries might sever relations with the United States. They respected the ambassador's judgment and remained occupied with the safety of missionaries without making legal commitments to do so.[25]

Minister of Foreign Affairs Ahmet Tevfik reiterated the government's determination to protect foreigners in times of peace and trouble. In this respect, he sought to appease US officials in his February 1896 address, reporting that "thanks to the steps taken" in Istanbul, "a perfect tranquility prevails in all the Asiatic provinces of the Empire." He also assured the US minister to Istanbul, Alexander Terrell, that "there is no room for any uneasiness" regarding "the security of the said religious men," the missionaries. Government authorities had already reached the critical security areas where local tensions were placing foreigners on a course fraught with serious risk and danger – especially the provinces of Bitlis, Harput, Erzurum, Sivas, and Diyarbakır. They instructed local agents to "watch with the greatest vigilance over the protection of the property and the lives of the American missionaries."[26]

While urging the protection of foreigners, however, Ottoman authorities discounted and concealed the extent of the post-1894 rebellions and massacres. Tevfik certainly contradicted his rosy depiction of perfect tranquility in Anatolia. In a follow-up address two days later, he discussed "the losses occasioned to the property belonging to the American citizens" during "the last disturbances." "Imperial troops" and "authorities" had "displayed all their efforts for the protection of the properties and the lives of the Americans." In fact, the sheer presence of imperial troops in Harput and Maraş defied the peaceful context he had previously portrayed. Beyond the centre's efforts, Tevfik noted that the Ottoman government, "not being in any way bound to make good the losses suffered," would not address "any question of the payment of an indemnity for the damage at stake."[27]

Official statements did not disclose what the authorities really thought of American missionaries. In fact, the internal debates indicated that Ottoman ministers suspected that the media and the missionaries themselves were the cause of their victimization. They took issue with their robust "allegation" that the Ottomans were "refusing to compensate" their losses. Also for Ali Ferruh, the Ottoman ambassador to Washington, the missionaries were pursuing a hidden agenda. In an October 1898 address, he noted that the missionaries had distorted the realities in seeking their government's intervention. US newspapers like the *New York Tribune* further supported their bogus claims by publishing "extremely deceitful articles" for which the missionaries had served as the main news source. The "falsified" information thus made its way into the mindset of the "ignorant" public in the United States. The ambassador concluded that the missionaries would continue to accuse the Turks of denying their "rights" and continue to advocate their own "convictions." In his view, this course of action was tantamount to organized propaganda against Istanbul – a uniform effort to "create solid [diplomatic] pressure on the Imperial State."[28]

The Ottoman ambassador identified how missionary stories had gained currency and publicity high enough in his government to sever the "invaluable" rapprochement between Istanbul and Washington. Despite Istanbul's "respectful" and "responsible" manners, the missionaries were "protesting" so vehemently that "diplomatic principles and standards have been trod under foot." Their suffering and losses had to be "their fault," as well, because they had "employed themselves in the work of confronting and conspiring," not "in the service of faith," as they were pretending. All "that gossip and noise" were being spread as a means of collecting "piasters" from Istanbul for the cause of missionary work. Like American journalists, the Ottoman ambassador's colleagues did not escape his criticism. If the staff of the Ministry of Foreign Affairs accomplished "the task" of making the ministry's points clear to Washington, the US government would stop showcasing its power by "navigating ships through oceans and seas."[29]

However, imperial authorities, including the ambassador, kept their opinions to themselves and adopted a cautious approach in US relations. At the highest diplomatic level, Minister of Foreign Affairs Ahmet Tevfik did not openly accuse the missionaries of following a treacherous agenda. In an August 1904 note to US ambassador John Leishman, he stressed the durability of "cordial relations" with the United States. Ottoman authorities "never" intended to treat "the Institutions, and the citizens of the United States" in any way differently from how they treated those of other favoured nations. Although they did not recognize the "legal existence" of American "establishments," their "competent department" would handle the matter "in conformity with the conditions and provisions of the regulations in force." Rather surprised, Leishman promptly asked whether "the terms and conditions of the settlement effected by the French Government in November 1901" would "apply in their entirety to American institutions." As a result of "assurances given" to him, the ambassador contacted the admiral of the US battleship moored in Izmir and asked him to leave the port.[30]

Besides the USS *Buffalo* and *Dixie*, twelve other battleships were sailing through the Mediterranean on "amicable" missions but half of them were fully armoured and ready for charge at anytime. In Istanbul, imperial authorities interpreted the pre-emptive manoeuvres of these ships as a diplomatic tool to pressure them on the missionary question. They became more alarmed when they heard that the Canadian Parliament had been discussing a "crusade-spirited" action to save Christian minorities in the region.[31]

At a time of internal crisis and domestic tensions, even casual incidents could incite a diplomatic crisis. In Alexandretta in December 1903, US consul W.R. Davis "intervened" in the case of Ohannes Attarian, a local Diyarbakır resident and a naturalized US citizen. Several weeks earlier in Aleppo, Ottoman officers had stopped and searched Attarian, found "$2,500 in his pocket," and suspected that he had returned home to join local insurgents. Davis had him "liberated" from prison and was prepared to accompany him aboard a steamer bound for New York "on condition of his leaving the country forthwith." But the bilateral agreements required that the US citizenship of former Ottoman subjects be revoked upon return to their native country. The officers thus did not let Attarian go. After a dogged pursuit, they also "assaulted and insulted" Davis and "rearrested Attarian." A *New York Times* editorial reported that the local "Moslems" had "seized on the occasion" and held "a hostile demonstration against the Consulate" and "against the Christians generally." The "military couriers" of the US Consulate reacted to the incident by surrounding the prison where Attarian had been held and breaking its windows. Consul Davis meanwhile lowered the US flag at the consulate and left Alexandretta for Beirut "for safety."[32]

The US ambassador, John Leishman, discussed the cause of "the trouble" in an urgent note to Secretary of State John Hay. His legation had obtained earlier permission for Attarian's wife "to emigrate to the United States to join her husband." Rather than her going, Attarian himself had "entered Turkey again by fraudulent means." The spouses met in Aleppo, where he was "arrested on suspicion" of being connected to the Armenian "revolutionary committee." The shocking "attempt to restrain the American consul in public" and "the assault committed upon him" by the officers "justified" the consul's reaction. The US Department of State reaffirmed that Consul Davis had acted appropriately by "resenting and resisting." His conflict with Ottoman authorities would have to be resolved in a manner determined by the department. As the secretary of state requested, the Ottoman government "officially called upon the American consul" and "expressed proper regrets." The US government dropped the case when the Ottoman government apologized to the consul and promised the "punishment of the offending police."[33]

In various meetings between Istanbul and Washington, US representatives expected Ottoman authorities to accept responsibility for protecting foreigners. Their particular request was a full transparency of the judicial processes that applied to American missionaries who had been prosecuted, deported, attacked, or murdered. The missionaries likewise aimed to secure the same standards as the Catholic missionaries – who, as citizens of France, were operating under the protection of the French Treaty of 1901. In his letters to Washington and Istanbul, Ambassador Leishman noted that the French missionaries had obtained privileges related to their "religious, educational, and charitable" institutions. He demanded that "an imperial [edict] be issued" to grant evangelical institutions "the same rights" as those accorded to the Catholic missionaries. In return, the Ottoman government wanted to obtain "the names of existing institutions for which Imperial firmans were desired."[34]

The American ambassador seemed content with the Ottoman decision to resolve the missionary issues. Unlike the enthusiastic missionaries, however, he predicted long processing times for obtaining further rights from imperial authorities. In a September 1904 address to the Department of State, the ambassador said that "the agreement is sure to be a long and tedious undertaking." Even "the French have not as yet succeeded in completing the formalities" of the institutions included "in their list." The Ottomans had only "accepted [it] in its entirety nearly three years ago." He also predicted that "the greatest difficulties [to be] encountered" might relate to the "transfer and registration of property" because the complicated "Turkish law" was already "causing a great deal of embarrassment and trouble."[35]

Ottoman authorities seemed rather defensive stance on the other side. They presented a long list of local petitions against missionaries and specific cases in which they had supported the suffering missionaries. Nevertheless, given that the existing treaties excluded the missionaries as a legal entity, they argued that their protection of American missionaries was *ex gratia*, not an obligation. Once again, the debates over the missionaries' rights occupied a central place in diplomatic parlance. Imperial authorities tolerated minimal interference and made no compromises in their position – except for guaranteeing the missionaries' safety in accordance with their standards.[36]

US authorities compelled Ottoman authorities to assume liability for the incidents involving American missionaries. From the outset, as a strategic commercial partner and a potential ally against Europe, their position had a serious impact on Istanbul. Imperial ministers restructured the state security network and allocated substantial resources to locating and managing local public crimes. Yet while striving to avert crimes, they devised their own tactics, as in the old days.

EMPIRE, STATE ACTION, AND CRIME MANAGEMENT

The Ottoman governance mechanism was based on the distribution of powers. It vested executive power in the dynasty, legislative power in bureaucrats, and judicial power variously in provincial governors, spiritual leaders, local judges, and security officers. This mechanism was centrifugal, being dependent on instructions transmitted from the state centre in Istanbul. As the supreme power-holders, the sultan and the Ministers Council trusted that this system could manage public security issues. But new conditions – coupled with the reform projects striving to emulate French standards and the provincial reports meant to avert local unrest – steered the centre to a conduit of greater control.[37]

To this end, intelligence reports generated extensive information on the missionaries and their students. In the capital, the bureaucrats returned to the provinces with further laws and regulations, instructing governors to "vigilantly monitor" suspicious activities and reminding the missionaries to "observe the law." The uniform message of incoming reports was the potential and actual threat of "sedition," an abstract term associated with any form of conduct prone to exacerbating local tensions. Even though sedition came in various shapes and forms, typical occasions involved an agitator and the missionaries becoming and abetting agitators, or at times suffering because of them. Some perpetrators conveyed a message of personal, social, and material salvation in lectures and talks, thereby pitting millets against the state, Islam, or one another. Several communities also attacked the missionaries for their potential to convert the population. At the state level, the authorities intervened when potential acts of sedition and actual incidents occurred.[38]

In localizing crime fighting, the central state pursued a carrot-and-stick policy by rewarding and punishing state agents based on specific cases. The Ministers Council dismissed several governors, including Haydar Efendi in Harput and Yannakıs Efendi in Haçin, as they had failed to control missionary activities in their region. In Haydar's case, in April 1899 the Ministry of the Interior's memorandum indicated that Harput had turned into a central district for receiving American missionaries and donations. Haydar was not reporting in and, worse, he did not know what was really going on. As a result, he was succeeded by Mazhar Bey, a trusted bureaucrat from the Court of Appeals. In a lesser-known case, imperial ministers removed Captain Hasan Pasha's title and deported him from Sivas because he had debated with an evangelical priest and beaten him up. The public security chief likewise discharged police officer Zekeriya because he had lowered the US flag in the Bandırma clubhouse on an Easter day, and given that he had been off-duty that day, the punishment was unusually harsh. Bigos Varjabedian, a popular city hall physician in Bitlis, also lost his tenure and left for a clinic in a distant village after collaborating with Armenian insurgents in the United States. In such cases, central bureaucrats punished local agents for causing incidents or failing to prevent them. They clearly preferred men of their own kind – loyal urban elite – to take charge and restore local order.[39]

The centre's priority to maintain public order benefited some individuals as well as costing others greatly. After courageously chasing and catching the murderer of an evangelical priest in Alexandretta, Musaddık Pasha was offered an administrative post. Several young men also won prizes and government jobs for their crucial service in arresting the infamous bandit Abdino, whose final offences in October 1909 included the stabbing of an unnamed American Board physician resisting his robbery attempt.[40]

In contrast, the governor of Kayseri made the mistake of not taking action when unidentified persons hung "flyers" on the walls of Talas American College in central Anatolia, threatening that "Muslims would kill Armenian neighbours." In another typical case, public security officers arrested Hasan Rakım, an Istanbul postman who "stole checks," "banknotes," and "valuables" from foreign residents. They relocated him from the city to the "countryside" where "no foreigner lived." But greater problems called for long-term arrangements. In a 1897 memorandum, Şakir Pasha exposed some other governors' misconduct and gross failure to avert public "nuisance" by emphasizing their "incompetency," "negligence," and "malfeasance." The Ministers Council discussed the local circumstances and how officials handled cases of sedition, concluding that the Ministry of Education should "directly monitor" all "foreign" and "Christian-owned institutions."[41]

The tendency to centralize the supervision of missionary institutions resulted from the repeated failure of provincial authorities to effectively handle public unrest. Indeed, many governors and officers did not go beyond blaming the missionaries for causing local troubles, such as provoking church affiliates to challenge the imperial authority and sheltering militant protesters in their colleges under the guise of students. Strikingly, in contrast, foreign diplomats and the media blamed these agents for siding with the Muslims and favouring them over minorities. Viewed from the state centre, the overall unrest was the total sum of isolated local rebellions, and the missionaries thus needed to be dissociated from possible contingencies. In the conflict-prone parts of the empire, then, local agents received specific directives to "vigilantly monitor" and "duly protect" them "in all circumstances." They had to "operate as instructed," satisfy security protocols, and take "responsibility" for the lives of the missionaries.[42]

The case of Bitlis indicates how the centre and provinces connected over breakdowns of the public order. In a 1895 survey of east Anatolia, Bitlis recorded 353,200 residents comprised of 238,000 Kurdish

Muslims, 104,000 Armenians, 6,000 Catholic Christians, 2,000 Protestant Christians, and 3,200 Orthodox Assyrians. An armed conflict erupted between the already hostile Kurdish and Armenian millets in October 1895 when some "neighbours cursed and shot" one another, leaving behind ten casualties. The public security minister, Hüseyin Nazım, met with local agents and notables to hear them and restore peace with their help. Although the incident involved several missionaries, he did not meet with them for a discussion.[43]

Born in Istanbul, Hüseyin Nazım (1854–1927) was the son of Tahsin Efendi, the secretary of the Ministry of War. He studied at French universities and interned in the prestigious Translations Bureau. He then published poems and news articles, taught in imperial colleges, and served as the sultan's secretary. He later governed Syria and several other provinces and led the Ministry of Public Security for six years until he retired in 1896 due to ill-health. Nazım described the Bitlis incident as occurring at a critical juncture in the rebellions and massacres. Such incidents erupted because some Armenians, invoked by rebellious ideologies, decided to revolt and fight. He presented previous incidents that had occurred in Gümüşhane and Trabzon as evidence, noting that no Armenian merchant had opened his store in these nearby towns after the outbreak in Bitlis. This being the situation, the Armenians had fired the first shot. The bureaucrat-turned-chronicler Nazım added to his anti-Armenian position a note on why local officers had failed in Bitlis. He claimed that, when the winds of sedition were blasting in east Anatolia, some officers were absent, tending to matters elsewhere. They had been serving posts outside the city on the day of the incident and thus could not have prevented the four-hour "revolt" in the city.[44]

In a deeper analysis, Nazım's narrative revolves around what scholar Patrick Hogan defines as "absolute moral culpability." This perspective implies that subsequent tragedies result from an agency's initial action. For Nazım, the Armenians were killed only after they rebelled. They took the first shot, which made them the antagonistic party. Grace Knapp, a female missionary born in Bitlis in 1870 when her parents were serving as missionaries with the American Board, contested this narrative, writing that "the Armenians did not fire that first shot." These emotionally engaged and cognitively biased perspectives are instructive when considering contemporary debates on the Armenian genocide. Whereas it is easy to identify the primary victims in these circumstances, it is much harder to discern how the specific choices of those involved amounted to a systematic mass murder. No matter how steadfast and worthy the attempt is to determine the initiating causal factors, massacres and conflicts originate from convergent and compound precedents – not from a single gunshot, a despot's lips, or his assassination. That is, nobody can justify heinous acts. This is indeed part of the point here. The Ottoman massacres continue to necessitate historical explanation. But because of the elaborate matrix of competing sources and stories, it remains difficult to explain the complex state of agents during the massacres.[45]

Charles Tracy and George White certainly harboured mixed feelings about official harassment and ethnic militancy. As the founders and presidents of Anatolia College in Merzifon, central Anatolia (1886–1933), they remembered the post-1890 unrest as "a dark time, trying to our souls." In January 1893 an anonymous person had mounted a notorious placard on the college gate inviting the British to colonize Turkey. Tracy "emphatically denied the charge of college complicity" and insisted that the college's board "was free from any knowledge of the affair." Regardless, the officers thought the native professors "were teaching sedition" in the college and thus arrested the professors and some Armenian students of the "revolutionary" kind. Two teachers, Hagop Tomaian and Ohannes Kayaian, appeared in the Ankara Provincial Court. The judge "released" them partly under pressure from Tracy and the US minister to Istanbul, Alexander Terrell, although this did not grant them a complete pardon. He forbade the teachers to stay in Merzifon and "exiled them to London."[46]

Yet another incident tried the souls of Anatolia College leaders. Around midnight on 1 February 1893, the Girls' School building went up in flames. Local officials hastily claimed that the rebels had done it to "foment trouble," "scapegoat Muslims," and "get attention." In reality, the Muslim neighbours had burned down the building, possibly with the tacit approval of the governor of Merzifon. The college president Tracy and US consul Henry Jewett found that the incendiaries had "evidently carried tins of kerosene" to the roof and "along the footwalks." After "pouring kerosene all the way and carrying the stream down the central ladders," they "dropped a lighted match and ran." Based on this evidence, not an insider group but outsiders had caused the incident. Then an Ottoman-American commission came from Istanbul and inspected the crime scene. The ministers of internal and foreign affairs, Halil Rıfat and Sait Halim, admitted their "failure to protect [the college] premises." The estimated "pecuniary loss" amounted to "$2,200," or 500 piasters, which was paid in full by the Ottoman government. This money was sent to Tracy along with an edict declaring that the Anatolia College administration was allowed to rebuild the Girls' School as early as May 1893.[47]

Despite witnessing criminal attacks, George White eulogized the essential qualities of the Armenian and Muslim communities. In fact, the Armenians of "reliable judgement" disowned the radical youngsters in their millet. They were displeased with "assassination in the streets," "paying levies of money to irresponsible parties," and "the leadership of nihilists and atheists." Most Armenians likewise "resented dictation from a remote clique of agitators living comfortably in Paris or Athens, provoking terribly dangerous hostility from the Turks but keeping themselves out of harm's way." The mainstream Armenians seemed rather "relieved" in 1895 when the officers had crushed "the hidden band of outlaws." They knew that the Muslims had control of everything: "the government, the post and telegraph, the army and all military supplies." But they still "hoped for justice" to be restored with "help from the concert of Europe." By comparison, the "common" Armenian and Turkish people were "steadily friendly," indeed, "as were most of the officials personally."[48]

As much as they appreciated the good status of local communities, missionary educators disliked the rebel youth ready to shed blood in order to change the status quo. One day, in 1900, Anatolia College president Charles Tracy met a band of young Armenians "fully armed with good weapons" and "bandolier[s] of cartridges." A college alumnus, the "fine, tall young" leader of the group was sporting "the well known headdress of a brigand or revolutionist." To President Tracy, he argued that "the Armenians had lived for generations as bondsmen under the unjust, oppressive, and cruel Turks." The British and French "had promised reform measures. But nothing was done." Thus "the Armenians themselves" had to "take the lead" and "create disturbances by insurrection." His band had already "pledged their lives, their all, to the sacred cause." Tracy understood that "they would shed blood if necessary, and they would not spare their own blood." Based on "wisdom, judgment, inevitable danger, [and] probable failure," Tracy "counselled peace, order, [and] patience," as well as reminding the band of his "natural sympathy with the oppressed." Not long afterward, these radical youngsters were "broken up and the leader … was slain."[49]

Peaking with the Armenian deportations from Merzifon, the tragedy made early encounters look trivial. On 10 August 1915 White had begun the day by reading Ezekiel 34:5–16, the verses on the wicked and good shepherds, when he heard "officials forc[ing] an entrance at [the college] gates." They demanded "the surrender of all Armenians." Having "parlayed" for two hours, White felt "further opposition was worse than useless." The deportation of his affiliates was seemingly inevitable. "Seventy-two persons from the College and Hospital" were taken.[50]

TRAGEDY, OTTOMAN OFFICIALS, AND THE CURIOUS CASE OF GEORGE KNAPP

American missionaries became a key item of imperial affairs in the 1890s. The exceptional case of George Knapp emerged around this time when local officials reported that he had sympathized and sided with the Armenian rebels. Born in Bitlis in June 1863, Knapp graduated from Harvard University in 1887 and Hartford Seminary in 1890 before being ordained in May 1890. Knapp then returned to Bitlis and served there for six years as a missionary with the American Board. Along with his missionary colleague Royal Cole, he operated five boarding schools. Reportedly, Knapp had provoked his students and their parents to show the same courage that their fellow Armenians had demonstrated in the Erzurum Revolt of 1890. He was accused of ringing the church bell to initiate a similar revolt in Bitlis. Just as he became the target of Muslim attacks as a notorious instigator, Ottoman authorities charged him with sedition and called him to stand trial in a state court in Istanbul.[51]

The US minister to Istanbul, Alexander Terrell, questioned the legal protocol by referencing "the provisions of the fourth article of the treaty of 1830." In a February 1896 address, he advised the Ottoman government that, if Knapp had "offended against the laws of Turkey," he would "be punished" in US courts or by "the consul-general of the United States." In a belated response in April 1896, Minister of Foreign Affairs Ahmet Tevfik clarified that "Mr. Knapp has not been a prisoner." The officers had simply given him "an escort on his voyage" to "insure his safety." The Diyarbakır governor general then welcomed him as a guest and sent him off to Alexandretta to be "delivered up to the United States consul in that town."[52]

3.2 Photo of George Perkins Knapp (d. 1915), 1886–87.

The governor of Bitlis, Ömer Bekir, called it no easy task when ordered to "relocate the missionaries to Van." The easterly walk of 177 kilometres would put in danger his officers and the Knapp family – the two companies equally disliked by the anxious locals. Mobs and unknown parties could strike a deadly attack while the companies were passing through several villages near the lake. Despite the risks, imperial ministers went forward with the initial plan and ordered the governor to "protect the property" of the missionaries after they had "moved" and even if "no news came about their whereabouts."[53]

Surprisingly, Ottoman bureacrats took two months to compile an official position on the Knapp case. During this time, Minister of Foreign Affairs Ahmet Tevfik changed his views several times in light of findings and further developments. In a June 1896 address to US diplomat John Riddle, he declared that George Knapp had "indulged in intrigues of a nature calculated to disturb public order and security in several provinces of Asiatic Turkey" and claimed that not only had

Knapp spoiled "the large hospitality" displayed by state agents and "the friendly relations so happily existing between the two countries" but he had also "brought about the Bitlis incident." Tevfik had "no doubt that the United States government will completely disapprove" of Knapp's actions and "will apply to this case the provisions of law." Attached to his address, the imperial memorandum further accused Knapp's contacts, such as chief insurgent Hany Sarsoun, of "forcibly abducting a Kurdish girl" and organizing meetings with local "agitators." It included the testimonies of three local Armenians, including Knapp's servant Mampre, who said they had wounded Kevark Bakkalian because Knapp had promised to "give £100 to whomsoever succeeded in killing one or more members of the Bakkalian family" and to "provide [for] the future of his wife and children in addition." He wanted the Armenians to "kill Christians," their own brethren, "in order that the crime might be attributed to Mussulmans." Based on these testimonies, Grand Vizier Halil Rıfat remarked that "Knapp would have been summarily executed" if he had committed these crimes somewhere else.[54]

US and British officials pursued the due process of law rather than summarily executing George Knapp. Philip Currie, the British consul to the Ottoman Empire, investigated the case. He found that Knapp, although "hot-headed," had not committed the treacherous crimes. He also noted that the testimonies cited by imperial authorities had been "wrung out of Armenian prisoners by force." Knapp himself denied all the charges by recounting his experience with Ottoman officials. In a May 1896 letter to the US ambassador, he made the counterclaim that the Bitlis officials, including Governor Ömer Bekir, had told local Armenians and Muslims to petition Istanbul for "the expulsion of the Americans from the country." If the Armenians "did not comply," "the fanatical Moslems" would "go bad" as the "populace renewed the talk of another massacre." He then asked for a "full measure of justice" to "prevent the Turkish Government from treating other Americans as they have treated me." While forwarding the letter to US secretary of state Richard Olney, the ambassador suggested closing this complex case in order to let "things quiet down."[55]

Between 1897 and 1899, George Knapp remained in the United States, and the Ottoman government dropped the charges filed against him. Knapp returned soon after and toured around east Anatolia. As the American Board's senior missionary, he settled in Harput, where he initiated extensive agro-industrial projects, taught the local students, and helped the needy. But "suddenly" one day, he died of an unknown disease on a trip to Diyarbakır, leaving the cause of death a mystery. Although two competing narratives about George Knapp's life and death emerge from US and Ottoman accounts, Knapp's return possibly crossed the line in terms of challenging the imperial authority and confronting local officials, for which he may have paid with his life.[56]

The case of Knapp was even more complicated as far as Ottoman-US relations were concerned. Ottoman authorities dropped the charges after extracting anti-Knapp testimonials under compulsion or after assessing the implications of this case for US diplomatic relations. Worth noting is that the authorities, generally abreast of important characters and their whereabouts, knew that Knapp had made a comeback and lived in Anatolia for sixteen years until he died in August 1915. Thus, although Knapp was guilty of resisting the authorities, he was virtually innocent of disrupting public order, despite siding with the Armenian millet during the rebellions of 1894–96.[57]

It is historically inaccurate to present Knapp's career as a measure of how imperial authorities treated other missionaries. For the Istanbul bureaucrats, the safety of missionaries was at the core of their agenda. In December 1895 amid local chaos in the eastern provinces, indeed, a state directive proclaimed an executive order to "safeguard" the missionaries "by any means deemed necessary." All provincial officials were thus charged with the task of monitoring and guarding the missionaries in specific regions where revolts and massacres posed high security risks.

The frequent communication between US minister Alexander Terrell in Istanbul and evangelical missionaries in the provinces indicates the Ottoman concern about the missionaries' protection. In east Anatolia in August 1896, when foreign institutions became the main target of arson and assaults, Terrell informed the Department of State that each American educational post in the interior provinces had hoisted "an American flag during the recent massacres and gave asylum ... to frightened natives." The missionaries were braving "future danger" because of their "wish to protect the natives." Terrell telegraphed all the missionaries at the same time. His urgent telegraph of 5 August 1896 was three anxious sentences: "Are you properly guarded? Do you wish guards to continue? Telegraph or write all your wants and dangers to me direct."[58]

Over the next three days, the responses reached the US Consulate. The missionaries in critical locations, such as Antep, Harput, Mersin, and Merzifon, wrote that "general anxiety" prevailed but that they were receiving "protection." Americus Fuller, the rightfully scared missionary in Antep, noted "talk of putting an end to our military guard" but added that "the demand for its continuance seems necessary." In Kayseri, James Fowle expressed his satisfaction with "the precautions of the authorities, everything being quiet." They were "safe."[59]

Not placated by mere assurances, the distressed US minister Terrell sent the missionaries another telegram a week later on 11 August. He calculated that the danger threatening "the security of all Christians in the interior provinces" would be "much increased if seditious outbreaks against the authority of the Turkish Government are renewed." So US citizen-missionaries who wished to "remain in Turkey can not be too careful in conforming their conduct." He felt "assured, however, that the Ottoman Government is exerting itself now to secure the safety of American citizens, and hope it will continue." Nonetheless, "the United States has for more than a hundred years pursued the policy of avoiding interference with the internal affairs of other governments." Even though seditious outbreaks would continue to put foreigners at greater risk, US officials refrained from intentionally interfering as a third party, remaining optimistic that Ottoman authorities would continue to protect the missionaries. However, their principle of nonintervention could change anytime. "The arm of our Government is long, and quick retribution would follow" if "citizens in Turkey who obey the laws are slain." The US minister certainly did not forward this note to Ottoman authorities, but they knew its sentiments all too well. This was part of the reason why they had empowered the Ministry of Public Security in the first place and mobilized central state funds to protect the missionaries.[60]

Additional motivations of the Ottoman state became clear in other intricate cases. In 1909 someone had fired at and hit staff residences around Talas American College in Kayseri. Notably, the Ministry of the Interior's Communication Bureau inquired first whether the shooters "intended" to kill or panic the missionaries. As striking as the bureau's questioning of the motives for the shooting was the fact that imperial bureaucrats placed this anti-missionary attack within the parameters of public security. Although many reports furnished no clues as to the motive in such cases – "unidentified assaults" – the bureaucrats applied their sense of what made a case a matter of "public crime." This interpretation extended the centre's criminal taxonomy to classify missionary-related incidents.[61]

Crime management and missionary matters were not remote struggles. Central directives correlated public disorder and missionary ideology from the 1890s onward. With a view to averting crime and restoring order, central authorities also punished local agents who failed to coöperate on this objective. Besides the failures of specific agents, the larger social dynamics had collapsed into a state of flux, and all the while the minister of public security was tasked with supervising and protecting the missionaries.

Imperial authorities worried about American missionaries, but their commitments were motivated by diplomatic concerns. In response to specific incidents, they also admitted "several material losses" from which the missionaries had suffered. The authorities nevertheless acquitted the Ottoman government of any liability, claiming that government agents had been working hard to manage numerous criminal cases at around the same time. In Washington, Ambassador Mustafa Tahsin reiterated the Ottoman state's perspective on what was going wrong. In a November 1896 note to the US secretary of state, he wrote that Ottoman "authorities were engaged in general in restoring at all points the public order," largely "disturbed by the Armenian" revolutionaries. They "hastened to assign troops and mounted gendarmes for the particular protection of the persons and property of American citizens." Indeed, disruptive incidents such as assaults and cases of arson in Kayseri and Merzifon had been "localized" and contained after causing "only slight damage." At any rate, these incidents "cannot be attributed to the negligence of our authorities," nor to a lack of effort "to prevent them as far as might be possible." Such incidents had been "nothing more nor less than the consequence of an abnormal situation," and thus "responsibility" for them "could not and cannot fall upon the Imperial Government."[62]

PUBLIC SECURITY MATTERS AND THE MISS GERBER OPERATION

Maria Gerber was an American missionary born in Sweden and educated at the Moody Bible Institute in Chicago. She came to the Ottoman Empire in 1898 and moved to central Konya with her companion, Rose Lambert, on a mission to collect and save the neighbourhood's abandoned orphans. In her view, the future of these orphans would be "macabre" if they were left to their fate. Christian neighbours covered her expenses and sheltered the orphans. But the

Konya governor, Mehmet Pasha, confronted Gerber's endeavours and classified them as "mischievous." In a May 1907 report to the Ministry of Public Security, he indicated that Gerber had been engaged in illegal activities. She had "adopted eleven Armenian girls" and "turned a house into a school without legal permission." As official investigations made the mission notoriously famous in the neighbourhood, Gerber moved again, this time 129 kilometres east to the Zincidere quarter in Talas, Kayseri, hoping she could care for orphans and widows in this distant area. She had placed the Konya girls in the custody of Lambert and failed to inform state agents of her departure. To the annoyed governor, this final act was a testament to Gerber's "secret agenda laden with illegitimacy."[63]

Urged to proceed as deemed necessary by Minister of Public Security Şefik Pasha, provincial officers barged into Gerber's house and "saved" eleven girls. Contrary to Gerber's claim, they found the girls to be poor and needy but not orphaned. They immediately "delivered five local residents to their guardians." Mehmet Ali, the police superintendent, identified the other "six girls" as originally from Istanbul and had them escorted home by his officers with the help of "an Armenian child-caretaker." Then the officers in Istanbul took the girls to aunts, brothers, grandmothers, uncles, and other relatives. Upon the "verbal and written" pledges of their relatives, Gerber's "orphans" were reunited with their families.[64]

The Miss Gerber Operation demonstrates that missionaries and officials articulated competing narratives of local realities. Even their rhetoric caused a clash over who needed support and who would provide it. Gerber considered orphans to be victims of tragedy and nursed them, whereas Şefik regarded them as captives of an evil-minded missionary and saved them. The families had mixed views on the whole story, but they admitted the girls when state officers delivered them to their homes, perhaps acting as the sultan's compliant subjects by refraining from causing trouble or partaking in state business.

In the late Ottoman Empire, spatial boundaries between itinerant missionaries and dislocated subjects became fluid and porous. The missionaries disdained imperial officials and dodged state pressures while passionately sheltering and protecting the subjects. The officials mutually disliked the missionaries and precluded their missions when legal conditions allowed for it. In Gerber's situation, the nursing of local girls in a residential home also conflicted with the long-held principle that imperial laws superseded individual virtues; the centre's authority reigned supreme over a missionary's personal judgment. Istanbul's orders promptly went into local effect as soon as Gerber had dissented. But Miss Gerber's case was not an insulated case after all. It served as a microcosm of how the Ministry of Public Security managed crucial pursuits of victim care and custody besides resorting to intelligence, surveillance, and interrogations. From the central state to the local agency, the Ministry of Public Security coordinated an extensive security network. In the post-1890 context, it was this network that the Ottoman government had depended on in its efforts to restore public order.[65]

Security agents arrested the offenders and averted public nuisance, thereby carrying out criminal and preventive policing at the same time. In these functions, the imperial network indexed case-based interrogations, memorandums, and surveys, all of which were forwarded to the Ministries of Public Security, Foreign Affairs, and the Interior in Istanbul. In the Ministry of Public Works, the Telegraphy Services Bureau facilitated this process by accelerating the exchange of classified information. Given the intelligence sensitivity of the central bureaucracy, the telegraph became the largest state investment in technology, the Ottoman telegraph network being the world's eighth-longest line in 1880 when it spanned 27,359 kilometres. In that age of innovation, communication agents such as Mustafa Şevket, the director of the Hamidiye Post and Telegraphy Office, came to function as conduits that linked the centre with provinces.[66]

As the wired intelligence information covered long distances in shorter times, central authorities developed a keener sense of public crimes. They defined several felonies, such as sedition and treason besides banditry and black marketing, as the most serious violations perpetrated "against the norm" and "against state interests." From their perspective, Maria Gerber had committed a public crime by violating public order on all grounds. She adopted local children without parental consent and sheltered them in her own house without official permission, ignoring the laws against such practices. In an alternative scenario, a law-abiding, elite Muslim missionary could deliver a noble service to the poor Christian children. But the unruly, American, evangelical missionary became a major concern when she reached out to the Armenian "orphans," rushing the authorities to handle her case. Thanks to bureaucratic concerns and the new medium, the Gerber news circulated across all state ranks in just two days, reaching the Konya governor, the Ministries of Public Security and the Interior, the Ministers Council, and Sultan Abdulhamid II. Minister of Public Security Şefik Pasha studied Gerber's situation from the reports telegraphed from Konya and discussed it with the Ministers Council the next day, 10 May 1907. The Miss Gerber Operation covered 483 linear kilometres between Istanbul and Konya and involved joint security procedures that included a house search, intelligence collection, and the delivery of Gerber's "orphans" to their families around Istanbul and Konya. Remarkably, the operation started and ended in two weeks.[67]

Imperial authorities orchestrated security operations, and provincial agents followed their orders. In the two decades around 1900, the agents encountered American missionaries on a daily basis while policing the neighbourhood. Their tasks overlapped with monitoring and protecting the missionaries amid social turmoil, which had been exacerbated in Anatolian towns, such as Adana, Diyarbakır, Erzurum, and Sivas, following the massacres of Armenian victims. Viewed from Istanbul, public crimes symbolized intended and imminent threats to state integrity – not merely a confluence of local responses to the threats to ethnic and religious liberties that had been proclaimed in an 1856 edict and discarded amid the post-1890s ethnic and religious revolts. Even local agents came up on the imperial state's radar for acts of misconduct. Police superintendents, army officers, and government officials became subject to arrest, exile, and penalties when they erred in cases of sedition and treason.[68]

As new state laws reflected the new realities of the region from 1880 onward, the Ministry of Public Security emerged as a vital government agency. Its minister and officers collected surveys, prepared memorandums, and led regional operations. The development of telegraph lines and significant cases expedited the whole process. Not surprisingly, missionary activities had become a serious public security matter by the end of the century, a correlation of which US officials were also aware. Later, in 1914, they tellingly asked about how the "imperial police and gendarmerie" had been operating since the 1880s. Minister of Foreign Affairs Sait Halim refused the request from Washington. Already skeptical about foreign interventions, imperial authorities defined security matters as a confidential item of internal affairs not to be shared with third parties. They also remained content with the standards of "imperial justice," which they considered adjusting only in line with the centralizing efforts and changing circumstances.[69]

IMPERIAL STATE, POLITICS OF JUSTICE, AND THE MISSIONARY PROBLEM

In the Eastern Mediterranean in October 1906, the Public Security Office of Alexandretta wrote a report on Mois Ashjian, a native employee of the American Board, who had been preaching at the local Protestant Church for several years. The appalled officials noted that Ashjian "had converted and shepherded about 30 Armenian youngsters into the new Protestant congregation." He had also "received from US agencies" money for his "expenses and taxes due to the central government," for his payment of fines, and for his services.[70]

Minister of the Interior Mehmet Faik Memduh solicited the Alexandretta Port Authority's view on the matter, adding that Ashjian's continued "habitation hereabouts" would "not be sensible." In agreement, the investigation committee advised that he "better reside in his hometown, Maraş." The minister then declared that Ashjian would be "relocated" to Maraş under the supervision of security officers. This verdict ended the exchange of information, shrouding the subject's fate in mystery. The unravelling of this story encapsulates how the Ottoman government framed and practised justice.[71]

The process started with security inspections and third-person complaints. Then local agents collected and indexed evidence before forwarding their findings to the central state. From there, imperial officials assessed the incoming data and proposed a verdict to the appropriate ministry. The Ministers Council typically trusted their judgments and drafted the verdict into specific directives. Resting on this bipolar model of exchange, the administration of justice constituted an integral and non-negotiable bastion of the Ottoman regime. It also laid the groundwork for diplomatic relations concerning the American Board's missionaries. Against the exclusive foundations of the regime, then, US authorities intervened in missionary-related matters insofar as imperial authorities tolerated third-party interference.

The post-1880 laws addressed multiple recipients in a holistic manner. Defining American missionaries as intruders into communal privacy and order, many local agents and communities turned hostile to the missionary enterprise and sometimes formed neighbourhood clans to sabotage it. Indeed, the missionaries suffered from physical and verbal assaults virtually in all major towns including Adana, Aleppo, Beirut, Bitlis, Diyarbakır, Harput, Konya, Mersin, Maraş,

Sivas, Trabzon, and Urfa. Even though imperial authorities were also skeptical about the missionaries, they created state directives with the goal of quelling local violence. Numerous decrees urged local communities "not to attack" the missionaries or "destroy their property." Further directives ordered local agents to "guard the missionaries" by "any means necessary" and to "protect their houses." Specific agents also had to "assign a sufficient number of security officers" to "watch," "guard," and "escort" the missionaries when travelling and to "protect their property." Coming from the central state, these decrees sought to endow "missionaries with safety." Although this was a brave effort, it proved too complex and difficult for the centre to maintain a balance between protecting missionaries and curtailing their impact on locals.[72]

In a deeper analysis, central authorities had blind faith in their justice standard. Against some "superfluous" allegations of bias and prejudice, the Ottoman government claimed that its "decrees and actions" thus far had "been completely effective." The accusations against it warranted no consideration and, in fact, the authorities took issue with them. In an October 1904 memorandum, the Ministers Council noted that all these accusations had originated from hostile partisanship and "concealment of the fact" that the imperial state could and should handle its domestic affairs "alone." This memorandum was an implicit statement of the authorities' absolute faith in their administration of justice.[73]

Imperial authorities believed that only they held access to objective and complete information. This assumption hinged on the state security network. By 1900 the capital had at its disposal massive records, including censuses, surveys, and reports. The minister of public security also received specific data regarding intelligence reports and field operations. These sources offered detailed information from the perspective of the state but nevertheless excluded many other perspectives. In a cumulative analysis, the incoming data also shaped the imperial concept of justice, in which local missionary cases merged with the larger incidents of public disorder. To the authorities, the objective of defending and punishing the missionaries made sense, as it served the homeland authority and external prestige at the same time. In rhetoric, the central government spelled out that the laws "approached non-Muslims" on fair terms so that they even "tolerated missionaries." With this line of argument, the Ministers Council aimed to shield the centre from criticism.[74]

The US government's position reflected a more complex situation. Although US diplomats pressured the Ottoman government for just and fair treatment of American missionaries and local minorities, Ottoman diplomats sought the cooperation of the US government in delivering criminals to imperial courts. For instance, the imperial Ministry of Foreign Affairs and the Ottoman Embassy in Washington discussed Albanian, Armenian, and Bulgarian "rebels" who had been "living in the United States" since 1895. Certain "mischief-makers" had lobbied against Istanbul and Islam, collected donations to purchase weapons, and sent these weapons to local insurgents fighting in Anatolia, Syria, and southeast Europe. Adopted by the Ottoman party, this position hinged on imperial sensibilities regarding "sedition" and "treason." The rebels were undermining local order; therefore, the US government had an obligation to extradite suspects accused of criminal public acts.[75]

By the 1890s, when American missionaries became the subject and object of public crimes, Ottoman authorities had identified three key priorities: protection of missionaries in security-critical provinces, monitoring and guarding their institutions against hate crimes, and surveillance of persons and buildings against ethno-religious propaganda. In routine and special operations, they likewise dealt with cases of murder and robbery. State directives urged security officers to pursue the villains who had hurt a number of American missionaries amid scenes of chaos and havoc in towns such as Aleppo, Bitlis, Harput, and Urfa.[76]

Muslims and some organized clans assaulted the missionaries and co-opted locals in their attacks. On several occasions, the mobs sabotaged, damaged, and burned the colleges in Adana, Aleppo, Maraş, and Sivas. Although imperial authorities transmitted messages instructing provincial governors to immediately control these situations, the proceedings following such incidents pursued the typical procedures of the administration of justice to resolve them. Local agents collected intelligence on each case, and the capital's bureaucrats discussed their findings and drafted ad hoc resolutions. In the last phase, the central government decreed how the convicts would be punished and the wronged redressed, as well as ordering provincial administrations to implement all necessary measures to avoid future incidents.[77]

Notably, staff of the Ministry of the Interior retrieved past cases for further review. In a January 1853 case, a local governor had imprisoned a Nestorian welcoming American missionaries to his village. The

Ministries of Foreign Affairs and the Interior revisited this case upon hearing the petitioners' complaints about the governor's arbitrary action. They found the governor to be "ignorant" of the laws because there was no law against meeting and greeting foreigners. To the Ministry of the Interior, that ill-informed governor owed an explanation for why he had jailed "innocent" people.[78]

The Bartlett incident offers deep insight into imperial justice and US intervention on behalf of the missionaries. Lyman Bartlett, a graduate of the Hartford Seminary, had come as an American missionary to Izmir, an urban coastal town in west Anatolia. The American Board tasked him with founding a mission farther east in central Anatolia in 1890. With his wife, sister, and children, he moved to Burdur, where Greek and Armenian residents received him rather coldly. Then the emotional resistance of the local community turned into open hostility and caused the Bartletts "constant challenges," even "everyday attempts" to "expel" them from the town. Two years later, their house was reported to have "collapsed suddenly," but in fact the neighbours had demolished it by "throwing dirt and stones" at it. The terrified family called on US diplomats to seek redress.[79]

In the violent context of the 1890s, the US Senate made it a priority to protect citizen-missionaries in the region. Several senators discussed whether to have battleships navigate the Mediterranean on a mission to demonstrate their support for the missionaries. Although Ottoman authorities advised US diplomats "not to attribute the utmost importance to that singular case," the Bartlett incident became an item of debate between Washington and Istanbul. Viewed from Istanbul, the show of force by US ships sailing around was certainly uncalled for. But the US diplomats still requested that the Ottomans extend to Lyman Bartlett $5,280, or "1,200 piasters," in compensation for his pecuniary damages. Additionally, they rendered "a certain demand" to "correct and replace the state agents" who had not prevented the hatred-filled violence against the Bartletts.[80]

Ottoman bureaucrats delayed responding to the request. Meanwhile, they initiated "correspondence" with local agents, collected "the existing information" from "Konya Province," and ordered "judicial authorities" to interview the eyewitnesses. Then Burdur's governor and its chief officer moved to "detain suspects involved in destroying Bartlett's house" so that a judge could "interrogate" them. The protocol progressed with ease, and the details reached Istanbul as a comprehensive record of documents. Finally, the verdict concluded that "there is not even a moment to worry" and ordered that several convicts be fined and the Bartlett family compensated. "Let Mr. Bartlett receive 400 piasters, the worth of the destroyed house as per the provincial estimate," and an additional "200 piasters for any other damages." For imperial justice to be fulfilled, the local governor "shall claim the total sum of 600 piasters from those who inflicted the damage." Based on this edict, Lyman Bartlett reserved "the right to rebuild the destroyed property." Also, "by taking the occasion to avert such problems," the edict delivered a requisite warning to stop disturbing foreigners.[81]

The Bartletts received 600 piasters, or $2,640, which was half of the requested amount but enough to rebuild their house. To resolve their case, central authorities issued a series of directives for the orchestration of regional operations. This practice became commonplace in the two decades around 1900, laying the foundations of late imperial standards of justice and security. The subtle policy of diplomatic resilience stemmed from the centre's unilateral conduct for the sake of public order. Central authorities developed a nuanced administration of justice and interpreted missionary-related incidents through the prism of state perspectives, public order, and a range of petitions transmitted from the provinces. In organized efforts to defend and punish the missionaries, state policies coverged over the perspectives of imperial authorities as much as the perspectives of provincial agents. By extension, diplomatic relations with the United States reflected the administration of justice and the operation of missionaries in the Ottoman Empire.[82]

CONCLUSION

Although overlooked by scholars of the US presence in the Middle East, the strategies adopted in Istanbul affected the ways American missionaries lived and worked in the Ottoman Empire. Imperial authorities redefined their rhetoric of justice and their policy of security in direct response to the new situations pertaining to the missionary problem. The rebellions and massacres of 1894–96 assigned further significance to the question of how the authorities coped with this problem. At a time when the missionaries and revolutionaries became a critical matter of public security, the authorities opted to handle these matters in a unilateral fashion. Although US diplomats and American missionaries held the Ottoman authorities accountable in local incidents, the authorities defined these incidents as domestic, not an item of diplomatic debate. Aiming to resolve the litigations without third-party interference, this perspective united the executive, legislative, and judicial branches of the central state. Viewed from within the state, the imperial standard of justice and security was fair and reliable, and at the central and local levels, the Ministry of Public Security seemed to be an agency equal to the task of guarding the missionaries and restoring the laws.

In fighting crimes and restoring order, Ottoman authorities did not exasperate any other missionary more than Ellen Stone. Stone believed that the authorities were subjecting her noble service to nonsensical formalities. Observing that even the Russians had come to her rescue, she felt that the Ottoman government had done nothing to free her after she fell hostage in September 1901. Perhaps she had learned about their failed attempts to save her, but she did not acknowledge them. Like most scholars on the subject, she herself remained silent on imperial efforts to guard her and fellow missionaries. For the aging Stone, Ottoman lands were fresh, not a distant memory. She still wanted to resume her unfinished work. On her fifty-ninth birthday in July 1905, she applied to Istanbul to go teach in the region. In the imperial Ministry of Foreign Affairs, the bureaucrats found her too popular and her endeavour too risky. In the name of public order, which they had struggled so much to retain, they rejected her application and turned Stone away.[83]

4

Institutional Regulations

Of New England Puritan descent, the Dodd family devoted several generations to the American Board of Commissioners for Foreign Missions. The family's story goes back to 1849, when Edward Dodd started preaching to three separate nations in three Ottoman towns. In his mid-twenties, he had departed from New Jersey to serve the Jews in Salonica, Turks in Izmir, and Armenians in Kayseri. His son William, born in Izmir and educated as a physician, worked in Kayseri. Then his grandson Edward Jr, born and raised in Kayseri, became a third-generation missionary. Following the family tradition, he studied at Cornell Medical School and Princeton Seminary and returned to his birth place. To observers, he showed an inclination for the Turkish language and the Gospel texts. "His Turkish accent and diction" sounded "so natural and so true" that he seemed "like the other little Turks." Edward worked in the region until his death in 1967. Based on his extensive experience of treating and preaching to Kurdish, Nestorian, and Turkish patients, he authored several valuable books on medical missions in the Ottoman Empire.[1]

Edward Jr wrote about the commitment of his father, William, to local missions. In his book *The Beloved Physician*, he recounted the dramatic events William had experienced while working in the Ottoman Empire. The four-year-old William had to leave Kayseri for New Jersey in 1865 when the cholera epidemic struck Kayseri and killed his father. This childhood tragedy had convinced him that there was still work to be done and that he needed to come back one day. He returned to the region in November 1886 after finishing his religious and medical studies in New England and Vienna. His son described him as a God-loving and talented physician with "miraculous powers."[2]

William first landed in Kayseri, the central Anatolia town where cholera had claimed his father's life two decades earlier. Soon thereafter, he founded the Talas Regional Dispensary in the neighbouring city of Konya. As desperate patients were lining up, his wife, Mary, and his colleague Wilfred Port helped him to construct a larger hospital. Surprisingly, in 1911 William parted ways with the American Board due to an implicit "difference of view." Following the split, he went ahead with his original idea and launched a noncommissioned forty-patient hospital 322 kilometres south of Kayseri. But the First World War wore on, and he stopped treating the British prisoners and Armenian exiles. William devoted the rest of his life to the local relief efforts of the Near East Foundation.[3]

The Near East Foundation emerged from the former American Committee for Relief in the Near East. It embarked on the largest "citizen philanthropy" quest to liberate the oppressed in the Middle East. William joined its several operations, such as the Red Cross's expedition to Palestine in 1918, and treated innumerable local patients.[4]

In the evangelical memory, William Dodd symbolizes an ideal missionary doctor. Besides the title of his biography, his gravestone in New Jersey defines him accordingly with the epitaph "Beloved Physician, 1860–1928." Other accounts attribute to him the divine qualities of commitment, compassion, forgiveness, and patience. He was "active among the churches" and "deeply interested in evangelistic work," and he exercised "a deep hold on the people this way." After all, he had devoted three decades to Ottoman bodies and souls. He had even palpated the least-deserving Turkish patients. He treated them because of his merciful personality and his unwavering "Love of God."[5]

The life and times of William Dodd read as a hagiography – a story in which he served the Turks like Jesus had served the Jews. Yet, somewhat glossy, this narrative has its gaps. A mystery is how "a difference of view" divorced him from the American Board. It is unknown whether the Boston headquarters of the board interpreted his departure as a solitary case. Ultimately, it is striking that William's narrative obscures Ottoman perspectives on his accomplishments. Its implications for the significance of missionary activities to imperial authorities and local communities are equally important. To begin, William's service was illegal because his hospital lacked imperial licences and because his surgeries raised local complaints. Likewise, even if we imagine that some missionaries possessed Biblical traits, the development of a similar conflict comes into question. How did the authorities, their supposed archenemies, tolerate board physicians like the Dodds? And in the special contexts of war and chaos, to what degree did imperial policies affect local missionary activities?[6]

To answer these questions, it is imperative to explore how the host parties viewed the physical expansion of the missionary endeavour. A key strategy that Ottoman authorities developed was the implementation of the "property certificate" – a special licence issued by the central state to recognize foreign institutions operating in service of charity, education, and healthcare. Such regulatory procedures replaced the earlier state position, which had been akin to an open-door policy. By using new directives as a tool to vet foreign enterprises, central authorities practised greater means of determining which institutions could open, close, and continue operating.

Ottoman views have not entirely escaped scholarly attention. In his pioneering book *Artillery of Heaven*, Ussama Makdisi concludes that missionary encounters encapsulated "the contradiction and struggle between two different and fundamentally antithetical readings of the world." Whereas American missionaries strived "to refashion the world on evangelical terms," the "Ottomans waxed and waned in their religious enthusiasm." Ottoman authorities were "always careful to couch their rulings within the highly-elaborated framework of Islamic law defined by the Grand Mufti in Istanbul." They produced "a violent refusal" to sanction the evangelical worldview.[7]

It is important to iterate the normative contradictions between religious worldviews. Evidence has yet to be found of a "violent" Muslim entity that denied the evangelical Christian enterprise simply on scriptural grounds. Indeed, the leitmotif of the Ottoman governance was bureaucratic calculation, not jihadic zeal. This situation was true even for grand muftis, who were the chief magistrates of Islam. In sanctifying the government's imperium by proclaiming faithful statutes, the muftis' agenda was secular and pragmatic, being less dependent on classical Islamic canons.[8]

Regulatory laws reflected the political choices made in the centre, but central authorities consisted of the bureaucrats who kept their watchful eyes on the American Board enterprises. They countered the expansion of the board's institutions by developing a strategy of containment. The authorities calibrated the laws in such a way that these institutions could survive and would eventually shrink and cease. Ironically, it was not the institutions but this political calculus that collapsed in the end.

Another irony was the unprecedented effect of centralist and libertarian principles on the central state. Laid out in the reforms of 1839–56, these principles paved the way for two correlated yet paradoxical paths – one to establish civil rights and the other to debilitate non-Muslim mobility. Although the rhetorical inconsistency and the double standards are now apparent, these incongruences made sense because they held the potential to appease the minorities and control the missionaries in the same vein. In efforts to stabilize the troubling post-1890 conditions, later policies also stemmed from the contradictory paths paved by central authorities.[9]

The definition of "philanthropy" was the crux of Ottoman evangelical encounters. American missionaries thought that childcare, education, financial aid, and healthcare were inextricably linked under the general umbrella of public services. But Ottoman authorities classified them as separate services and accordingly determined who could receive and provide them. For them, subjects of the imperial state should undertake these projects with the supervision of local agents and notables.[10]

Even communication mediums acquired a political tone over time. Church and tower bells, as insignificant as they may have sounded to accustomed ears, created debates that the missionaries were using them for nefarious means. Authorities attempted to mandate that the bells be used exclusively by the Orthodox Church. This device caused serious conflicts, echoing the desires of the involved parties.

Evangelical and Muslim worldviews posed contradictions. However, it is also important to note that Ottoman laws changed algorithms in the post-1890 context. One such example relates to property transactions. As a common practice until 1900, missionaries violated the public regulations by purchasing private houses and converting them into home schools. The Ottoman government reacted to it as an illegal practice, and the successive ministers of the interior blamed provincial officials for failing to avert it. In the view of these ministers, official neglect caused home-school conversions to continue and expand in the provinces.

For the closure of property transactions, legal protocol required a realty licence granted by a state agent. To remain legal, the missionaries also had to consult with the agents when purchasing and renovating buildings. Such requisites laid the groundwork for revising the tax status of the American Board's enterprise and eliminating US diplomatic interference.[11]

A salient feature of legal protocol was a double standard that affected the identity of the owner and the location of the real estate. Although all foreign establishments were compelled to register with the central state at some point, the Beirut and Istanbul colleges were not on the state's radar because central authorities had relaxed these colleges' commitments. In this legal context, a look at the formation and efficacy of state regulations is instrumental to understanding the Ottoman narrative of American missionaries in the Ottoman Empire.[12]

IMPERIAL REGULATIONS AND MISSIONARY INSTITUTIONS

The Ottoman government enacted a land code in 1858 with particular reference to property rights. Third parties were renting the names of resident subjects, purchasing and obtaining title deeds of public lands, and constructing buildings on these lands. Legitimate on paper, such transactions favoured the interests of foreign missionaries and businessmen. The new code represented a landmark in this matter. It still exempted nonprofit transactions from regular and one-time fees, such as estate taxes and customs duties, but it also removed the intermediaries by allowing non-Ottoman parties to purchase and use public lands as long as they complied with state protocol. The amended land code of 1864 complicated the matter by requiring that foreign charitable institutions apply for their operational status. These stipulations laid the legal framework by which to monitor American missionary institutions.[13]

Another set of procedures, the Regulations for General Education of 1869, standardized public education by declaring that officials would authorize only the schools "monitored by the state." The ambitious article 129 stipulated that privately owned schools could not "use books" "that run against the higher moral values" and "the state's political position." Printed materials would "be inspected and approved in advance by the Ministry of Education's experts or local education agencies." Additionally, private institutions would be recognized after they had obtained a licence of operation, and the future faculty would "have to have their certificates approved." The Ottoman government reserved the right to close them "unless each of these conditions were met." These conditions applied to the American Board because it was a foreign, private, and charitable enterprise.[14]

The local failure of regulatory laws led the central authority to transform itself from a distant entity into a strong-arm bureaucracy. A wide range of problems initiated this historical shift, but the centre's overall frustration with the local status quo accelerated it. Political and social tensions being immanent, the authorities aligned internal challenges with the advent of ethnic nationalism, the failure of local administration, and the spread of missionary propaganda. Local officials roused the ire of central authorities because the increasing volume of ethno-religious propaganda outpaced the slow-moving execution of new instructions. In this perspective, illegal missionary activities were possible only with tacit approval at the provincial level. Central authorities thus imposed their control of such matters traditionally left to provincial administrations.[15]

Missionaries experienced official failures on the other side of the spectrum. George White, the president of Merzifon Anatolia College from 1913 to 1933, felt disturbed when "the General and the Judge" once made a surprise visit to the college. To him and his "legally-minded associate" Theodore Riggs, these officials "seemed" malevolent and "eager to find some incriminating evidence, something that would implicate or compromise us Americans." After studying "two maps hanging on the wall on which they read the word, 'Pontus,'" they turned to each other and said, "These are maps of the province of Pontus, which they aim to establish." They also noted that "the Pontus boundaries are not the same" because "on one map they are larger than on the other." Apparently, the publishers would "enlarge the boundaries as their ambitions increase."[16]

The maps hanging on White's office walls had come from Chicago and illustrated the Roman provinces. Quite astonished at the ignorance of visiting officials, White said that these ancient maps belonged to "the time of the Apostle Paul!" The facts did not affect any change, as the officials had already made up their minds. Their reports made their way into Istanbul newspapers, claiming that the Pontus club, led by the college's revolution-minded Greek students, were working to have the Pontus province "annexed to the Hellenic kingdom." Although imperial authorities made no statement on this matter, local officials rushed to act and arrested "the Executive Committee of the Greek Literary Society," which consisted of "three teachers, one alumnus, and two students." Indeed, "much was made of the Pontus Society seal, as rebellion" – even though the seal in fact "carried a device clearly showing a school boys' club for 'musical, literary, and athletic' exercises." Although the archival documents are silent on White's experience, local officials affected his perspective as much as the bureaucratic mindset in Istanbul.[17]

In Istanbul the ministers had the means to discipline officials who failed to meet their expectations. In a January 1893 directive, Minister of the Interior Halil Rıfat denied the American Board's application to expand the Euphrates College campus in Harput. The Harput officials had asked for his opinion on a specific petition to renew the college's licence for a high school for boys and girls, its thirty-year-old lower division. In fact, they had previously neglected the state directives by permitting the enterprise. This type of incompetence precluded the feasibility of institutional expansion under local authorization. However, the new prerequisite – the official certification of property and justification for the continued activity of specific institutions – seemed effective. The denial of Euphrates College's request captured the Ministers Council's multipurpose objective to curtail missionary expansion, dampen public unrest, and assert the centre's writ against local officials.[18]

At the critical post-1890 juncture in missionary expansion and public unrest, the centre tightened its grip on local agency. Imperial directives laid great emphasis on legal procedures, reminding local officials that foreigners had to obtain state permission to found and operate "charitable institutions." On several occasions, Ottoman ministers notified US diplomats that their citizens "shall not open foreign institutions anywhere" unless they held "an Imperial Decree" issued for specific plans.[19]

In executing procedures, all state officials had to answer to the sultan and ministers who had made these laws. In a November 1893 report, the officials of Istanbul's Gedikpasha municipality discussed the changing status of the American College for Girls. The college campus had moved to Üsküdar several years after its foundation in 1871, but the older college building was still operating without a valid decree. Whereas the officials requested its closure, Rıfat ordered them "not [to] shut it down" and to "wait" until the Ministers Council discussed this case. Surprisingly, the council gave the benefit of doubt to the college and reminded its board of the licensing requirements rather than slamming its gates.[20]

While the case of the American College for Girls was in progress, the local caretaker, Grigor Efendi, planned on renovating the college's older building in Gedikpasha. He submitted a quick application, perhaps to have an inkling of the legal status of the building. Rıfat told him to wait until they completed the assessments because the procedures in such cases required that a thorough inspection be made by multiple layers of government, involving the Ministries of Internal Affairs, Education, and Public Security. Strikingly, Rıfat's response reinforced the supreme authority of the centre and rebuked the Gedikpasha municipal officials, who had acted as though they were more authoritative than the ministers themselves.[21]

Although state laws prohibited arbitrary conduct, many other agents followed suit, likely choosing to err on the side of caution. In the south Anatolian towns of Mersin and Aleppo, officials once closed three American schools and then reopened two of them. In an April 1902 directive, the central government emphasized this problem. It urged the officials not to act independently or talk with US diplomats who might want to discuss imperial policies in person with them.[22]

In the midst of all that was going on in the provinces, strategic circumstances dictated juridical changes. In a 1906 case, the Tarsus American College's administration started building additional halls on campus in 1906 before obtaining an imperial decree for this purpose. In fact, the college's building plans called for a specific sanction from the authorities based on its strategic location. The campus had been properly situated outside the town, but it bordered the state's ammunition store, thus remaining within the radius of a safety-critical area. Central authorities thus overruled a previous decree by suspending the campus expansion. When the authorities urged the Haçin governor to halt a missionary building project because the construction site was near the army barracks in Sivas, such imperial sensibilities were again at work.[23]

Sacred realms symbolized another area where legal procedures staved off missionary expansion. Ottoman millets created, respected, and frequented graveyards, convents, and saints' tombs as their "sacred landscapes." Imperial instructions venerated these places in the summer of 1903, declaring that archeologists, missionaries, and other foreigners shall stay clear of the areas known traditionally as "sacred."[24]

Regulatory laws affected a wide spectrum of property contracts, their general patterns hinging on two crucial principles. First, imperial authorities retained absolute authority in all circumstances. Second, American missionaries had to accept this fact and adhere to it. In an October 1911 directive, the authorities repeated that the missionaries could not "establish schools without an imperial decree." Given the persistence of this matter, they also reminded provincial agents "never [to] fall back on the old ways of letting missionaries" open institutions before checking with them.[25]

Although frustrated, American missionaries tried to obey the laws by submitting applications and obtaining authorizations for their institutions. Certainly, William Dodd, the director and physician of a hospital in Konya, fulfilled the requirements for expanding its premises. With his colleague George Post, the director and surgery professor at the Beirut American Hospital, he submitted a "written declaration" and pledged that their purchase of local estates had been for "personal use only." They would "not establish a church, school, etc." and would "not import prohibited goods and not settle prohibited persons" on them. This was a hard commitment intended to ensure the success of their transactions.[26]

While trying to rise to the occasion, local officials found the centre's shifting perspectives troublesome and inconsistent at times. For example, missionary institutions other than orphanages and architectural schools would be subject to taxes. This simple law was difficult to enforce because some missionary institutions incorporated within the same premises both taxable and nontaxable units. Additionally, although the tax-exemption protocol still applied to the existing institutions, property taxes would be imposed on them if their licences were invalid or if their status changed to that of a profit-making enterprise. Profit here meant the revenues collected from the parents and donors in efforts to subsidize an institution's costs for facility maintenance, faculty salaries, and student tuitions.[27]

Merzifon Anatolia College is a typical case in point. Established in 1886 by American missionaries through a $221,790 fund raised variously from external and local donors, the college divided its students into grammar and mathematics sections and offered rewards for their individual performances. Following the monitorial method developed in the early nineteenth century by British educator Joseph Lancaster, the college's administration also believed that students would learn a subject better when teaching it. The talented seniors thus served as assistants to other students in self-help workshops.[28]

Administrators were pleasantly surprised to see their revenues increase in the coming decades. The 1910 fiscal year recorded that the college owned two campuses, thirteen faculty houses, two halls under construction, an orphan house, a rich research library, and a living museum. In detail, donors had funded most of these assets in Merzifon, valued at $149,644, whereas tuition payments generated only 0.6 per cent of its annual income. All this was alien to the Ottoman Empire because, traditionally, the central state funded educational initiatives that the public attended free of charge. Such significant figures convinced central authorities to strip the self-expanding missionary institutions of their tax-free status.[29]

In the final analysis, central authorities sought to assert power, standardize education, and control the institutions owned and operated by American missionaries. However, their rhetoric and the related choices created debates rather than solutions regarding the legal status of missionary institutions.

THE LEGITIMACY OF MISSIONARY INSTITUTIONS

The key to grasping the authority-missionary dialectic in legal debates is to explore the definition of "philanthropy." For American missionaries, the work of childcare, charity, healthcare, education, and soup houses formed an integral part of their universal vision of enlightening nations. For Ottoman authorities, this was a disturbing sight because orphanages, churches, hospitals, and schools were legally separate areas of public acvitiy. The laws had to address and manage these areas in a manner exclusive to each case in its context.

In the absence of tougher enforcement of the existing laws, missionaries operated with relative ease. In a May 1884 case, imperial ministers issued an imperial licence for a seminary in Mezra, east Anatolia, and ordered local agents not to hamper the educational activity therein. Even though the construction of this seminary had happened without permission, the Ministers Council allowed the seminary to operate with the proviso that it would "serve the Protestant community" and not provoke the Christians against the state and Muslim neighbours. Ordained by the American Board, the native bishop was also recognized as the caretaker of the seminary. Albeit conditionally, the Ottoman government was sanctioning establishments owned by foreigners.[30]

Post-1890 interstate correspondence reflected a policy change caused in part by the incompetence of local administrations and the magnitude of missionary operations. Still dependent on local agents to collect intelligence and enforce the law, the authorities in Istanbul adopted a stricter reactionary position to cope with the decade-long public disorder, bringing about a surge in regulatory directives. But the question remained of whether new regulations would effectively resolve disputes over the legitimacy of missionary institutions.

State directives addressed local inquiries about missionary buildings in the cities and villages of Adana, Aleppo, Harput, Konya, and Sivas. In recognizing the legal status quo in these locations, imperial decrees certified numerous colleges, hospitals, schools, and seminaries, including the Beylan church-school complex in Aleppo and the Protestant college that replaced a thirty-six-year-old church in Çorum. Specific decrees likewise acknowledged the active status of American Board institutions as long as there had been no record of seditious activity in them. In a June 1894 case, an imperial decree voided Euphrates College's initial permit, given by the Harput administration, and then a second decree ordered that the college's board must renew its licence to retain tax-exempt status.[31]

Even though religious judgments nurtured official responses to missionary enterprises, it is inaccurate to attribute state sensibilities to a greater commitment to the Islamic laws. Given the difficulty of measuring religiosity, it is hard to understand how Ottoman authorities practised their faith and whether they were more or less religious than their predecessors. Kemal Karpat's analysis in his seminal book *The Politicization of Islam* indicates that it was bureaucratic calculations that pitted the authorities against the missionaries. In fact, while solidifying the late imperial power, the authorities did not Islamize their position; it was Islam that they politicized.[32]

A substantial product of bureaucratic calculations was a type of containment strategy. Imperial decrees granted individual missionaries state protection and their establishments legal permission to operate as long as they did not strive to expand. Specific decrees did not prohibit the local distribution of foreign aid, for which they required permission. Essentially, these directives defined the missionaries' status as a legal matter.

Legal rights came with certain limitations based on two assumptions. American missionaries had to abstain from preaching to students, patients, orphans, and the poor and from provoking people against Istanbul and Islam. They would also register their institutions following a thorough inspection. These conditions were toughened during the post-1890 rebellions. Indeed, a specific decree went so far as to prohibit the US flag on school premises because it became a symbol of sedition at this time. Not at all trivial, these decrees hardly warranted a portrayal of central authorities as downright hostile. Additionally, the authorities sought to avert undesired exchanges by putting resources in competition with missionary institutions. Then, not coincidentally, the imperial state treasury funded public schools and numerous students to study in France and come back to teach in these schools.[33]

Even though state authorities linked missionary home schools with local ethnic revolts, this situation did not overly concern them because they were confident of their means to intervene. Notably, the authorities called the Armenians a "faithful nation" that was traditionally loyal to the eternal state. This judgment rejected the possibility of an inward-driven Armenian rebellion against the state. According to this logic, when the Armenians revolted in east Anatolia towns after 1894, the external force of American missionaries must have led them to stray from the faithful path. Based on serious accusations that some American missionaries were inciting disloyalty, imperial authorities deemed it necessary to stop missionary operations. In several decrees, the Ministers Council ordered the American Board's agents to sign a binding declaration that they had not converted houses into home schools and would not do so. Additionally, its instructions charged provincial officials with the duty to monitor any suspicious activity in their region. The officials had to be vigilant in this task if they were to avoid "dismissal, imprisonment, and punishment." However, the council's assumptions and measures were somewhat naive given the complexity of local circumstances.[34]

Specific decrees allowed foreign establishments to retain tax-free status. Despite the general laws against the idea, the decrees used the tax card as an incentive for collaboration. Foreign schools and hospitals would "be granted tax exemption" if they "promptly completed the process" of applying for a licence and registering with the state. Reports in February 1910 indicated that most of the institutions owned by the American Board were maintaining tax exemptions. Many schools and hospitals were legitimate and free from criminal records while registered with the state. To eliminate legal problems, regulatory directives also reminded local officials that these institutions would continue to be "accordingly exempt from property taxes, customs duties, and other taxes."[35]

In return for rights, the missionaries had to operate within the limits of the law. When Parsen, the American Board's native bishop in Burdur, requested the approval of his recent property purchase, and Ateşli, his colleague in Mosul, applied to build "a house" on his land, provincial governors applied the same protocol, obliging them to swear on oath that they would not use their property for a public purpose. In these transactions, institutional legitimacy came with legal liability.[36]

A red line did exist between housing sedition and housing needs. Central authorities took it seriously when reports identified the occurrence in private houses of some public activity, or "inconspicuous act," as many officials suspiciously called it. In an 1894 case, a municipal report found that the missionaries had secretly designated a newly constructed house for "schooling purposes," and the governor of Aleppo shut it down immediately. When the defendant raised objections with support from US diplomats and local churches, the authorities in Istanbul supported the governor's verdict with certainty, ruling that the defendant had "violated the law of the land."[37]

Restrictive regulations controlled both individuals and institutions because intelligence inspections assessed the status of institutions based on the profile of the individuals who were leading them. Local reports revealed the staff's identity, credentials, and function in a specific location, and central authorities determined the legality of the persons reported. Viewed from the centre, legal opinions reflected a fine balance between imperial, regional, and religious norms. In a December 1904 directive, for instance, the Ministers Council forthrightly refused to authorize Ms. Elizabeth and her colleague, two female physicians with US degrees, for employment in south Anatolia because it was illegitimate for female physicians to see male patients. They might nurse patients but could not treat them.[38]

Foreign institutions bore the brunt of some partial reports transmitted from the provinces to the capital. These reports tapped into the fears of central authorities typically by complaining about missionary transgressions into the public mindset, and they registered a profound impact because they came at a time when American Board missionaries were secretly repurposing residential houses as public institutions. Some reports claimed that the houses-turned-schools, or "home missions," as the board called them, were targeting young Armenians and "brainwashing" them into hating imperial law and public order.[39]

Regulations mandated personal and institutional assurances that missionaries would not host social gatherings in private houses. A subject's notoriety affected future policies in certain circumstances. In October 1896, for instance, the Ottoman government did not render assistance to Euphrates College even though a Kurdish Muslim mob had burned it down. The Ministers Council refused the college's application to rebuild because its operation had only worsened how Ottoman authorities were perceived by its Armenian students, who were already set to hate them. The college also had enough influence to ignite new hatreds between Armenian and Kurdish locals. Released months later, the construction permit imposed some oddly harsh procedures.[40]

The legal case of Edward Haskell, a pioneer of the American Board's missions in western Anatolia, illustrates how personalities impacted the outcome of imperial policies. In an August 1898 letter to the Ministry of the Interior, Haskell asked to register his house in Thessaloniki, Greece. In fact, the Haskell family had already been preaching in private homes for about two decades. Minister Mehmet Faik Memduh likewise took note of the family's unfriendly attitude to local officials and rejected Haskell's request, noting that "the registration and approval" of his new house shall "depend on the condition of not turning the house into a church." Based on the existing judgments, Haskell readily failed to prove that this would not happen. Later, in November 1903, the Ottoman government also "prohibited" Haskell "from constructing a school of industry and agriculture."[41]

Property laws framed the centre's responses to many other missionaries. William Dodd and Mary Garbis, two of Haskell's colleagues, received a similar note upon applying to open a hospital and a girls' college in central Anatolia. After a long wait, they were instructed to guarantee their compliance with regulations, to regularly report to state officials, and not to interfere with public affairs or to proselytize the local youth. In a note to the US Senate, Ambassador John Leishman complained that the complicated "Turkish law" was causing "a great deal of embarrassment and trouble" and that the "procedures" regarding "the missionary claims [and] rights" took a long time to process. In fact, the processing of missionary cases was lengthy not because the laws were complicated or problematic but because imperial authorities needed a long time to factor political concerns, intelligence records, and local circumstances into their final decisions.[42]

Other missionary groups had their own reasons to complain about the slow-moving Ottoman bureaucracy. In 1893 when the latecomer Ohio Missionary Society requested the reopening of a church, the bureaucrats had a lengthy discussion about whether this church, which was to be operated in Maraş by the Ohio missionaries, would become a site of sedition. Ultimately deciding that it might create a public platform for Armenian Christians, a quarter of the local population, to revolt against the capital, they sent a delayed rejection of the application, noting that it had simply failed to meet imperial standards.[43]

A TALE OF TWO COLLEGES

The exceptional stories of Robert College of Istanbul and the American University of Beirut deserve to be told. The Ottoman government treated these two colleges with leniency unknown to other colleges. Strikingly, Robert College was the first college established by Americans outside the United States. It was also the first American college established in Istanbul. Founded in 1863 by pathbreaking missionary Cyrus Hamlin and recognized by an imperial decree granted by Sultan Abdulaziz, Robert College consistently "acquired a worldwide reputation as a model American Christian College." George Washburn, co-president of Robert College from 1877 to 1903, noted that "all the Christian churches of the East are in sympathy" with the college's educational and ethical standards.[44]

Washburn forgot to mention that various branches of the government, too, were in sympathy with Robert College. In a March 1903 survey, the Ministry of Education began its complete assessment of foreign schools with Robert College. Home to 32 professors and 320 students consisting of Americans, Britons, Bulgarians, Greeks, Romanians, and others, the college offered education at the elementary and higher levels, both of which were licensed by the state. Like the Christian churches, the ministry's surveyors admired Robert College, calling it an "outstanding" school.[45]

The high regard for Robert College had a long history. Minister of the Interior Ahmet Münir raised no qualms in February 1889 when Washburn applied to create faculty houses and an outdoor-activity space by "clearing the schoolyard." He ordered municipal officials to monitor the project and ensure that it complied with the existing regulations – the main criterion being that construction was to be confined to the college's "existing boundaries." Caleb Gates, the president of Robert College from 1903 to 1932, also checked the validity of the building permits secured by his predecessor Washburn and asked whether they could use "gunpowder" in excavating the college's yard in order to make more space.[46]

Many other construction projects secured no permission from the Ottoman government. It is worth recalling that the Ministers Council's

October 1896 decree postponed Euphrates College's legitimate right to reconstruction after local mobs had burned down eight of its twelve buildings. Although it was a clear case, the ministers left the college's board in limbo for several months, and then the official approval came with some conditions. The phases of construction had to "comply with the existing conditions," and the buildings under construction could "not function as additional classrooms." While construction was in progress, the authorities added the requirement that a cap be put on admission numbers so as not to exceed the previous size.[47]

In comparison, Robert College obtained virtually boundless permission to expand their campus and enrolment. The college's president even received a state permit to use chemical explosives in order to "clear the land," despite strict measures restricting foreigners' use of gun powder. This exception seems remarkable given the college's physical proximity to the imperial Yıldız Palace. Six and a half kilometres away, the sultan and ministers could literally hear the construction progressing on its campus.[48]

This missionary college in Istanbul remained free of additional requirements. In an August 1915 correspondence, Bebek municipal agents inquired about the right course of action regarding "the newly constructed buildings on campus." The college's expansion was in violation of "the construction law," yet imperial authorities advised that its new buildings shall "incur no penalty." Although the municipal agents had already revoked the college's licence of operation, they quickly reissued it.[49]

Like Robert College, Syrian Protestant College was often spared the stringency of the Ottoman bureaucracy. Founded in 1866 by energetic missionary Daniel Bliss and later known as the American University of Beirut, Syrian Protestant College rose to pre-eminence and became the desired venue for public education. Even though the Beirut governor once advised Istanbul to "counter" its impact by reopening the inactive "imperial college," imperial authorities did not follow his advice, except that they ordered the Muslim parents not to send their children to non-Muslim schools.[50]

Under President Bliss (1866–1902), Syrian Protestant College expanded its campus and student body. In October 1904 an imperial decree also allowed it to construct an obstetrics and gynecology hospital. In the liberal arts and medical sciences, the college graduated many students proud of their alma mater. Wadad Hamdan, a nursing graduate in the 1940s, said she would gladly "follow the footsteps" of her predecessors by making "a future of the nursing profession" in the Middle East.[51]

Although Robert College and Syrian Protestant College remained off the state's radar, their exceptionality lay in the favours they obtained from bureaucratic leniency. These urban colleges had been visible, transparent, and in close contact with Turkish Muslim authorities. Several authorities even sent their children to these colleges. For instance, the daughter of Ottoman treasurer Mehmet Edip, Halide Edip (1884–1964), studied at the American College for Girls, Robert College's sister institution at Üsküdar. Graduating in 1901 as the college's first Turkish Muslim alumnus, she established a remarkable career as an avant-garde novelist and political activist at the critical juncture between the end of the Ottoman Empire and the beginning of the Republic of Turkey. The life and times of Halide Edip further indicate that imperial authorities valued these colleges so much that they broke the laws they themselves had made. Additionally, at a time when French schools in Beirut were benefiting from priviliges under capitulations, the authorities may have intended to prevent tensions with US officials by avoiding double standards in relation to Syrian Protestant College. In a deeper analysis, preferential treatment was premised on a shared assumption that, unlike other schools across conflict-prone east Anatolia, the colleges in Istanbul and Beirut posed no imminent challenge to the imperial law and public order. Thus the centre's negative judgments bypassed the campuses of Robert College and Syrian Protestant College.[52]

LEGAL DISCOURSES AND ILLEGAL CONSTRUCTIONS

The authorization and refusal of missionary proposals hinged on the local reports and circumstances surrounding the applying colleges themselves. The policies varied as to what specific constructions were permissible or illegal. After the 1890s a real problem was the issue of whether the missionary institutions might legally expand on virgin land. Ottoman authorities pursued the strategy of containment on this issue and aimed to confine the missionaries' activities to the space where they were already operating.

The Ministry of the Interior found that an extension proposal, submitted by Tarsus American College in central Anatolia, was "unacceptable" and "had to be declined." In an 1893 directive, Minister of the Interior Halil Rıfat predicted that the proposed project would run the risk of exacerbating ethno-religious tensions in the region, a consistent worry of the authorities in regard to missionary expansion. "No licence," their decision repeated, could "be issued in the absence of an imperial decree." This response came as a reminder that central authorities had adopted a strictly bureaucratic position around this time. Their procedural requirements had increased, resulting in the rejection of missionary constructions on the basis of illegality.[53]

Whereas American Board institutions were expected to remain within their existing boundaries and were deprived of territorial expansion, the state's "Muslim institutions" were seriously contemplated by Ottoman bureaucrats as a means to compete with them. An "urgent plan" proposed that state schools, such as the old imperial college in Beirut, "combat" missionary schools. Imperial and local officials would thus retrieve local students and enrol them in these schools. The Ministers Council also somewhat naively expected provincial governors to fund these schools in their region. This creative attempt to curb the missionaries' expansion by limiting enrolment in their schools was an exception for its time, and its Ottoman version failed due to organizational, financial, and other obstructions. The ministers then focused again on curbing the illegal expansion of missionary institutions in other ways, returning to their emphasis on a legal approach.[54]

Minister of the Interior Mehmet Faik Memduh issued regulatory instructions on how local agents could effectively monitor the unlicensed missionary establishments. A symbolic incident occurred in Kayseri, central Anatolia. For several years, the Parker family had "directed the Haçin orphanage," where they "took care of some students." In October 1910 they applied to open a second orphanage in a nearby town. The Ministry of the Interior made a thorough assessment and rejected the application, all the while confirming the legal status of the existing orphanage in the absence of any criminal reports. The ministry staff also compelled the Kayseri governor to "warn Parker." He had to cancel the proposed idea in order to avoid the consequences of violating the diktat. A later directive sealed the fate of the Maraş Orphanage on account of its administrative misconduct. In this case, the British missionaries were operating the orphanage even though it was owned by the American Board. The applications submitted by other missionaries drew little attention from imperial bureaucrats. For instance, state procedures disappointed the German missionaries to such an extent that they did not question the status of their building application when the bureaucrats denied even the legality of their advanced property purchase in line with their school and orphanage project.[55]

The legal status of institutions changed when the Ottoman government recognized the American Board as a legitimate entity, proving to be a pivotal move. Late government authorities abandoned the earlier notion that the board's missions were a discrete unit and now required that sister institutions register under the board. They did not simply submit to the demands repeatedly expressed by US officials. Rather, they aimed to engage with the American Board as a corporate legal party that could serve as an interlocutor for its missionaries. Individual missionaries transferred their property titles to the board over the course of two decades after 1900. The whole series of "transactions" took a long time, as US officials had predicted. Once the process was completed, however, the board's headquarters in Boston emerged as the registered owner of all American hospitals, schools, seminaries, orphanages, and other institutions in the Ottoman Empire. The board even reclaimed the land in Tripoli, owned by a missionary named Wilson Nelson, and built a new college there.[56]

The Istanbul authorities urged the American Board's leaders to abide by imperial directives in return for having granted the board legal ownership of local enterprises. The board's headquarters in Boston moved forward and received further permission to renovate and construct buildings in various institutions – such as hospitals and schools in Adana, Beirut, Kayseri, Mardin, and Van. The October 1914 instructions allowed the International College to purchase "state land" and expand its campus in Buca, a major district of Metropolitan Izmir. Such instructions always noted that the board's institutions had to "comply strictly with the existing laws." Additionally, the 1911 directive had already proclaimed the prerequisite that these institutions pay "compulsory taxes" to be appraised by provincial agents. Property transactions and new projects would be cancelled if they held outstanding debts and fines owed to the government. As a state-of-emergency measure, imperial authorities also proclaimed their right to requisition foreign institutions, or "rent" them, as they said in Istanbul, in their efforts to render public and military services in the First World War. Most missionaries suspended operations as instructed, although many also stayed in the chaos-stricken eastern provinces.[57]

The legal work regarding missionary institutions distracted only some of the attention from various activities being held in these institutions. In the 1910s, the period marked by some scholars as the peak of Ottoman-Islamist reactions, imperial authorities discussed the missionaries' "destructive effects" on local communities and aimed to "prevent their growth." They nevertheless continued to vest the American Board with the basic rights to property, petition, and security. At the same time, the bureaucrats kept abreast of local incidents, which they strove to examine and resolve rather than readily confirming and punishing the suspects presented by local agents as culprits.[58]

Successive regulations reiterated that the legal certifications of specific institutions were still conditional upon the observation of "the due process of law" set forth by the Ministers Council. In two striking cases, Tracy Atkinson acquired Ottoman subject Numanzade Konstantin's real estate in Harput to establish the Harput Dispensary on behalf of the American Board, and Bishop Robert Chambers led the expansion of the board's college campus in Izmit. The directives allowed the creation of only a garden yard for the dispensary patients and the establishment on the Izmit campus of only a single, one-storey building for noncurricular activities. Besides setting these terms, local officials would also monitor and report on the progress of these projects. The directives sounded more extreme in other cases. For instance, in response to the board's illegal school expansion in Adana and unauthorized multistorey construction in Tripoli, the provincial governors cancelled the projects and issued a stern warning to the board not to violate their existing contract with the imperial state. In the Tripoli case, they had constructed a four-storey complex although only two storeys had been preapproved.[59]

Local surveillance of foreign institutions exacerbated tensions between the capital and the provinces. In September 1890 Minister of the Interior Ahmet Münir bitterly rebuked provincial officials for having closed the American school in Afyon. The frustrated minister noted that the licence granted to the school was still valid and inquired as to why it had been shut down. He ordered all provincial governors to halt their "arbitrary" treatment of foreign-owned institutions and to check in with Istanbul whenever he deemed necessary. The minister's strong admonition came at a time when arbitrary actions had become commonplace at the local level.[60]

Some local officials did the right thing in bypassing the law in order to operate quickly. In November 1891 the Burdur Municipal Administration suspended the house construction of Lyman Bartlett, an American Board missionary. The Ministers Council had no qualms about this act and confirmed it until further notice. Bartlett had obtained authorization to construct a residential building on his land. But, in reality, the construction had "commenced on state land" adjacent to his estate, contravening the legal limits set for him.[61]

Bartlett's case was in line with similar cases. Local agents shut down many institutions and cancelled several construction projects in other towns. When handling these cases, imperial authorities first aimed to assert their supreme position and to resolve the matter in a non-confrontational manner. Regarding Bartlett, for example, the Ministers Council notified the Burdur governor that Bartlett had to "pay the state tax," as his project had transgressed the licensed construction site. The governor would "register the buildings that he was constructing" after "the due taxes" had been collected from Bartlett. To authorities, this was the most effective and appropriate method to employ so as not to cause people any "suffering." Bartlett eventually registered his residence.[62]

After all, Ottoman authorities nullified local verdicts against missionary investments, justified the integrity of state laws, and helped to moderate reactions, all the while aiming to stave off US diplomatic interference. However, imperial regulations did not always reiterate the local judgments. In another symbolic case, the governor general of Adana stopped the construction at Tarsus American College before reporting it to Istanbul. His February 1895 telegraph mentioned that he had cancelled the construction because it was happening near the imperial ammunition storage. The location of institutions mattered so much that the authorities in Istanbul gave local agents tacit approval to act on their own without punishment or warning. Burdur, Adana, and other cases indicate that local arbitrary decision making was possible when predicated on a faithful, strategic premise.[63]

FOR WHOM THE BELLS COULD TOLL

In the Middle East and eastern Europe, church and tower bells embodied state authority, communal spirituality, and the auditory landscape. Besides crosses, flags, and other icons, they likewise held a public value in the Ottoman Empire. In his pioneering book *The*

Well-Protected Domains, Selim Deringil explains that Ottoman authorities regarded the foreign equivalents of these objects as "rival symbols" when imported to the imperial realm. Exploring the "coat of arms" of an enemy power, "illustrated plates" coming from Russia, and even the race between "clock towers" and "the minarets" to regulate time from the earthly and celestial realms, he finds that these symbols were more than simple objects of identity. State authorities and foreign missionaries attributed conflicting meanings to them, claiming these objects for themselves and thus inventing another layer of debate about them.[64]

To imperial authorities, foreign access to identity symbols, especially bells, signalled a breach in the public order. It held the potential to enflame local hatred against foreigners. In the troubled 1890s, the American missionaries' symbolism bothered the locals, except for those who studied and worked with them. The authorities argued that only Ottoman subjects could use symbols of this kind. Strikingly, the more urban and religiously diverse the location, the less tolerant the authorities became of the missionary bells.[65]

When the American Board's missionaries requested permission to purchase school bells for their institutions in Amasya, Beirut, Burdur, Merzifon, and Tokat, the officials raised the issue that they were already using the bells in their schools and seminaries. A February 1893 report dwelled on this situation, mentioning that the bells at the board's institutions were "ringing untimely at any hour." Even though imperial laws authorized the announcement of classroom periods with bell ringing, some local reporters said that they knew the difference between school routine and missionary intention. They argued that the missionaries were ringing the bells as a means to challenge the customs and religions of their communities. Imperial authorities still endorsed the law, yet they issued further regulations for prospective cases. The new policies distinguished between "foreign-made" and "superfluous" bells and cautioned missionaries to avoid tolling the bell outside of school hours.[66]

The Ministers Council shaped the state's perspective by addressing the primary motives for using bells. The size of the bells also became a source of debates. When the American University of Beirut's administration applied to import a 300-kilogram bell in November 1911, the council rejected the proposal, stating that it was "superfluous," as the university did not need it. Three years later, the Ministry of Public Works noted that the missionaries had installed a bell tower in the Burdur Church under permission from Istanbul. The applicants had purchased a smaller bell and made the claim that the tower would benefit public interest by showing the local time. Where missionary institutions occupied official debates, the symbols of identity being used in these institutions afforded central authorities a venue to manifest their power. In the flag case of late September 1919, the public security chief also discharged from duty an officer named Zekeriya who, apparently for no reason, had gotten angry at the American flag and lowered it at the Bandırma Clubhouse in west Anatolia.[67]

The 1911 provincial report pointed out that the American University of Beirut's administration had built a clock tower before the bell-importation request reached Istanbul. The authorities in Istanbul eventually had to authorize the project, but they did so by sending a letter of reprimand to local officials, noting that their ignorance had caused the problem in the first place. The issue of local ignorance prevailed in Beirut and other locations throughout the 1910s. As noted above, in a case dated August 1915, the missionaries constructed a four-storey school complex in Tripoli with a permit for a two-storey structure. No matter how much the Istanbul bureaucrats admonished their agents to observe the law, the storied Tripoli college hosted students for the coming year. Eventually, the American Board's clock tower began showing the time in Beirut – the activity of its hour and minute hands limited only by the evangelicals' clockmakers, not the imperial decision makers.[68]

ANOTHER TALE OF THE BELOVED PHYSICIAN

Dedicated to healing the Ottoman soul and body, the thirty-year career of William Dodd was said by some to have summoned the love of God and accomplished the evangelical "medical task overseas." But Dodd's service produced a competing tale among the Ottoman authorities. Local officials doubted his intentions, physicians disliked his arrival, and patients petitioned against his malpractice. These reactions quickly reached the capital, prompting imperial authorities to punish him and close his hospital.[69]

Prepared by an unnamed official, a January 1894 report made serious charges against William Dodd. It claimed that Dodd was performing "unscientific surgical operations" in his "fifteen-bed" house-turned-hospital in Talas. In absence of evidence of the alleged crimes, however, imperial authorities did not punish Dodd or revoke his medical licence. Minister of the Interior Halil Rıfat instead ordered some detailed information, including interrogations and inspections, regarding this case. A second report then presented the extent of Dodd's activities alongside the testimony of a "state doctor" and other information collected by police officers.[70]

"Mr. Dodd, the Representative of the Talas Protestant Community," had acquired his medical degree from the United States before coming to work in the Ottoman Empire. According to the state doctor's report, he practised medicine generally "in compliance with the regulations of the Ottoman Medical Science Association regulations." But he was "incompetent" and "incapable" of properly fulfilling his professional duties. He had been "unnecessarily cutting parts of the body" of his patients and causing some patients' untimely deaths. His practice was "not a good practice of the medical science." Some local residents noted that Dodd was doing all this "on behalf" of the American Board. They hated him and urged that he "be stopped" and "stripped of his licence."[71]

The police report, one of Dodd's most notorious reviews, mentioned the patients were grumbling about excessive wait times. The in-patients were cooking their meals and receiving unfair bills in his hospital. Several patients also claimed to have been "crippled" on his operating table. Hearing about these complaints, imperial authorities found the case of Dodd too serious to ignore. But despite these severe concerns, they did not punish Dodd in a July 1902 decree, opting to merely close down Dodd's hospital.[72]

Further instructions targeted other physicians. The legal status, capacity, and function of missionary hospitals occupied the state agenda when prompted by local complaints. Specific decrees likewise rejected missionary-trained doctors' proposals to open dispensaries. Finally, in a July 1902 decree, the Ministry of the Interior proclaimed that the Ottoman government would no longer consider the establishment of "dispensaries" that would be "privately owned" by missionary physicians and others not affiliated with the state. Effective on this date, provincial authorities had to "close down unlicensed hospitals as soon as possible."[73]

The closure of the American Board's medical missions in Konya and the deportation of William Dodd's colleague Wilfred Post from this town were incidental, as the residents of this conservative province were discontent with the missionary presence right from the beginning. Some locals claimed that Post had "politicized" and "proselytized" his patients. The dual objective of medical missions – physical and spiritual treatment of patients – then induced central authorities to restrict healthcare licences and institutions. The eventual closure of the board's services in Konya was mandated in an April 1917 decree.[74]

Occassionally, local officials disrupted the long-term policies of imperial authorities when they "coerced" the missionaries into closing their institutions although these schools had state authorization to keep operating. In bureaucratic terms, imperial authorities called such complex cases *actio quod jussu*, as these were legal matters regarding the missionaries and the locals alike. In the face of such malpractices, they strained to explain these incidents to US diplomats. This difficulty partly explains why the authorities urged the Adana officials to reopen one of the two institutions they had closed in April 1902: it was a "college approved by the state." The follow-up directive required additional information on the second case and ordered local authorities not to "close these institutions" and not to "allow US consular intervention" in the second case.[75]

Besides the officials' misconduct, the missionaries' legal violations manifested in the local context. Indeed, many missionaries clearly disrespected state directives to "obtain property licences" and "stay away from Muslim children." In the Karataş district of Adana, for instance, Meteni, the board's native missionary, whose last name the sources left unmentioned, had established a neighbourhood school and operated it off the state records in 1887, its inauguration year. Then the residents complained, saying their children were "coming away" from this school "denuded" of their customs and traditions. The Ministers Council pressured local officials to investigate and report on this case. The petitioners included a party of local Christians – whom the American Board's missionaries called "nominal" Christians ignorant of real Christianity. The governor of Adana reported that this institution would do no good, especially for the petitioning party. Remarkably, after a July 1887 directive ordered the permanent closure of his school, Meteni did not even try to apply for an "official permit" the next year. The directive likewise urged the arrest of a teacher, identified as David, who had "indoctrinated local Muslim and Christian children" with anti-state ideas. The governor's reference to Muslim children struck an additional nerve in the capital. The governor was advised to proceed "as is expected."[76]

CONCLUSION: LAWS, INSTITUTIONS, AND WILLIAM DODD

Ottoman authorities crafted complex perspectives to curtail ambitious missionary investments and arbitrary provincial actions at the same time. Post-1890 laws matched the principles of political centralism, religious conservatism, and public justice. Hinging on these tenets, state directives granted rights to American missionaries but allocated no space for their institutions to expand.

Unlike the American Board, the Ottoman government defined social programs such as aid, education, healthcare, and guidance as independent services, rendering foreign agents unfit to deliver them. This foundational difference precipitated the idea that if the American Board's institutions were permitted to survive but not thrive, they would shrink and then cease. As a scare tactic, government authorities also warned of punishment for those who might violate their instructions. Their overall objective was to reinstate state power, replace public ignorance with loyalty, and impose sanctions on the board's construction schemes. General instructions soon frustrated the recipient parties because they called for submission to the centre's demands one way or another. Missionary institutions failed to flourish against the backdrop of specific requirements even after the board started to defend its rights in legal cases.

Lasting wars, outstanding debts, civil unrest, and the meddling of the US government might have defeated the centre's bureaucratic calculations. Additionally, Robert College of Istanbul and the American University of Beirut, two favorite institutions in the minds of central authorities, established a long-lasting legacy and rose to eminence above their counterparts in the Middle East and eastern Europe, the erstwhile Ottoman world.

The tale of William Dodd captures the perceived realities and real perceptions of Muslim imperial and Christian evangelical actors. On one side, Christian Americans loved Dodd, remembering him as a merciful visionary who had cared for and caressed the sick and the needy. On the other side, Muslim locals hated him, remembering him as a merciless impostor who had overbilled and killed his patients. After all, Dodd and his missionary colleagues did occupy a mental and territorial space even though the contrasting recollections overstated their qualities. To this day, Ottoman-missionary tales remain too publicized for the distinction between reality and fiction to be easily determined. Although it seems impossible to decipher the historical truth behind faithful encounters, it is still possible to conclude that Ottoman authorities largely failed to curtail the missionaries' expansion in actual and spiritual ways.

5

Ink Saw the Daylight

Henry Dwight, the prolific lead editor of the American Board of Commissioners for Foreign Missions, was a second-generation missionary born in the Ottoman Empire. In 1872 at the age of twenty-nine, he became the director of the Bible House, an Istanbul-based publishing press. He relocated the press to a convenient site in the Eminönü district, purchased new machines, and began publishing books day and night. As his colleagues continued to set new records in output, the Bible House became a blockbuster. Its machines printed millions of pages every year.[1]

Dwight recounted the story of a "printer's boy" in his book *Constantinople and Its Problems*. That boy, one of the American Board's 2,500 local workers in 1900, was amending proof sheets and turning "the wheel" of the Bible House machines. Soon enough, he proved industrious at printing work and studious in studying religion. He even made up his mind to deliver the prayers from the chapel in the Bible House to the public in the countryside. One day, he visited Dwight carrying "not a trace of ink about his person." He had "learned to know Jesus Christ" and asked for "prayers" that he "may be helped" while trying to tell people what Christ meant to him. This anecdote ended as a story to be continued and as though only one particular aspect of it seemed interesting. Dwight refrained from rating the boy's chances against the troubled conditions in east Anatolia. He did not spare any more words to describe the boy's persona, except to note his intention of "entertaining an angel unawares." Instead, the boy's narrative aimed to raise the missionary spirit by suggesting that divine wonders were coming about through service and time.[2]

By the boy's last workday, the ink soon to be scrubbed off his clothes had imprinted 8,319,200 pages each year from 1880 to 1902. The printing press served as an exogenous instrument with the potential to maintain or alter the spiritual fabric in the Ottoman Empire. Imperial authorities and missionary publishers observed the odds on each side. The authorities required the publishers to be vetted by state agents, who would also evaluate book proposals and suggest a range of revisions. As Dwight concluded in his book, "The printer may print neither book, newspaper, nor picture" without "the signed approval of the censors of the press." Virtually all publishers encountered official censorship at some point.[3]

The censorship protocol served as a catalyst to counter anti-Islamic and anti-regime propaganda. Numerous directives ordered inspections of the publications in a search for "forbidden words." Literature experts indexed and updated these words, including "anarchy," "assassination," "bomb," "cruelty," "nation," "rebellion," "reform," and "revolution." Central bureaucrats likewise banned or censored globally themed periodicals, just as they stripped public readers of access to regional news on the post-1905 development of revolutionary and parliamentary changes in Iran and Russia. As well as restricting the flow of information in the Ottoman domain, they crafted an alternative reality of the fate of world leaders in the eventful years following 1894. Whereas in reality their lives were taken by assassins, in the Ottoman narrative French president Sadi Carnot died of a heart attack, US president William McKinley died of carbuncle, and the Austrian empress Elisabeth died of heartache. Patently absurd, imperial censors even crossed out the term "big-nosed" when the publishers used it as a veiled epithet in their criticisms against the reigning sultan. Considering that Abdulhamid II did have a big nose, and finding this epithet to be pointed and insulting, a censor instead ordered the use of "prominent" as a substitute word.[4]

Ottoman censors were unnamed officials hired by the Inspection and Examination Committee, a bureau of the Directorate of the Foreign and Internal Press. Although their numbers increased tenfold from 1878 to 1907, registering fifty-nine agents on the payroll, these censors remained overworked most of the time. They examined all book proposals, suggested various corrections, and determined whether the revised books had sufficiently satisfied imperial standards. Failing to meet state standards, certain books had to be "burned" and "destroyed." But the censorship work was not an isolated state service and certainly not arbitrary, as Dwight imagined it to be. It entailed a meticulous literary assessment in accordance with state perspectives and local circumstances. As another salient feature of Ottoman-missionary encounters, the interactions between censors and publishers also reveal the glaring discrepancy between what the missionaries desired to publish and how the authorities allowed them to publish.[5]

On usual workdays, the censors skimmed through publications for references to authorities and religions. By associating religious and political slander, they blacklisted missionary books that conveyed four core messages: Ottoman Muslim officials were oppressors, Christianity was a better religion than Islam, the path of Jesus was the only path to salvation, and American missionaries had come to salvage the locals. In fact, the implications of these messages hold stunning relevance for recent encounters between authorities and missionaries. In a February 2002 case, Turkish police arrested Ahmet Güvener, the pastor of the Protestant Missionary Church in Diyarbakır, southeast Anatolia, allegedly because he had "slandered" Islam while delivering the Bible "illegally." Then a regional criminal court heard the testimony of Kemal Teymür, Güvener's Protestant-convert assistant. Tellingly, in the presence of the US consul in Adana, who had attended the hearing in person, the defendants were released on probation.[6]

Besides missionary books, US newspapers went through content checks. On 21 December 1894 the *Washington Post*'s editor cited a missionary source's claim that Ottoman authorities had been prowling around with an intention to "destroy" their "entire Christian population." The censors forbade the circulation of this piece, urging that the government take to court the masterminds behind the claim and forestall their "weapons of sedition" so that they would no longer "infect the masses." Provincial agents likewise alarmed the centre by identifying similar texts within the libraries of various American Board schools. Although the censorship agency was understaffed, its findings convinced central authorities to curtail the freedom of the press.[7]

Missionary presses had no other choice but to adjust to state sanctions. In one case, an official censor required retranslation of John 4:20 in a booklet on Christian ethics. The author had to change the direct object from "brother" to "sister" so that the verse would read, "If a man say, I love God, and hates his *sister*, he is a liar." Apparently minor, this change was not arbitrary at all. To Henry Dwight, the booklet's editor at the Bible House, the use of "brother" in the original verse might admonish the readers by alluding to the Armenian massacres of 1896. The required revision would vindicate the imperial honour because Armenian "women were not commonly killed in the massacres." Although the Inspection and Examination Committee later overruled specific suggestions of its censor, the missionary editor noted that an "inward turmoil of conscience" continued to pervade the Ottoman government from high-ranking bureaucrats to the book-ranking censors.[8]

Prominent scholars acknowledge the impact of missionary publications on local communities. However, they often overlook the perspectival meanings of the printed texts, particularly how Ottoman authorities challenged the discourse of these texts. The American Board's presses benefited their audience even though they failed in the final mission of conversion. The existing narratives likewise address missionary publishers by aptly examining their publications yet partly obscuring the receiving parties from view. In Çağrı Erhan's analysis, the Ottoman government "took an attitude of negligence" toward American missionary literature. Erhan's conclusion hinges on US archival documents, but it precludes any possibility of looking at Ottoman archival documents and does not acknowledge the existence of an organized state policy on the matter. Because the print media posed an imminent threat to the crisis-ridden regime, state authorities thought long and hard about ways to curb the missionary literature.[9]

Little is known about the history of the printing industry in the Ottoman Empire. In several pioneering studies, Johann Strauss finds that the missionary editors became noticeably productive, with the censorship officials emerging as a self-made "cultural worker" class who "controlled and supervised" their projects. Meanwhile, in the *fin de siècle* context of internal developments, state-funded editors prepared inventories regarding railways and telegraph lines and indexed topical lists of the books allowed and approved by the Ministry of Public Education. In detail, the works of these editors seemed as though they were measuring the sprectrums of imperial power in distances and minds. Additionally, as indicated in Mehmet Murat's catalogue of publications and handbooks, American and Ottoman book editors met state standards by adjusting their projects to such an extent that their combined production listed 4,000 book titles in Turkish from 1881 to 1901.[10]

Although the press laws restricted words on paper, some loyalist authors and officials embraced the print culture being imported by

American missionaries. Paradoxically, then, the domestic press countered missionary publishers by emulating their mass-printing technology. Indeed, the state-sanctioned presses had been printing newspapers and almanacs since the provincial reforms of 1864. Their half-century growth showed 136 printing facilities in Istanbul alone. These presses were owned variously by local and foreign publishers, comprising 49 Armenians, 45 Turks, 38 Greeks, 10 Jews, and 7 American Board members. The printing business likewise appealed to provincial governors, such as Giritli Sırrı and Abidin Pasha, to create a vast publishing network in Istanbul and other urban centres, including Ankara, Beirut, Izmir, Rhodes, Salonika, and Trabzon. The first illustrated Turkish newspaper, *Mirat-ı alem* (*Global Mirror*), had copied the American Board's printing style and form since its inception in 1883, showing that Ottoman and American publishers exchanged aesthetics and techniques as much as they all coped with censorship to varying degrees.[11]

Given the state's resilience against outside influence, the American Board's publishers encountered a greater degree of skepticism. In fact, the 1877 press law restricted them further by mixing reactive improvisation with pragmatic inference. Mandated for the missionaries in particular, the intricate procedures and heightened screenings induced an effective interdepartmental collaboration. The Inspection and Examination Committee received censorship reports and publication copies from other departments, including the Press Services, Communications and Telegram Centre, customs offices, and Ottoman Embassy in Washington. Then the committee's agents assessed the incoming information to weigh the impact of publications on potential readers. Strikingly, they found that some "Muslim families" had started "reading the Bible" and "attending the Church mass" held by the missionaries. Appalled by their findings, they noted that much of the missionary literature was disorienting the "malleable" folk, so it had to be restricted until censorship experts decided what books could remain in circulation.[12]

As far as Minister of the Interior Mehmet Faik Memduh was concerned, "ignorance" had already "plagued entire communities" before American missionaries entered the scene. In a May 1898 memorandum, he concluded that missionary activities had political overtones and actual potential to "nurture sedition," as "the complete ignorance" of the rural public would readily "invite such abnormal activity." The minister did not define what he meant by "abnormal activity," as though it was obvious. The Ministers Council shared his concerns and agreed on the importance of the matter.[13]

Despite seeking to minimize missionary engagement with the rural public, which was extremely "susceptible to imported ideologies," imperial instructions did not deter missionary literature from reaching the more informed urban readership. New instructions also separated the literature by content, granting access to religion-themed pamphlets in western cities while making them inaccessible in eastern villages. However, several problems challenged this strategy when put in practice. Provincial agents struggled to catch up with the centre's instructions, missionary presses continued to print at fast rates, and all the while missionary college libraries still held numerous collections not yet seen by state officials.[14]

During a routine investigation in the spring of 1888, local officers found in Antep American College's library "numerous books" that defamed the Ottoman government and Islam. In a somewhat suspect report, they noted that some maps therein showed east Anatolia as "Independent Armenia" but hesitated to interrogate the library staff without advice from Istanbul. Minister of the Interior Ahmet Münir ordered the seizure of all the publications and warned the college's board not to acquire anti-Ottoman books.[15]

Viewed from Istanbul, such incidents appeared to be an aberration from traditional norms and a failure of administrative planning. The imperial state clearly failed to prevent missionary transgressions in a later incidentin Ioannina, northwest Greece. There, exposure to the American Board's "seditious books and pamphlets" had reportedly shattered the faith and loyalty of the Muslim community. In a May 1907 note, Governor Seyfullah Efendi said that, "this being the case," he was working hard "to eliminate the possibility of these books and pamphlets" reaching the locals. He thus aimed "to pursue and prosecute the people deliver[ing] anti-regime speeches in cafes and out in public."[16]

The governor of Ioannina did not state that anyone was under surveillance. His shocking note nevertheless induced central authorities to enforce restrictive policies against local missionary engagements. The stringent regulations urged extreme monitoring of the American Board's presses and vetting of their books. Once again, new directives impeded the dissemination of missionary publications in the countryside but did not necessarily prohibit it in town centres.[17]

In efforts to impede the dissemination of missionary publications, Ottoman authorities abstained from banning them all. Also, by allocating responsibility to the publishers and local agents, they wished to check the printed materials at the source. This policy allowed the missionary media to survive but not thrive. However, educational materials were regarded as an exception, as various textbooks went through multiple editions without procedural setbacks. In a deeper analysis, this nuanced perspective was the specific result of a larger bureaucratic desire to monitor, censor, and control the views and works of publishers in the Ottoman Empire.[18]

MISSIONARY PUBLISHERS, MONITORING PROCESSES, AND THE LOCAL CONTEXT

The publishing agenda of American missionaries posed a risk of disrupting public order and tarnishing the Turkish-Islamic image. Just as Ottoman readers read and heard the evangelical message from the American Board's missionaries, American readers learned of the Turks and Islam through monographs and articles written by the same missionaries – especially Charles Tracy, Cyrus Hamlin, George Knapp, George White, Edward Prime, Henry Dwight, and Henry Jessup. The press policies of the Ottoman state stemmed from coordination between the Ministries of Education, Foreign Affairs, the Interior, and Public Security, the Communications and Telegram Centre, the customs offices, and the Ottoman Embassy in Washington. At all ranks and levels, these government units sought to track and control the authors by exercising enhanced vigilance.[19]

Earlier book proposals had usually secured permission from Istanbul without much formality. The centre's lax policy had allowed the American Board's publishers to print and distribute literature for general readers. Facing the exponential expansion of their network, central authorities espoused a rather defensive position to safeguard the imperial edifice by curtailing the board's publications.[20]

Amid a state of emergency against the local interference of foreign nationals, the Ottoman government exhorted provincial officials to survey missionary propaganda in their region. But new directives, precipitating attention to any type of literature, entailed too much work for local agents – given that even the imperial language experts, a total of eighty men by 1890, were failing to abstract and translate

5.1 Photo of the American Board of Commissioners for Foreign Missions, Istanbul, 1859.

strategically important documents into Turkish. By means of a mass recruitment in August 1893, the Ministers Council strengthened the Inspection and Examination Committee's ranks by hiring anglophone censors. These new hires started to "scrutinize" non-Turkish literature, spending their time mostly on examining and censoring American missionary publications.[21]

Neşet Efendi, the director of the Inspection and Examination Committee, remained concerned about the duties of his subordinates even though new hires had joined them. In an August 1895 memorandum, he made a bleak presentation of the committee's performance because the assessment procedures for foreign books had become completely overwhelming. Regardless of how hard his subordinates had been working, they were failing to catch up with the rising demand for their services. The director admitted the failure of his understaffed yet overworked unit, all the while noting that the duty to assess all the existing literature was simply beyond their capacity.[22]

Minister of the Interior Mehmet Faik Memduh admitted that various bureaucratic challenges were no doubt exacerbating the problem of dissemination of missionary materials. Yet at an 1898 council meeting, he interpreted the complaints of lower-ranking officials as a sign of their poor execution of new state directives. His colleagues nonetheless absolved these officials of their reluctance and failure to act and concluded the meeting by issuing a decree to reject new book proposals. The reason for this decision was threefold. The distribution of missionary publications was already rampant, a representative number of these publications contained "provocative" elements, and the shortage of "trained staff" rendered it impossible to effectively process the publishing demands. Imperial authorities orchestrated an empire-wide surveillance at the same time, hoping the decree might help to debilitate the impact of the missionary literature already in public circulation.[23]

If the decree of 1898 stipulated no specific criteria on how to analyze a written work, supplementary instructions instilled in state agents a sense of what publications would be deemed provocative. Typical directives mandated the removal of literature that criticized the imperial state, Islam, and the local status quo. In a March 1899 directive, for instance, a specific clause noted that American missionaries had been proactively involved in rebellions in Alexandretta, south-east Anatolia. They had distributed various leaflets to the locals – Alawi, Assyrian, Christian, and Jewish residents – and had blamed the Istanbul government for causing regional conflicts. The Communications and Telegram Centre forwarded such propaganda materials to Istanbul, showcasing them as evidence of the board's "ulterior motives." Then the ministers, finding an ancillary to public unrest in such propaganda, issued further directives against missionary publications. Additionally, some civilians took upon themselves the task of hunting for foreigners who were distributing pamphlets about their town, essentially deputizing themselves as guardians of the law.[24]

Provincial officials in Harput receieved a series of orders to exercise caution against international communications. In an August 1905 directive, central authorities sought to diminish the missionary impact on east Anatolia by instructing them not to release any type of correspondence to "unauthorized" persons whom they knew nothing about. In a coded fashion, "unauthorized persons" alluded to American missionaries, the most visible group of foreigners regularly in contact with families, friends, and reporters in Europe and the United States.[25]

For the American Board's publishing houses, surprise inspections became routine inspections, no longer surprising amid an empire-wide surveillance. In cases where these inspections revealed any sign of illegal activity, imperial authorities did not hesitate to punish the parties involved. In many cases, indeed, the publishers lacked authorization, imported printing machines without authorization, or printed "seditious works" – and in the late Ottoman context, they engaged in a range of physical, verbal, and written activities against state "norms" and "public order."[26]

The Ministry of the Interior harked back to the critical issues previously articulated by the Inspection and Examination Committee's director, Neşet Efendi. In a February 1902 memo, ministry officials offered a good excuse for why the director might have given up the hassle. His censorship staff were largely underqualified for the task of processing foreign publications. Additionally, ministry officials confirmed Neşet Efendi's honest diagnosis as much as they lauded some censors as "competent" and "meticulous." These few censors had been screening the publications and properly identifying them as "permitted" or "prohibited." Although such qualified agents were appreciated and sought after in Istanbul, they were rare talents and remained exceptions in their field.[27]

To central authorities, miscommunication with provincial agents was a constant challenge even after the telegraph network endowed the centre with the latest technology to communicate with the provinces. Indeed, the Ministry of Public Works had linked the Ottoman realm by laying a 27,359-kilometre telegraph line, the world's eighth-longest line in 1880. Despite having access to these facilities, many provinces did not submit assessment reports to Istanbul, and those reports that were submitted came in "rather late." By extension, this problem meant that the censors failed to receive foreign-language literature in a timely manner. Although the censors knew "occidental languages and the geography of those countries," these materials were "nearly impossible to decipher." To facilitate the process, central authorities ordered the hiring of polyglot agents by provincial governors. A major credential for the job was a reading "knowledge of English," which the existing staff usually did not have.[28]

An October 1903 edict bid local governors to draft new recruits to their payroll. This executive order – which encouraged the central government to "hire and pay for agents" to screen foreign publications – echoed the administrative objective of consolidating central and provincial power. Yet those on the receiving end claimed that the centre had discounted local circumstances in proclaiming the edict.[29]

The governor of Kayseri, Mustafa Hilmi, grumbled about increasing his white-collar population and stressed two impediments to this assignment. "Nobody" in Kayseri truly "knew languages," but even so he could not hire more agents on account of "inadequate funds." Given that the American Board's correspondence and publications were being shipped and printed through the western ports of "Izmir and Galata," he thought that they "may better be handled" there, not in his province in central Anatolia. Rather than preaching to Istanbul about how to deploy imperial resources, the governor was showing how impractical it would be to recruit anglophone experts in Kayseri. His comments eventually served their purpose, effectively shifting the centre's pressure to other provinces.[30]

Where the central ideal of "vigilance by any means necessary" prevailed despite the intractable problem of inadequate resources, field reports signified manifest desperation in keeping missionaries in check. Justifying the fear of imperial authorities, several cases revealed that missionary literature had swarmed the countryside as well as western cities, causing local agents to waver over what kind of publications were "legitimate" or inclusive of "seditious gossiping."[31]

HENRY JESSUP, BOARD PUBLICATIONS, AND STATE INSPECTIONS

The career of Henry Jessup, the American Board's lead editor in Beirut from 1856 to 1910, embodies the story of how missionaries interacted with authorities over their publishing enterprise. Jessup contacted the central government in Istanbul several times when local officials shut down and reopened his press between 1887 and 1904. Like his colleague Henry Dwight at the Istanbul Bible House, he criticized Ottoman authorities because "all books entering the empire were examined by the censor, and if objected to, were either confiscated or sent back to Europe and America," as though foreign publishers were "under their paternal scrutiny." In speculating about the regime's stringent control over the media, Jessup cited Dwight Moody's book *To the Work! To the Work!* (1884), which official censors had "refused to sanction." In this case, the censors "suppressed" the manuscript's "lessons drawn from the story of Gideon" and "any map of the Holy Land showing the divisions made by Joshua among the twelve tribes of Israel." In Jessup's view, such an ignorant perspective could result only from the "perilous suggestiveness of the possibility that such an event might occur again."[32]

In December 1886 Jessup had a first-hand encounter with the Ottoman state when Beirut customs officials "seized" seven outgoing boxes of the "Arabic Scriptures" even though the boxes contained "the stamp of imperial approval." The city's unnamed director of public instruction "declared that their export" outside the state was being "interdicted." Two months later, the director revisited his press and "examined all publications" therein. This time, he "placed on every one the seal of approbation."[33]

The standard procedure obliged the editors to "send to [Istanbul] two manuscript copies of every book to be printed." Then "one copy" would be "returned" to the editor's press with "correction and sometimes mutilation." The revised manuscript had to be "mailed" again to Istanbul "after printing and before publication" so that the censors could compare the original and corrected text. Certainly, "woe to the press that varies in printing from the corrected copy!" Much to Jessup's dismay, the American Board's editors had to go through "this same precautionary process" for "every daily, weekly, and monthly journal." The presses would really suffer that "woe" if they dared to print postscripts. Jessup was so preoccupied with censorship requirements that he constantly brought it up in his monographs, such as *Fifty-Three Years in Syria*.[34]

An intense discussion centred on the *Weekly Publication*, an Arabic-language journal launched by the American Board in 1871 and edited by Jessup between 1889 and the early 1900s. He contacted the Ottoman government frequently throughout this journal's chequered existence. In June 1890 Minister of the Interior Ahmet Münir accepted his appeal for a certificate to resume the journal after the Beirut officers shut it down because it had printed literary translations without consulting with officials. This time, the minister reopened the journal and granted him a second certificate to publish a "Supplementary to the Publication." Whereas Beirut-based censors recorded mixed reactions to Jessup's publications, imperial authorities believed that these publications did not manifest an intent of sedition and contributed to the readers' "advancement of knowledge."[35]

Nonetheless, in an August 1898 decree, the skepticism of central authorities regarding missionary editors caught up to Jessup. As the *Weekly Publication* underwent enhanced monitoring in line with the state-wide search for instances of "obscenity" and "sedition," the censors identified provocative articles in the journal three times – in February 1900, July 1903, and February 1904 – and the Ottoman government revoked the journal's licence. One final act effectively silenced the journal without an explanation, and Jessup began to ponder over how the journal's legal status had changed overnight.[36]

The select use of references could have been the reason. Until 1904 the *Weekly Publication* had printed Bible verses such as Ezekiel 21:2, which invited "all Christians to unite" and to "speak ... I am against you; and I will draw my sword ... and cut off from you the righteous and the wicked." In the presence of religious tensions escalating in the region, such verses emitted the same signal as Henry Dwight's reference to John 4:20, which alluded to Muslim injustice, thus instigating non-Muslim communities to refuse allegiance to the Ottoman authority.[37]

Lacking further evidence, Istanbul and Beirut officials overreacted to Jessup by labelling the later issues of his journal as "title-tattling" and idle gossip instead of responsible journalism. This radical shift explains the complexity of rigorous publishing standards to curtail the American Board's spreading literature and to deal with the possible contingencies of these standards in specific contexts. Surprisingly, the Inspection and Examination Committee reconsidered its former ruling once more, for Jessup got around the July 1903 order of closure and recovered his journal in February 1904.[38]

Even so, the stubborn Jessup was fortunate, unlike other editors. In the dialogue with authorities, he benefited from his contacts – the friends under whose influence Washington officials also offered him the position of US minister to Persia in 1883 – whereas other editors waded through a sea of directives that curbed their enterprise more stringently. Although imperial directives were meant to restore law and order, the American Board's editors perceived them as bellicose threats against their publishing agenda. When imperial bureaucrats offered up the term "seditious" – that oft-quoted and abstract word in the late state lexicon – it sufficed to warrant the legal prohibition of the literature in question and the closure of its source.[39]

The expansion of missionary publications in inverse proportion to imperial resources led to greater coordination between government branches and a stricter vigilance against the dissemination of these publications. But imperial authorities, still discontent with the execution of regulatory standards, considered alternative ways to control missionary editors. They turned to movable type and printing machines that the editors had been using in printing their work. In the 1890s an innovative policy of monitoring printing devices went into effect that expanded the regime's attention to the medium of publishing itself.[40]

CHALLENGES OF PUBLISHING HOUSES AND DEVICES

American missionaries reached their largest audience when their importation of printing equipment soared in the 1880s. Ottoman authorities correlated these developments and responded by creating a policy of restriction on the ownership and use of printing machines and movable type – the devices that potentially allowed missionaries to reach the less educated populace. To curb the course of the missionary publishing enterprise, provincial agents monitored local presses, confiscated printing devices that lacked official licences, and deterred the publishers from moulding printing type.[41]

General directives did not endorse summarily closing American missionary presses and confiscating all their assets. They instead warned the editors of the legislative intent, stating that the criminal record of certain authors and the seditious content of certain books would bear legal consequences such as closures and confiscations. In practice, these directives precipitated a constant round of on-site inspections. Following a February 1893 decree, for instance, provincial agents inspected virtually all the establishments owned by the American Board and confiscated unlicensed tools of operation, such as the copy machine in Merzifon Anatolia College.[42]

The degree of an author's "notoriety" determined whether specific sanctions would be definitive or could be repealed at a later date. In an August 1893 case, local agents red-tagged an Istanbul-based press and confiscated the printing machines in the building. Then central authorities discovered that the owner had no publishing licence but did not have a criminal record either. Minister of the Interior Halil Rıfat annulled the act of closure and seizure. He also urged the agents to return the machines "as soon as" the owner "forfeited to the Internal Affairs Fund the required fee" for operating without a licence.[43]

In tracing the legal status of active presses, local records made central authorities even more anxious about the state of public order. Several presses, like the publishing house of Manukian, an American-turned convert and Ottoman editor, were publishing a series of provocative pamphlets. In a February 1899 directive, Rıfat sought to tackle this matter by ordering the closure of the presses that lacked an official licence to operate. To complicate the matter, state officials, including the minister's own staff, ignored his instructions and continued to copy even "confidential state documents" using Manukian's press because it was cheaper that way. The Ministers Council ordered the officials to revoke Manukian's licence, shut down his publishing house, and abandon such "ignorant" practices.[44]

The restrictive printing policy affected the typesetters and editors near and far away from the capital. Based in Beirut, Khalil Sarkis and Khalil Badawi were publishing Arabic pamphlets and circulating them among the residents in the greater Syrian province with an imperial certificate. But early in 1900, their certificates were revoked allegedly because they had been using Arabic type that they themselves had moulded despite an official warning to discard it. The Ministers Council evaluated provincial reports, and as a result, Minister of the Interior Mehmet Faik Memduh issued a February 1900 order urging a "definite" confiscation of the printing machines of both publishers.[45]

It is a mystery why Sarkis and Badawi caused an immediate reaction from the Ottoman government. Local reports projected a scandalous image of them to the centre, and perhaps the authorities wanted to make an example of them. Further instructions to Syria and the other provinces reminded the publishers that they must notify provincial officials of "every step of their work" and must not import printing type without the necessary paperwork. The instructions also reminded the officials that they must "caution" and "enhance vigilance" against the typesetters and editors in their region.[46]

Whereas local officials found imperial decrees to be ambivalent, missionary publishers thought they were unfair. When Syria officials caught wind of the American Board's importation of a printing machine to the Beirut American College's library in August 1905, they double-checked whether to confiscate the machine and learned that the machine could stay in the college premises to copy course materials. Additionally, Minister of the Interior Mehmet Faik Memduh ordered Beirut officers to inspect all the presses in the region and to send a comprehensive list of them to Istanbul. Like his minister colleagues, Memduh suspected that the board's missionaries had an ulterior motive and that all the while they had been neglecting the binding decrees.[47]

In Istanbul municipal authorities bore the brunt of imperial orders because they were within arm's reach of the central state and because many publishers were clustered in the American Plaza, a multistorey complex in the Eminönü district on the capital's European side. Specific conversations between imperial and municipal authorities show the degree to which publishing restrictions impacted the plaza's occupants, even that "humble" and "inculpable" Ottoman merchant named Agop Matosyan. Matosyan had obtained permission to import European-made printing type to his press earlier in August 1899. But in November 1903, when he showed up at the Galata Customs Office to receive several boxes of type that he had ordered from Liverpool, the main print-technology exporter to Istanbul, he was surprised to learn that municipal authorities had already checked his invoice through the office and had confiscated his type in keeping with "the executive order of vigilance." Much to his dismay, they had even transferred his type to "the Imperial College of Industry" in order to make it a public good.[48]

Matosyan was a seasoned Istanbulite merchant, not born yesterday, and he petitioned for reparations of his grievances. Imperial authorities responded to his case by admitting that it was clearly a bureaucratic "error" and proceeded to do "the right thing" – that is, to return his printing type and admonish the municipal agents responsible for the error. The case of Matosyan reveals that the authorities had no qualms about reversing specific decisions arbitrated at the local level and making redress to the defendants if deemed necessary.[49]

Local authorities were grasping at straws or acting more royalist than the king. Their arbitrary measures persuaded the press owners that, in order to maintain their legal status and avoiding bureaucratic errors, they had to "seek permission" and complete the paperwork in advance. Even though the government's tactic of suasion continued to fail in resolving specific cases, the American Plaza publishers checked in with the authorities, just as Matosyan had completed the necessary formalities well before the Galata Customs Office received the invoice regarding his next order of Greek-letter type.[50]

Strikingly, the story of Matosyan outlived the Ottoman Empire. In the National Assembly of Turkey, several senators suspected that the government had extorted his printing devices. In a November 1949 parliamentary question, they asked the Cabinet members why his expensive assets had been leased out for much lower than market value to Yunus Nadi – a pro-republican journalist whose national newspaper, *Cumhuriyet*, had been advocating for centre-left views since its inception in May 1924. Entering into the debate, Finance Minister İsmail Rüştü Aksal started by refuting the allegation that the Abandoned Property Commission had usurped the Matosyan Press and delivered its inventory to the state treasury, but then the minister confessed, arguing that it was the right thing to do. Matosyan had died in 1889 and the inheritors – his son, Vahan, and three daughters – had not paid off Matosyan's debt to the Ottoman Bank. Instead, they had "escaped" to Switzerland upon the proclamation of the Turkish Republic. Eventually, when more corruption cases drew the senators into a whirlpool of polemics, the inheritors lost Matosyan's assets to the republican statesmen, who expropriated these assets to spread their views, possibly bribing a like-minded publicist to help with the task.[51]

In the late Ottoman Empire, specific regulations targeted what came into missionary presses and what came out of them. This is why various debates took place at the port of entry, where the common attribute of officials was an extreme sense of duty to track the inbound freight traffic. Indeed, from Istanbul to Anatolia, customs officials inspected the printing machinery and type so distrustfully that they started causing problems rather than solving them.[52]

In a June 1902 case, customs inspectors received "two boxes of foreign language type" and another "box of rubber-coated, cast-steel type" at the north Anatolia Port of Samsun. The manufacturer's invoice asked for delivery of the first shipment to American Board missionaries and the second shipment to a local merchant named Ohannes Kürekian. Rather hesitant, the inspectors contacted the provincial head office in Trabzon, which turned to the Ministry of the Interior, and the communication eventually made its way from the customs authority to central authorities in Istanbul. In detail, the itinerary of this case captures the fluidity within the layers of the imperial state and a sense of doubt in the lower layers of authority, a side effect of the imperial caveat that it would be better to err on the side of caution.[53]

Inspectors had to confiscate printing type on account of "missing documentation." However, the inspectors in Samsun used caution because the act of confiscation would induce grievances and become an issue of liability. Thus only after being instructed to do so by Minister of the Interior Mehmet Faik Memduh did the inspectors store the boxes in their warehouse until further notice.[54]

The missionaries and Kürekian wanted to petition for redress, so they approached P. Bogognano, a respected merchant who owned a knitting store in Istanbul. An expert broker, Bogognano contacted the sultan on their behalf and pleaded that the boxes of printing type stored in the Samsun warehouse be "returned to the recipients," as doing so would be "in accordance with the law." To "price and package" merchandise, he himself used "this sort of printing type," which was "sold ubiquitously." Bogognano preferred not to explain why the boxes had ended up in the warehouse.[55]

Since the 1890s, when non-Turkish printing type had flooded the local markets, the merchants of Istanbul had used it to label their merchandise. In a June 1902 report, the Galata Customs Office noted that imported type generally lacked a "promissory note," which would have certified the contracting parties. Additionally, the director of the internal press, Mustafa Efendi, studied the marketing trends while his staff were working on Bogognano's petition. In a letter to the sultan, who "would very soon give the final words" on this matter, he said that such petitions "should be treated as others had been" treated in the past. But a serious discussion was started because the latest case had epitomized practical problems and offered a legal model for solving them.[56]

Given the inefficacy of the existing laws, central authorities drew up a new protocol to regulate the importation of printing devices by land and sea. Individual applicants first had to record in the state registry the movable type and printing apparatus "prior to shipment" by notifying authorities of the "intended purpose" and "reason for importing" these devices. Then the applicant party would swear a written "oath," acquire a "promissory note," and attach these documents to the records. In good practice, these stipulations could streamline the work of customs officials and avert a range of legal encounters between authorities, publishers, and merchants.[57]

Immediately effective, the new protocol affected the cases in progress. Not only did the Ministry of the Interior's Communications Department tell local agents about the importance of the new regulations, but in an August 1902 memorandum, it also specifically ordered that the printing type confiscated in Samsun be delivered to the missionaries and Kürekian. Yet the transaction was contingent on the submission of a written oath that the recipients would use the acquired type only for "commercial purposes." A "promissory note" and then the delivery followed the oath. Even though an oath had not been submitted prior to the shipment, a belated oath satisfied the necessary steps. The memorandum ended with an approval of the perspectives presented by the petitioner, Bogognano, and the internal press director, Mustafa. In detail, it ordered no exceptional treatment of any recipient party and the handling of printing type purchases "in compliance with the law." Besides these instructions, the processing of Bogognano's petition indicates that state authorities actively sought to control the ownership and local use of printing devices.[58]

Given the variety of circumstances, stringent regulations did not create the rights and remedies desired by the central state. In November 1903 local officials reported on the transaction of an individual who had already submitted a promissory note to purchase a copy machine. This was an unusual case because the applicant was not a merchant in need of a copy machine at work. Minister of the Interior Mehmet Faik Memduh responded by saying that the applicant would not be "allowed to vend the machine" or "share the right to use it" with a third party. Then the owner had to apply in person to state officials for separate permission to sell or jointly operate printing devices. Specific decrees thus emerged when needs arose, but they carried legal implications for many other applicants.[59]

Where central authorites defined the rules of conduct, missionaries and merchants procured ordinances with a view to importing more tools to colleges and presses. But the clarity of directives did not bring certainty to practices in the local context, as state agents faced particular situations and erred on the side of caution. When in doubt about the right course of action, they confiscated printing tools and held them in a customs warehouse unless instructed otherwise. This behaviour became the norm and a mere formality in the early twentieth century. Additionally, the August 1902 memorandum failed to resolve legal disputes even though it allowed the law-abiding parties to claim printing type and machines. What imperial standards eventually created was a formal dialogue with third parties and a range of documents to be used in legitimate disputes. As recipients of movable type and printing devices, American missionaries recognized the importance of legal documentation to Ottoman state bureaucracy and their publishing activity.[60]

CHALLENGES OF PRINTING AND CIRCULATING BOOKS

George Herrick, the American Board's veteran missionary in the Ottoman Empire, had much to say about the field. In a September 1904 issue of the *Boston Daily Globe*, he explained that "there are three hundred American educational and philanthropic institutions in the Ottoman Empire whose property interests exceed seven million dollars." These endeavours could have easily multiplied if state officials had not "held up" their "building" applications "for months." Indeed, state vigilance became so ubiquitous that "customs agents" held "any book" whose title had "the word 'America' in it." This editorial informed the readers of missionary operations by way of reducing the imperial state to an intolerant, jaundiced entity.[61]

Vigilant officials monitored foreign publications. Perhaps inadvertently, Herrick also claimed that the Ottoman government permanently closed the route from press to readership. In reality, the officials undertook inspections under certain instructions. They certainly did "not hamper the publishing and distribution" of the literature already "registered in the imperial index" – an official list that the Ministry of Education compiled by classifying the approved and forbidden books in the spirit of medieval *index librorum prohibitorum*. Books might be seized and destroyed, but the decision hinged on a range of state sensibilities, not arbitrary judgments. By the early twentieth century, imperial authorities had established specific criteria for assessing the content and impact of missionary literature.[62]

In inspecting books citing America, the key criterion was "sedition," an abstract concept that charged such books with making "anti-state" and "anti-Islamic" statements. As political and religious criticisms could be marked as provoking local subjects to question the state authority, the elements of sedition varied in accordance with the circumstances in which these books found themselves. In the post-1890 context of public disorder, provoking Armenians in eastern Anatolia to revolt against the state was a type of sedition, and slandering Islam at missionary-run Central Turkey College was another. Imperial regulations authorized missionary editors provided that they did not denote such types of sedition in their literature. This rule reflected a conversative bureaucratic response to the simultaneous yet not directly related emergence of ethno-religious tensions and missionary operations in Ottoman lands. State authorities began by searching for possible missionary links with local rebellions and adopted various tactics that scoured the American Board's publishing projects for a particular type of sedition. Any other criteria for authorizing missionary projects, such as an author's reputation and intent, teetered on the axis of sedition.[63]

All authors could publish for an Ottoman readership unless their words fell under the anti-state and anti-Islamic rubric. From 1880 onward, the procedures for publishing proposals warranted a thorough examination of the author's reputation and the book's content. Typically, the submission of a proposal started the process of publishing the book under question. In the Ministries of the Interior and Education, staff ranked and filed these submissions, checked to see whether the authors had a criminal past, and registered their written oath. For criminal records, they consulted provincial administrations, the courts, and the customs offices and embassies when necessary. It was local agents who completed the procedure by registering the oath as an appendix in which the authors swore to respect and reckon with Ottoman rules and norms.[64]

Notoriously detailed, these procedural steps cancelled some book projects and prolonged the processing times for others that needed major revisions. In other cases, the imperial paper and seal conceded the distribution and copy rights of "benign" projects. Noncontractual by design, such a method of authorization afforded the Ottoman government legitimate grounds to oversee the American Board's publications and to censor those books already in press. It likewise shrank the margin of bureaucratic error by allowing the officials to double-check the substance of books and by exposing the publishers to the perpetual risk of liability.[65]

The success of the state's control mechanism remained contingent upon coordiation between the centre and provinces. Whereas the magnitude of earlier administrative coordination had fluctuated, the perspectives of central authorities were synchronized with provincial perceptions after 1880, when the publishing activities took off in the provinces. Some agents disrupted the mechanism and went beyond the three orders of business that the centre assigned them – inspecting publishers, reporting cases, and enforcing the law – by confiscating publishers' equipment without legitimate grounds. Again, the centre intervened by amending their arbitrary course of action.[66]

A dialogue between the capital and provinces illustrates the degree to which local agents subjected the American Board's editors to a stalemate by suspending the centre's peremptory edict. In a May 1892 directive, the Ministry of the Interior updated Anatolian governors regarding the list of "certified" missionary books. Suprisingly, the agents had red-tagged missionary presses and seized the books circulating in their region although these books were already on the list of allowable materials. Minister Halil Rıfat ordered all agents to report in immediately.[67]

In an August 1892 meeting, the Ministers Council discussed the issue of administrative incompetence and drafted an additional decree to subordinate aberrant practices to the centre. The decree endowed imperial authorities with absolute power over foreign publications. The Ministry of Education's experts would examine them and include in an index the books that they approved so that "they will be published." Arbitrary actions such as confiscating indexed publications subsided gradually as power was consolidated by the centre.[68]

Coupled with the local mistrust of merchants contracted by foreigners, government decrees did not end the unfair treatment of American missionaries who had been trading books in public spaces. To clarify the matter, US diplomat Pendelton King contacted the Ottoman Ministry of Foreign Affairs. In a January 1887 letter to Minister Sait Halim, he noted the rise of "frequent interference" with the "colporteurs employed by the American Bible Society." These booksellers were involved "in the sale of books," but they were selling only the books "submitted to and authorized by the Board of Public Instruction." This being the case, he demanded that the Ottoman government "issue positive instructions to the competent authorities" and "prevent further interference with said colporteurs." Seeing three more booksellers arrested, King contacted Halim again. Strikingly, he reiterated the matter without mentioning the latest Bible House incident – wherein "the minister of police" charged an officer "to search the *book-store* opening on the street, forming a part of the Bible House" in Istanbul. The officer had wanted to "search not only the book-store but the entire building." Rather worried, the Bible House staff told him that he could "go through the entire Bible House *alone* and search it as carefully as he desired; this he refused to do."[69]

Ottoman authorities collected specific incidents under the general subject of "the colportage of the books." In a March 1887 letter, Minister Halim explained that the US government had "incomplete" information on this subject. Police records indicated that American missionaries had "commenced the spreading of certain tracts" against the Islamic faith, which the Board of Public Instruction would never authorize to be sold by the colporteurs. This being the case in reality, the imperial government "decided to enforce the seizure" of such "injurious and calumnious" books. Regarding the specific Bible House incident, the "search" of its bookstore "brought the discovery of many volumes of those tracts" alongside "others not less injurious." The legal translator "opposed their seizure by the agents of the authority," but his "opposition" was "the less justifiable." Additionally, "the action of the police" was not to be hindered and "must be exercised freely and without reserve." Given that the Bible House constituted "a vast establishment, containing a printing establishment, a book-store, an editing bureau of a journal, and a school – the whole making a public place," Ottoman officials reserved the right to "free access" and would "practice, in case of need, a direct supervision."[70]

Diplomats made a rich polemic out of book sales. In an April 1887 response to Sait Halim, Pendelton King said that the party "totally devoid of truth" was the Ottoman government, not the United States. American missionaries did "not offer for sale, either at the Bible House or through their colporteurs, a single book or pamphlet which they are not ready to have examined by the proper authorities." They possessed "no book nor pamphlet" that had not been "sanctioned" by the Ministry of Public Education or had not "passed the censorship of the custom-house." More importantly, the missionaries had for sale "nothing against the Mussulman religion or public order." King thus urged imperial authorities to support "a grave charge of this kind" with "definite facts" such as "what books or pamphlets have been offered for sale to which objection can be made?"[71]

King dragged up specific incidents to show "the erroneous information furnished" for the Ottoman government. The missionaries once "offered for sale some copies of a Greek book" published in Athens. This book "proved to be objectionable" only after it had "passed the censorship, and paid duties." Even then, the Bible House editors "immediately withdrew them from sale" and "struck the title from their catalogue." Additionally, King brought up the latest incident, which he had not brought up in his previous letters. He called the missionaries "our missionaries" for the first time and noted that they were already in contact with Mehmet Tahir Münif, the minister of public education, who had himself worked long years as an author, editor, and polyglot translator fluent in English, French, and several other languages. He added that the Bible House was "free to be visited at any time by officials in an unofficial manner and without police." So were other presses and bookstores owned and contracted by the American Board. In return, King asked for respectful treatment of his fellow-citizen publishers and booksellers – "many of whom have already been arrested and hundreds of books taken from them." He finally assured Sait Halim that the "cessation of such interference" would not only "remove a chronic cause of complaint" but would also be of "great convenience to your Government" authorities in Istanbul.[72]

Ottoman authorities thought that doing so would be extremely dangerous, not "a great convenience," because American missionary publications would then soar and reach the malleable masses. Besides further qualms raised by Minister of the Interior Mehmet Faik Memduh about this matter, a November 1904 resolution rejected the American Board's petitions in clear terms. It cited as the reason a shortage of personnel to monitor the bookstores and protect them against mob attacks – which happened often when local neighbourhoods heard rumours that missionaries were kidnapping and converting children. The undisclosed reason was that the imperial centre decoded the colportage of books as a potentially "seditious venture," an enterprise that would complicate the process of separating the good books from the bad books. As this polemical debate continued into the next decade, imperial authorities worried about the books' quantity and mass distribution as much as they worried about their quality and content. They thus aimed to curb public circulation of the books, including those that the censors had checked and approved.[73]

The American Board's representatives urged the Ottoman government to reconsider the resolution, making it a matter of protracted confrontation. Because of their perseverance, Mehmet Faik Memduh and Mustafa Haşim, the interior and education ministers, compromised and supplanted the previously solid refusal with a conditional approval. In an April 1905 decree, they granted missionaries the right to circulate the copies of the Bible and other books approved by the Ministry of Education. But the decree retained the custom of suppressing such intrusions upon the minds of the masses by cautioning that the Ministry of Education's staff would reject "controversial" pamphlets and that local officials would monitor the literature's distribution. Again, new regulations applied to the entire print media, as the native publishers would also be held accountable for violating them. Additionally, a publisher's reputation became critically important during this time, but the status of specific publications depended largely on their content. Legally, then, the American Board's publishers could print and circulate literature without hindrance as long as they did so in accordance with state laws. Most of their pamphlets nevertheless violated the regulations and became an object of further restrictions.[74]

Imperial ministers relied on local reports transmitted to the capital, and the agents had a penchant for treating the missionaries based on personal judgment, not on the capital's midcourse guidance. In an early 1887 case, eastern Anatolia officers detained an unidentified missionary who was carrying a bag full of notes, which they sent to Istanbul. Ministry of Education personnel examined the notes, which consisted of sermons and a pamphlet, and found in them radical "criticisms" against the Ottoman state, "falsified news" on Christian oppression, and "a call for rebellion." In a February 1887 decree, the Ministers Council agreed that such notes would confuse the minds of local subjects, so they required the Ministry of Education to "destroy these seditious notes," although they ordered the officers to "free the missionary."[75]

Articulated in specific decrees, enhanced vigilance and detailed instructions showed variations in scope and practice. As local conditions nurtured imperial positions, missionary incidents engaged central authorities in diplomatic tussles with US diplomats and brought them into serious conflict with local interest groups, such as press owners in the Eminönü district's American Plaza and the Christian community leaders who disliked the missionaries and the officials at the same time.[76]

Situated at the nexus of diplomatic and social encounters, local interpretive action received one of two reactions from the imperial centre. First, if arbitrary practices averted an impending crisis that otherwise might have posed complex problems, the centre either demonstrated a tone of appreciation or remained silent, which was the traditional sign of affirmative feedback. In a September 1890 incident, central authorities praised the agents for their timely reaction to the illegitimate activities in north-central Anatolia. These agents had no time and no choice but to "inhibit" missionary pamphlets from reaching the "country folks" by confiscating them on site and then reporting them to the centre. Minister of the Interior Halil Rıfat responded by validating their act and encouraging them to "keep on doing what they did." Second, if arbitrary practices caused more harm than good, the centre expressed frustration. In a September 1892 incident, several agents broke the law by seizing the books that the American Bible Society had shipped to Kocaeli in northwest Anatolia. They had not examined these books in advance because they did not know that the Ministry of Education had already certified them. Exasperated, Minister Rıfat directed these "irresponsible agents" to apologize to the society, release the books, and submit an incident report. The centre's responses to such cases hinged on a pragmatic inference – the perspective that the late Ottoman authorities espoused to compensate for contextual variations. In a deeper analysis, the sultan and ministers activated an encoded sense of authority, faith, and order over the American Board's corpus.[77]

Some texts in the missionary corpus were "illegal" *ab initio*. Informed by preliminary reports, state decrees targeted malevolent authors who had a palpable interest in public outreach and pre-emptively prohibited their activity. In a late 1896 report, for instance, censorship agents criticized two Arabic pamphlets, *Selected Reviews in Geographical Science* and *Commensurate Answers*, that American missionaries wanted to circulate. These pamphlets slandered the imperial state and agitated local Christians to revolt against it. In a January 1897 decree, Minister of the Interior Mehmet Faik Memduh studied further inspection of these pamphlets and ordered local officials to inhibit the importation and distribution of such "obscene" and "seditious" publications. The officials understood the significance of "seizing and destroying them on sight" when found, but the decree presented no detail about what elements of obscenity and sedition the mentioned pamphlets had enveloped.[78]

The course of imperial action did not register measurable change in the next century. Without going into detail about transgressions, executive instructions urged local agents to seize seditious pamphlets such as the Turkish sermons "On Miracles" and "The Place of the Virgin Mary." Indeed, after 1900 the stringent guidelines on literature restrictions prevailed and signified the sum total of a machine bureaucracy, which George Herrick claimed was opposed to all missionary books reaching local readers. From an outsider's vantage point, Herrick and fellow missionaries did not really grasp the Ottoman *modus operandi*, particularly the ways that central authorities executed anti-literature decrees and interacted with local officials.[79]

Higher degrees of sedition conduced greater scrutiny, hence a greater effect on the status of publications, and almost always the minds of rural folk were most at stake. In a February 1902 landmark decree, the Ministry of the Interior outlawed "the pamphlets in villages." Albeit less effective than the centre expected, this decree came at the right time, as missionary pamphlets abounded in the villages, pitting the missionaries against the officials checking their activity. Given that much of the American Board's literature could potentially exacerbate public disorder, its dissemination necessitated stricter sanctions.[80]

Several cases served as a pretext for the prohibition of literature in the countryside. In January 1895 police patrols in eastern Anatolia saw an uneventful day disturbed by a passenger who, on his way home for holidays, was carrying two suspicious letters in his briefcase. Around noon, they stopped the passenger and identified him as Garabet, the son of Mesih, who was the American Board's locally hired preacher at Euphrates College. Somewhat furious, the patrols took him to the office of Rauf Bey, the Harput governor, who turned to the imperial government for advice on "what to do" in this case.[81]

Based on further investigation, foreign and internal affairs officials detected in the preacher's letters "seditious" content and a clear example of anti-regime literature. These letters claimed that the constant oppression of the Armenian subjects called for the imminent fall of the Ottoman Empire. The target audience was the college's Armenian students coming from the marginalized neighbourhoods in eastern Anatolia – the frontier region that had been plagued by political, economic, and communal crises since the 1870s. Inspired by American missionary teachings and European nationalist movements, the audience seemed ready for such a wake-up call.[82]

To the Armenian students, the preacher said, "Rise up, my sons," for now "I deliver to you not paper and pen, but something else. Cross your sword and run to the battlefield. You unfurl the flag while I load your guns." This battle cry against the six-century old Ottoman yoke was presented as legitimate. "Long have they eaten the Armenian bread and drunk the Armenian water yet returned with cursing us in five languages." Since the beginning, he wrote, "the vile Turks amused themselves while destroying the Armenian millet once and for all." The Turks would not hear or see the effects of their cruelty, as "their ears were the deafest, and their eyes the blindest." So it was time to return Armenia to the Armenians because "thy homeland is Armenia in Turkey," the lands where the Armenians had "survived" with their traditions "to this day!" At a time of high and deep emotions, the American Board's preacher cursed the Turks, claimed eastern Anatolia

– ancient Armenia – for the Armenian people, and called for an armed uprising against the imperial regime.[83]

A second letter addressed the larger public, urging the Armenians to join in bearing arms and exacting revenge. They had to claim "Even the mountains." Near and far, the Armenians should "come to Armenia," "form the ranks," and "fight the Turks like they are going to a wedding." They must "unite," "be saved," and "save thy land with blood." Let everybody "shout 'Damn Turkey' and 'long live Armenia'!" With the preacher Garabet predicting that "now is the time" to reclaim Armenia, such militant words hurriedly reached the Ministers Council in Istanbul while Garabet defended himself in a court in Harput and pleaded "not guilty." These letters carried elements of "sedition" and "militancy," he admitted, but "the content" therein had originated "from news clips and an American missionary," not from his pen.[84]

The provincial court found Garabet to be guilty until proven innocent, whereas the unnamed missionary colleague he would drag into the case remained innocent until proven guilty. Sait Halim, the foreign affairs minister, would have called the missionary to a court hearing. He nevertheless did not think it would be necessary because the experts' phraseological analysis of the letters convinced him that Garabet was lying. The quoted letters could not have been copied from an outside source. Then Halil Rıfat, the interior minister, told the Harput officials to keep the letters as evidence and advised Grand Vizier Kamil Pasha that the imperial government should allow the local court to handle the trial in progress. He also suggested that American missionaries stay out of this case "unless decided otherwise." In a deeper analysis, the preacher Garabet had known about the culpability of American missionaries in the minds of Ottoman authorities, and thus he possibly planned on getting away by pitting the authorities against the missionaries.[85]

After all, the issue of printing and circulating books challenged the authority of Ottoman officials and the activity of American missionaries at the same time. Preoccupied with the idea of restoring order by way of fighting sedition, the officials displayed uniformly vigilant behaviour that sought to disconnect publishers, preachers, and many others from the public. Amid the rise of public disorder, this behaviour was coupled with an unapologetic manner even in cases where the conduct of officials was difficult to justify. In a January 1893 case, placards hanging on the gate of Merzifon Anatolia College urged "the Turks to rise and apply the same medicine for the ills of the country that the people of India had employed." These placards – "revolutionary and incendiary" and commonly found in American Board institutions – advocated that only a British occupation of the Ottoman Empire would end local chaos. Although the college's president, George Herrick, "emphatically denied the charge of college complicity," the officials focused on the placards being printed using a "cyclostyle," a printing instrument at the college's disposal but "rarely found" anywhere else. Police officers then arrested Hagop Tomaian and Ohannes Kayaian, who were members of the college's local faculty, and imprisoned "many persons" for "alleged revolution," "deceit," and "violence." Based on field inspections by an international committee, Ottoman officials "released" the local faculty members and "exiled" them from the country. Despite an apology due to the American Board, they closed the case without apologizing for their overly vigilant behaviour against the evidently innocent missionaries. But George White did not forget about this story. He recounted its end with incredulity, asking readers to pause and "imagine it all!"[86]

PROSPECTS AND CHALLENGES OF SCHOOLS AND SCHOOLBOOKS

Charles Tracy, the principal of Merzifon Anatolia College in central Anatolia from 1886 to 1912, was passionate about public education. "The work of translation and publication is one mission very eminent among others," he said, because "the fruitage of their influence" was infinitely "large." Indeed, "the greatest contribution to the American Board's Turkey mission" was the printing presses, not the colleges or hospitals. In May 1893 he called the presses "our main business as missionaries." Ottoman authorities reflected on the simultaneous benefits and liabilities of the missionaries' fruitful enterprise. They approved of schoolbooks because modern education would benefit the young generation in the countryside, yet this was paradoxically the same generation that had to be kept away from the negative influences of religious propaganda.[87]

By the 1890s the education minister, Ahmet Zühdü, had compiled inventories of the American Board's curricula, textbooks, teachers, and staff. These inventories recorded the legal name, country of citizenship, and educational background of employees and included the bibliographical information and educational value of textbooks. The inventory of Merzifon Anatolia College illustrates how imperial authorities interpreted the quality of missionary schools and the materials they were using in the classroom. Developed from the provincial government's reports and the Ministry of Education's studies, the inventory opened up a panoramic view of the school's premises and conduct.[88]

American Board missionaries founded Merzifon Anatolia College as a four-year boarding college for the liberal arts. In 1886–87, its inaugural academic year, the college admitted over a hundred students from Armenian and Greek communities. In the two decades until the First World War – a crucial period for state officials to monitor the college's development – missionary founders filled administrative positions and hired local graduates as faculty and staff. Most of the textbooks came from the United States.[89]

The inventory of Merzifon Anatolia College listed the college's core faculty as Director Edward Dickens (1864, Princeton, English and philosophy), Frans Geech (1889, Carlton, mathematics), George White (1887, Iowa, English), and Suzanne Dickens (1890, Elmira, mathematics). The local faculty members made a longer list: Akilef Yoanidis (1892, Anatolia, Greek), Anna (1859, Istanbul, advisor), Arail Sivaslian (1891, Carlton, mathematics), Arusban (1893, Merzifon, music), Aspasia (1891, Bursa, Greek), Avadis Gelinjian (1886, Anatolia, Armenian), Dimitrios Theoharidis (1887, Anatolia, Greek), Lucy (1890, Merzifon, diction and handwriting), Ohannes Agopyan (1886, Anatolia, Ottoman Turkish), Ohannes Manajian (1882, Antep, physics), Seyak Toumaian (1891, Anatolia, music), and Yerapion (1868, Merzifon, Armenian).[90]

Compiled in June 1896, the inventory of Merzifon Anatolia College presented the American Board's hiring process as well as the administration's and faculty's profiles. Indeed, the native workforce at this college had soared throughout the century. There were 88 American missionaries and 30 local employees in 1820, 376 missionaries and 787 locals in 1860, 422 missionaries and 2,183 locals in 1885, 593 missionaries and 4,723 locals in 1910, and 656 missionaries and 4,777 locals in 1915. The inventory noted that no Muslims studied or worked at the college. But Armenians and Greeks graduated and sought employment from the American Board, all the while gaining an upward and lateral mobility that did not exist elsewhere in the Ottoman Empire. Many local students obtained teaching positions through personal connections, and since their degrees were commensurate with official standards, specific inventories and reports did not take issue with their tenure.[91]

Compiled by the Ministry of Education, school inventories compelled attention to the classroom materials. They classified the textbooks by subject matter, not by their content, and indicated that students who were enrolled at American colleges studied English, engineering, and science from textbooks imported by the colleges' boards. Other courses in Turkish, law, and arts adopted textbooks assigned by state authorities.

The particular book collection of Merzifon Anatolia College was up to date, with one-third of the total not older than five years.[92] The inventory recorded textbooks by citing the author's family name, the book title, and the publication date and place. Foreign books came from New England, mostly from New York and Boston. In detail, students at the college studied six science books printed in Boston, including Winters's *Applied Engineering* (1888) and *Analytical Engineering* (1892) and Eastwool's *Science of Sanitation* (1890). They studied seventeen books printed in New York on grammar and science, including Lewis's *Engineering* (1889), Sonton's *English Grammar* (1893), and Berry's *Economics and Politics* (1890). In the absence of alternate sources for these subjects, and the absence of seditious elements in these sources, the Ministry of Education invariably authorized the importation of these textbooks to Merzifon Anatolia College and other missionary schools.[93]

As required by imperial authorities, American schools assigned Ottoman textbooks for local languages, religions, and sensitive subjects such as geography, history, and law. Students at Merzifon Anatolia College studied these subjects from thirty-three domestically printed books, besides the following titles: *A Brief Ottoman History* (Ali Nazım, *Muhtasar Tarih-i Osmani*, 1892), *History of Islam* (anonymous, *Tarih-i İslam*, 1893), *Science of Speech* (anonymous, *Fen-ni Belagat*, 1891), *State Law* (Hasan Fehmi, *Hukuk-u Devlet*, 1883), and *Readings in Ottoman Turkish* (Muallim Naci, *Talim-i Kıraat-i Osmani*, 1886). A deeper analysis shows that the college board imported half of the textbooks used for science and English – thirty-nine of the seventy-seven items – and used domestically produced books in the arts and humanities.[94]

The variety of course materials exposed students to a curriculum that was modern and traditional at the same time. Students typically kept abreast of Western sciences, studied Ottoman languages and laws in a classical sense, and acquired English as a medium and French as a second language along with Ottoman Turkish and either native Armenian or Greek. Not coincidentally, Merzifon Anatolia College's graduates proactively engaged with global and local developments in much the same way as imagined by the college's first president, Charles Tracy.[95]

In a May 1893 speech, Tracy discussed the missionaries' publications in the Ottoman countryside. Religious and educational publications had become their "main work," which could reap the desired benefits of civilizing and evangelizing locals. Recorded in state inventories, the breadth of Merzifon Anatolia College's faculty and textbooks provided this missionary college's students with an internationally diverse curriculum. This diversity was permissible as far as Ottoman authorities were concerned. In essence, they resisted the idea of religious, community-oriented publishing activity but tolerated instructional materials that could benefit the community at large without changing their political and social views.[96]

Given the issue of schoolbooks, central authorities refrained from banning missionary literature as a whole. Their specific tactics combined pragmatic inference and reactive improvisation and were developed against the backdrop of a contextual understanding of authority, faith, sedition, and order – the terms that defined and reflected what the central state did and did not accept. State instructions, then, outlawed some publications that could have a combustible influence at the local level, but they permitted others that offered scientific information, a time-honoured commodity in the late Ottoman Empire. This strategy, based on a particular judgment of a book's author and content, prompted American missionaries to redefine their target audience for both religious and educational purposes.[97]

CONCLUSION

Ottoman press laws owed their origins to the political dynamics in the capital and to a mixture of incidents in the provinces. Coupled with the capital's attempt to restore public order, the process of screening and licensing missionary publications precipitated the strategy that imperial authorities wielded over the missionary operations. This strategy created subtle tactics revolving around instructions that called for vigilant censorship. Official inspections, which proved rampant and were conducted by numerous agents, solicited constant state intervention.

In the troubled post-1890 era, the American Board's publishing agenda signified an existential challenge to the central state and local order. Against the backdrop of manifest ignorance at the provincial level, critically important cases moved forward under ministerial concessions. Throughout these cases, the common thread was the centre's determination to exercise absolute power over the production and dissemination of the printed materials.

Central authorities improvised a wide range of decrees in ways meant to curtail and counter missionary editors. In addressing the means of printing, such as movable type and printing machines, their reactionary perspectives revealed various sensibilities being articulated in the Ministers Council. So that their overall message was clear, they declared that publishers could not import, print, and circulate any books deemed by the state to be seditious. For censors and other agents, however, there existed some degree of discretion when applying the centre's instructions to a standard practice of screening, identifying, and outlawing certain books that challenged Ottoman integrity and the Islamic faith.

Imperial laws drew a qualitative line between textbooks and religious pamphlets. No evangelical pamphlets reached the countryside without official authorization, whereas educational books circulated in cities and schools with ease. Additionally, state directives enforced this pragmatic and targeted strategy with a view to regulating the publishing industry and compelling the editors to consult with officials and to publish what they said was publishable.[98]

American missionaries continued to print and distribute books and pamphlets on and off the record, and thus their enterprise had crossed the mark of 21 million pages by 1914. This impressive accomplishment became possible due to the work of frustrated yet motivated editors such as the director of the Bible House, Henry Dwight, who printed more than half of these publications. Additionaly, Dwight edited the Turkish translations of the Bible and chaired the publication committee for *Redhouse* – the Ottoman-English dictionary that the British author James Redhouse had produced under the American Board – which had been the most popular lexicon since its first edition was published in 1890. If imperial authorities had been less hostile, missionaries might have accomplished a lot more.[99]

The print media also revealed its complex history by staging a public feud between Ottoman and American editors. Ahmet Mithat, the prolific author and founding editor of the Ottoman Imperial Press in Istanbul in 1879, was not shy of expressing outrage against the missionary views. In the daily newspaper *Tercüman-ı Hakikat* (*Interpreter of Truth*), he explained that "all faiths and sects are exercising full rights" to such an extent that imperial authorities did not even "outlaw the missionaries" who were "roaming freely" in Ottoman lands, "distributing books to people from all walks of life," and "calling them to Christianity." Likewise, these "books and articles that they published against the faith of Islam" did "open new theatres of war," making "attacks so vicious that other peoples suffer when restraining their audacity." Seeing the Ottoman Islamic identity and the American evangelical message as essentially incompatible, Mithat appointed himself to defend this identity against missionary encroachments. His editorials popularized the central state's perspective on the dangers associated with the missionary message by making it accessible and meaningful.[100]

Henry Dwight, the prolific editor and director of the Bible House, could not disagree more because imperial authorities were always causing trouble with his books and articles. Indeed, each year since 1859, the American Board's presses had published "10 million pages of Christian and educational literature" in "the Turkish, Armenian, and Greek languages." But this was not close to what they were really capable of. "Millions more would be eagerly welcomed" if there was more "money" and less "suspicion" toward missionary literature. More publication funds could be raised in New England, but it was virtually impossible to satisfy the officials in Istanbul. In a private meeting in Istanbul, Dwight once confided to a European ambassador that he had been placed in a particularly "difficult position … through the suspicions of Government officials." He asked, "Can you suggest any changes of policy or method that might somewhat forestall such suspicions?" To "console" Dwight "even in the delicate position which you sometimes occupy," the sympathetic ambassador summarized the missionaries' situation with a Turkish proverb: "The dogs run out and bark, but still the caravan goes on!" Carrying tons of pages loaded with ink, the missionary caravan went on. But the dogs not only barked; they trailed the passengers and bit them, too, at times hobbling the caravan itself.[101]

EPILOGUE

The Mighty Have Fallen

Three missionaries encounter three cannibals alongside a river. They must cross the river on a boat for two, but the cannibals cannot outnumber them on water and land. How can they do it?

An instance of God's algorithm, this riddle reckons that an omniscient being knows all the moves. It solicits a minimal number of steps to preclude the bad from eating the good. It is an exercise to sharpen your logical skills (see the answer in note 1). Its context, however, evokes actual drama rather than a puzzle. In the late nineteenth century, encounters with man-eaters compelled flesh-and-blood missionaries to take the right steps to move on. Their journey was a matter of life and death, a venture painful and rewarding at the same time. The original scenario lurked in the heart of *Hudson Review* author Diana Webster on her 1987 trip to the Fiji Islands, where the "last missionary had been eaten" a hundred years ago. Tragicomically, she felt that the cannibals' progeny could "celebrate the centenary" by eating her right there and then.[1]

In the Ottoman Empire, imperial authorities met the criteria for a villain. This assumption became an essential item in US newspapers and a household staple in New England. Ruling from Istanbul, the sultan and his ministers had obstructed the evangelical journey since year one. In the 1890s they were said to have manifested their darker emotions by regressing to those "savages," who were prowling round to slaughter the humans. The entire human race faced peril at their hands if they remained unchecked. But in reality, the authorities featured more than "bloodthirsty" qualities. They had their own stories to tell. A critical look at the imperial perspective is long overdue.[2]

The Ottoman world resembled a well-worn galleon, an old ship that drifted into a tragic realm of the unknown. It consisted of five components: the cabin, the deck, the hull, the gunnel, and the keel. The cabin hosted the sultan as captain and the ministers as the crew members who swung the compass and measured the water's depths. On deck, local agents served as conductors, and the communities travelled as passengers. The hull represented the eternal state. The gunnel contained the state laws. The keel comprised faith and order.[3]

Westerly storms and dwindling supplies defied the galleon as it set sail. The catastrophic conditions traumatized the passengers, diminished their trust in the cabin, and stirred up some bitter recriminations. Conscious of the situation, the captain and his crew instructed the conductors to defuse growing discontent. When the galleon's mass and load could barely sustain the water density, evangelical missionaries came aboard as transit passengers with their bags and baggage. The crew members expected the hull to withstand the increased pressure. They warned the new passengers that the harsh conditions – not of their making – might deteriorate. As mortal fights erupted and the storms battered the galleon, the cabin reinforced the gunnel by increasing reliance on the keel, subdued the minority passengers, and limited their mobility. The transit passengers joined the throng by ignoring specific instructions, by traversing the compartments, and even by challenging the conductors. They also incited the reactions of other passengers and clamoured for outside intervention. In response, the cabin crew wanted them stopped and the captain's authority restored.

This scenario captures the context as Ottoman authorities viewed it. It reveals how they addressed local disorder and missionary activity. Eventually, in both fictional and actual contexts, the journey itself became their terminus. In his study of late Ottoman governmentality, Selim Deringil traces a *mission civilizatrice* – a type of modern centralist discourse that the imperial regime adopted by challenging Europe's political tenets while embracing its societal norms. Ironically, as well, the regime sought to protect the missionaries against local assaults and the locals against missionary activities. With a view to restoring state power, the Ministers Council targeted public crimes in which the missionaries had been suspects or victims. By treating religious interactions as security matters, central regulations invented a legal pretext for handling them. Not coincidentally, a coded lexicon arose over high-frequency crimes such as sedition and treason.[4]

Pioneering European missionaries deserve to enter the metaphorical scenario as additional transit passengers. The French Jesuits, for instance, had been operating in the Ottoman world for two centuries before American missionaries came on board. Yet by 1880 the latecomers had surpassed their predecessors in every area of the holy venture. Also worth considering is what went wrong *within* the cabin. In debates over the problem of the division of the sultan's house against itself, the authorities in Istanbul wavered between conservative and liberal solutions. In a symbolic case after the 1908 Young Turk Revolution, Mehmet Faik Memduh, the elite, centrist, and moderate minister of the interior, worried about his own fate more than the sultan's and went into voluntary exile.[5]

An anti-missionary consensus, however, transcended political camps. It stood the test of time and united the ranks of the state. The reactionary perspective borne against the missionaries who transgressed the red lines drawn by the state also forged a bond *within* the state bureaucracy.[6]

Against one storm after another, the Ottoman galleon persisted. When the restless passengers criticized the captain, the crew members advised him on the right course of action, which entailed announcing that the coast was clear. They fortified the gunnel and keel, restricted general mobility, and rebuked several conductors. The crew also tried to mute the voices of transit passengers, which were echoing near and far.

State instructions succumbed to the fiercest storm, which erupted in Sarajevo in July 1914 and raged for five winters. Already fissured by inner cracks, the galleon took hits, shifted sideways, and splendidly capsized in the water. As the survivors were jumping into lifeboats, Turkish shareholders began to mull over the question of why their galleon had foundered, wondering ever after at "how have the mighty fallen!"[7]

It had to be someone else's fault. In 1913 prominent scholar Ahmet Hamdi Aksekili published his interview of American missionaries in the Islamist journal *Sebilürreşad* (*True Path*), warning that their agenda would destroy the Muslim nation. Five years later, the Ottoman war minister, İsmail Enver likewise berated the missionaries, concluding that their agenda had destroyed the eternal state. Adopted by towering figures such as Aksekili and Enver, this arbitrary conviction reflected and shaped the public mindset after the mighty state was gone.[8]

In a 1939 editorial published in the popular newspaper *Yeni Sabah* (*New Dawn*), Musa Kazım Karabekir added new currency to the reactionary consensus. Coming from an outstanding commander, a co-founder of the Progressive Republican Party, and the future speaker of the Turkish Parliament, his words carried a lot of weight.[9]

Karabekir's views melded the past with the present. Foreigners could "easily herd" those nations that were "trapped in a mood of intrigue and intoxication." In the Ottoman Empire, evangelical missionaries had created such an atmosphere of sedition. They had disturbed the public order, slandered the Turkish nation, and "precipitated the collapse." If the missionaries sustained their activities "by stealth" and "in public," this type of a "catastrophe" would recur in the Muslim world. Karabekir thus declared open season on the missionaries. He regarded them as evil-minded outsiders and blamed them for having initiated the tragic events in east Anatolia. On the receiving end, the Turkish Muslim public espoused his narrative because it exonerated them and reduced their burden of responsibility for the past.[10]

Post-Ottoman identity politics hinged on a collective self-deception. Its development resembled the blame game. By design, Turkish players defined themselves as lily-white characters and others as natural-born criminals. They invented a new, idyllic past and then came to believe in it. The game then became larger than they could have expected. Today, in modern Turkey, it has become reality.

The 1923 Treaty of Lausanne acknowledged the Republic of Turkey and tacitly allowed the republican founders to build a somewhat uniform state. Article 41 of the treaty recognized Turkey's right to make "the teaching of the Turkish language obligatory." The 1924 law on the unity of education then came into effect with deliberate efforts to centralize and nationalize "public instruction." Indeed, all foreign institutions were subordinated to Turkish state authority. Robert College – whose president, Caleb Gates, tellingly represented foreign institutions in the region during the Lausanne peace talks – also became state property. The Ministry of Education took over its century-old campus peacefully in 1971 and renamed it Bosphorus University. Sooner or later, the republican authorities claimed the bags and baggage of the American missionaries, those transit passengers who had sailed with their imperial predecessors.[11]

Although historical records refute Karabekir's claims, the dominant state ideology of modern Turkey continues to obscure the truth of history. It ignores some hard-learned lessons by whitewashing the stains of corruption, injustice, massacres, and poverty. When things go wrong, scapegoating a third party seems a viable choice, as well. Broadly, the modern Turkish state – represented nationally by 600 Parliament members and locally by 3,390,738 agents as registered in the latest state statistics – defines officials and citizens by distinguishing between insiders and outcasts or outsiders, like those traitors and missionaries who once disrupted law and order. The history of the Ottoman state embodies the salient features of a cautionary tale. Troubled times left the central state notoriously prone to abusing powers, violating civil rights, and when coupled with a postwar survival mode, making critical errors leading to undesirable horrors. This tale is also a subtle reminder that state officials saw minorities and missionaries through the lens of profane interests, not from a purely religious perspective. They politicized religious interactions as much as they politicized anything else.[12]

Faith matters in the present, as it mattered in the past. As late as 2007, in the massacre at the Zirve Publishing House, some savages murdered evangelical missionaries, compelling the state to do something about it. In the future, political reaction or inaction will make such tragedies preventable or inevitable. As a start, we should recognize the actual potential of the state and the inalienable rights of the faithful at the same time – even though many narratives that counter this recognition still exist and will persist. Optimistically, the savages will cease to exist. After all, the cannibals' grandchildren should not prevent us from following in the footsteps of Diana Webster in the South Pacific and reckoning with the history of American missionaries in the Ottoman world.

Notes

PROLOGUE

1 The 1909 report of the American Board of Commissioners for Foreign Missions contains comprehensive figures – except for those largely "destroyed by the April 1908 uprising" in central Anatolia. In Ottoman missions, the report identified 61 single and 49 married women, while locating 7 colleges, 38 boarding and high schools, 8 seminaries, 9 hospitals, 11 dispensaries, and 4 east-Anatolia kindergartens. Virtually until 1918, the board's administration committed its resources to Ottoman and China missions. *Annual Report* (1909), 52–80, 111–27; *Annual Report* (1917), 62–95, 145–91. The board's missions appeared in Ottoman sources, including *A. Mkt. Mhm.* 536/14, 14 Şaban 1313 (30 January 1896); *A. Mkt. Mhm.* 615/9, 30 Safer 1324 (24–25 April 1906); *Y. Prk. Myd.* 20/87, 9 Ramazan 1315 (1 February 1898); and *Y. Prk. Myd.* 21/42, 29 Rabiulevvel 1316 (17 August 1898).

2 Yurdusev, *Ottoman Diplomacy*, 5–35; Kazıcı, "Osmanlı Devletinde Dinî Hoşgörü," 75–81. Fernand Braudel, the historian of the French Annales school, derived an influential socio-historical approach from his "long-term" concept. See Braudel and Wallerstein, "History and the Social Sciences"; Lee, *Longue Durée,* 1–7; and Shami and Millet-Idriss, eds, *Middle East Studies*, 4–7.

3 In November 2015 in Ankara, Mehmet Görmez, Turkey's president of religious affairs, delivered a keynote speech at the opening ceremony of Konrad-Adenauer-Stiftung, a Germany-based Christian foundation that promotes freedom and justice in global and local politics, in which he lauded Ottoman religious tolerance by mentioning the above edict issued by Sultan Mahmud II.

4 For further examples, see Quataert, *Ottoman Empire*, 64–8; and Barkey, *Empire of Difference*, 226–63.

5 See the literature review in Şahin, "American-Turkish Relations." The cited works include Makdisi, *Artillery of Heaven*, 276; Şafak, *Osmanlı-Amerikan İlişkileri*, 59–79, 172–3; Erhan, "Ottoman Official Attitudes"; and Grabill, *Protestant Diplomacy*, 286, 294–5; as well as DeNovo, *American Interests and Policies*, 8–9, 96–9; Salt, "Trouble Wherever They Went"; Kocabaşoğlu, *Kendi Belgeleriyle*, 219; Erhan, "Main Trends"; and Provence, "Ottoman Modernity, Colonialism, and Insurgency," 208. For an excellent study of Ottoman perspectives in a global context, see Aydın, *Idea of the Muslim World*, 1–13, 65–132.

6 On Ottoman elitism, Mardin, *Religion, Society, and Modernity*, 1–19; on Plato's allegory of the cave, Weiss, *Virtue in the Cave*, 171–84; Harvey, *Spaces of Capital*, 271. On Ottoman elitism, see İnalcık and Quataert, eds, *Economic and Social History*, 759–933; and Moran, *Türk Romanına Eleştirel Bir Bakış*, 6–34. On Ottoman elitism in literature, see Ertuğrul, "Reading of the Turkish Novel." My analysis of governmental elitism draws on archival documents, including *Dh. Mkt.* 1765/117, 15 Safer 1308 (30 September 1890); *Hr. Sys.* 66/82, nos 1–2 (12 May 1900); and *Dh. Mkt.* 948/42, 15 Safer 1323 (21 April 1905). It also draws on informed studies in the field by Fleischer, *Bureaucrat and Intellectual*, 214–31; Findley, *Bureaucratic Reform*, 51–2, 251; Hanioğlu, *Osmanlı'dan Cumhuriyet'e*, 98–101, 129–32; Göçek, *Rise of the Bourgeoisie*, 3–43; and Karateke and Reinkowski, eds, *Legitimizing the Order*, 111–29, 195–232.

7 Kurşun, "Mehmed Memduh Paşa."

8 Memduh, *Mirat-i Şûûnât*, 54, 87, quoted in Aslantaş, "Bir Osmanlı Bürokratı," 198–200.

9 Nick Birch, "Three Murdered," *Guardian*, 19 April 2007; "Christians Killed in Turkey," BBC *World News*, 18 April 2007; Laura King, "3 Men Slain," *Los Angeles Times*, 19 April 2007; "Turkish Believers Satanically Tortured for Hours before Being Killed," *International Christian Concern*, 25 April 2007. On the ongoing debates and religious crimes, see "Misyoner Saldırılarının Şifresi" [The code of assaults on missionaries], *Posta*, 14 March 2016; Kılıç, "Türkçe İnternet"; and Akyıldız, "Misyonerliğe Karşı Yasal Tedbirler." Turkey's Association of Protestant Churches recorded the post-2005 hate crimes. Launched as a "representative committee" against the 1990s anti-Christian assaults, this organization has been defending local Christians since 2009.

10 "Zirve Ergenekon'a Bağlandı" [The Zirve case merged with the Ergenekon trial], *Milliyet*, 17 March 2011; Mikail Pelit, "Tolon Paşa'ya Zirve

Davasından Tutuklama Kararı" [Arrest warrant for General Hürşit Tolon in the Zirve case], *Milliyet*, 18 January 2013. See also "Zirve'de 9 Yıl sonra karar çıktı" [The verdict passed on Zirve after 9 years], *Hürriyet*, 28 September 2016; and the records of the first ninety-seven sessions at Malatya Heavy Penal Courts 1 and 3 in "Duruşma Tutanakları" [Hearing records], online at Zirve Davası ve Gerçekler. On the Ergenekon trial, see Margolis, "Turkey's Violent Storms"; Esayan, "Ergenekon"; and Taş, "Turkey's Ergenekon Imbroglio." On the post-1980 Kurdish guerilla warfare, see Bozarslan, "Kurds and the Turkish State."

11 "Sıra Bize de Gelecek" [Then our turn will come], *Sabah*, 19 April 2007; "Turkish Believers Satanically Tortured for Hours before Being Killed," *International Christian Concern*, 25 April 2007; "Emre Günaydın Azmettirici İddiası" [Emre Günaydın's allegation of an instigator], CNN *Türk*, 23 April 2007.

12 "Malatya'daki Vahşet Dünyayı Ayağa Kaldırdı" [Savagery in Malatya has raised alarm in the world], *Hürriyet Daily*, 19 April 2007; on Turkish government and society, Haynes, "Politics, Identity," 317–22; and Corke et al., *Democracy in Crisis*, 1–18; on the implications of the "Report Card approach" adopted by Europe's so-called Turkey experts, Deringil, "Turks and 'Europe,'" 709–10.

13 Chomsky-Erdoğan debates in "Chomsky Hits Back at Erdoğan," *Guardian*, 14 January 2016; "Noam Chomsky Responds to Erdoğan," interview, *Al Jazeera*, 21 January 2016. The Middle East Studies Association of North America published "Letters on Turkey" after the Academics for Peace platform announced the January 2016 petition "We Will Not Be a Party to This Crime." On post-August 2015 developments, see Human Rights Foundation of Turkey, "TİHV Dokümantasyon," 1–34; Yanmış, *Resurgence of the Kurdish Conflict*, 17–24; and Yeğen, Tol, and Çalışkan, *Kürtler Ne İstiyor?* 59–86. On governmental deficiency and mentality, see Habermas, *Legitimation Crisis*, 61–75; Bobocel et al., eds, *Psychology of Justice and Legitimacy*, 151–72, 251–324; and Reidy and Riker, eds, *Coercion and the State*, 77–94.

14 "Attack on Christians in Turkey," *Der Spiegel*, 18 April 2011; "Group of Young Muslims Murders 3 Christians in Turkey," *Florida Baptist Witness*, 25 April 2011. See also Nick Birch, "Three Murdered," *Guardian*, 19 April 2007; Laura King, "3 Men Slain," *Los Angeles Times*, 19 April 2007; and "Turkish Believers Satanically Tortured for Hours before Being Killed," *International Christian Concern*, 25 April 2007.

15 World Evangelical Alliance, "I Simply Cried."

16 Ibid.; World Evangelical Alliance, "Martin Bucer Seminary."

17 On how Turks remember the Armenian genocide and how past tragedies affect Turkish politics, see Göçek, *Transformation of Turkey*, 38–61, 211–40.

18 "Conditional Release of 5 Suspects," *Hürriyet Daily*, 10 March 2014.

19 Mikail Pelit, "Zirve'de Hizmet Kusuru" [Defective service in the Zirve case], *Milliyet*, 27 January 2016; European Court of Human Rights, *European Convention on Human Rights*, 10–11.

20 "Zirve Yayınevi cinayetlerinde 9 yıl sonra karar çıktı" [Verdict passed on the Zirve Publishing House murders 9 years later], *Cumhuriyet*, 28 September 2016. See also issues of national newspapers in Turkey dated 28–31 September 2016.

21 On the reasons for studying Ottoman history, see Quataert, *Ottoman Empire*, 1–12; Finkel, *Osman's Dream*, 428–525; Aydın, *Politics of Anti-Westernism*, 15–38; and Faroqhi, *Approaching Ottoman History*, 18–22.

22 Kafadar, *Between Two Worlds*, 1–19; İnalcık, "Istanbul," 4–18; Göknar, Kafadar, and Aydın, *Istanbul*.

23 Worringer, "'Sick Man of Europe.'" On Ottoman ideologies and conflicts, see Berkes, *Development of Secularism*, 208–70, 359–410; Kayalı, *Arabs and Young Turks*; and Uyar and Erickson, *Military History of the Ottomans*, 175–279.

24 For a comparison of Ottoman, Safavid, and Timurid state formations, see Findley, *Turks in World History*, 93–132.

25 On Ottoman expansion, see Kafadar, *Between Two Worlds*, 29–59.

26 Barkan, "İstila Devirlerinin"; Deringil, *Conversion and Apostasy*, 28–66.

27 Tezcan, *Second Ottoman Empire*, 79–140; Isom-Verhaaren, *Allies with the Infidel*, 23–48; Casale, "Ottoman Administration."

28 Findley, *Bureaucratic Reform*, 41–220; Casale, "Ottoman Administration," 194–8.

29 Eldem, "Ottoman Financial Integration," 143–5; Karaman and Pamuk, "Ottoman State Finances."

30 Shaw and Shaw, *Osmanlı İmparatorluğu*, vol. 2, 178–329; İnalcık and Seyitdanoğlu, eds, *Tanzimat*, 127–49; Grandits, Clayer, and Pichler, eds, *Conflicting Loyalties*, 1–12. On Ottoman centralism and modernization, see Göçek, "Ethnic Segmentation"; Karpat, *Studies*, 27–74; and Polk and Chambers, eds, *Beginnings of Modernization*.

31 Ortaylı, *Osmanlı Barışı*, 45–7, 66–154. On Ottoman intellectuals and ideologies, see Akşin, *Turkey*, 82–8; Akçura, *Üç Tarz-ı Siyaset*, 19–36; and Meyer, *Turks across Empires*, 21–47, 171–8.

32 For a succinct analysis of the Young Turks' Union and Progress Committee and Turkey's political transition, see Ahmad, *Making of Modern Turkey*, 31–51.

33 Zürcher, *Unionist Factor*, 1–117; on the Turkish "syndrome," Göçek, *Transformation of Turkey*, 185–210.

34 Dale, "Ibn Hhaldun," 431–51; Darling, *History of Social Justice*, 127–54.

35 İnalcık and Anhegger, *Kanunname-i Sultani*, 83. On fratricides and politics, see İnalcık, *Osmanlı İmparatorluğu*, 319–23; and Dağlı, "Limits of Ottoman Pragmatism."

36 Genç, *Osmanlı İmparatorluğunda*, 43–96; Genç, "Ottoman Industry," 59–86.

37 Kafadar, "Question of Ottoman Decline"; Barkey, *Empire of Difference*, 226–96; İnalcık and Quataert, eds, *Economic and Social History*, 759–933. On the late Ottoman state, science, and society, see Yalçınkaya, *Learned Patriots*, 1–16, 180–205.

38 Findley, *Bureaucratic Reform*, 163–90.

39 Ibid., 255–65, 301; Akşin, *Turkey*, 38–81; Ortaylı, *Osmanlı Barışı*, 148–54; Özdemir, *Osmanlı Devletinde Bürokrasi*; Shaw and Shaw, *Osmanlı İmparatorluğu*, vol. 2, 195–9, 217–35, 264–79; Weiker, "Ottoman Bureaucracy." Ahmet Tevfik served as grand vizier several times between 1909 and 1922.

40 Shaw and Shaw, *Osmanlı İmparatorluğu*, vol. 2, 161–6; Karpat, *Studies*, 611–46. On local millets and for the 1895 Ottoman map, see Campos, *Ottoman Brothers*, 8–12.

41 Barkey and Gavrilis, "Ottoman Millet System," 25–8.

42 Shaw and Shaw, *Osmanlı İmparatorluğu*, vol. 2, 293; Setrakian, "Armenians," 32–66; McCarthy, *Muslims and Minorities*, 2–115.

43 Karpat, *Studies*, 644; Göçek, *Transformation of Turkey*, 185–240. For an extensive study of 2,000 in-person interviews with citizens of twelve cities that have a visible Kurdish population, see Yeğen, Tol, and Çalışkan, *Kürtler Ne İstiyor?* 125–42.

CHAPTER ONE

1 Eddy, *What Next in Turkey*, 86, Houghton Library; "Eddy, David Brewer," in Marquis, ed., *Who's Who in New England*, 364; Eddy, *Eddy Family Collection*, Houghton Library. On the American Board's global expansion, see Hutchison, *Errand to the World*, 38–124; Chang, *Citizens of a Christian Nation*, 65–98, 153–65; Putney and Burlin, eds, *Role of the*

American Board, 11–48, 142–92; and Reeves-Ellington, *Domestic Frontiers*, 108–74. For a view of the board's records, see Coakley, "ABCFM Collection."

2 The American Board's reports recorded 9 colleges, 4 seminaries, 437 high and elementary schools, 9 hospitals, 10 dispensaries, and native donations of $196,627, of which 63 per cent was drawn from the richer western Anatolia neighbourhoods. For more details on missions to the Ottoman Empire and Imperial China, see *Annual Report* (1917), 62–95, 145–91; and *List of American Educational, Religious, and Charitable Institutions*, American Research Institute in Turkey.

3 Quataert, *Ottoman Empire*, 62; on Ottoman elites, Findley, *Bureaucratic Reform*, 40–333; Deringil, *Well-Protected Domains*, 19–21, 166–70; Ortaylı, "Tanzimat Adamı"; Shaw and Shaw, *Osmanlı İmparatorluğu*, vol. 2, 263–73. On early Ottoman elitism, see Atçıl, "Route to the Top," 499–502; and Atçıl, *Scholars and Sultans*, esp. 83–210. On the Beirut elites' gathering in the spring of 1909, see Campos, *Ottoman Brothers*, 1–19.

4 Kuran, "Küçük Said Paşa," 125. For a comparison of Mehmet Sait and Mahmut Kemal, see Findley, *Ottoman Civil Officialdom*, 152, 211–92.

5 Besides archival sources, this analysis benefits from various studies, including Barkey, *Empire of Difference*, 242–61, 277–89; Deringil, *Well-Protected Domains*, 16–43, 68–92, 135–49; Fortna, *Imperial Classroom*; Göçek, "Ethnic Segmentation"; Karpat, *Studies*, 604–10; Kasaba, ed., *Turkey in the Modern World*, 38–111; Kieser, *Iskalanmış Barış*, 155–329; Quataert, *Ottoman Empire*, 54–74; and Yalçınkaya, *Learned Patriots*, 152–206.

6 For examples, see Hamlin, *Among the Turks*, 180; Edwards, "Sinners"; and *The Problem of Turkey*, Andover-Harvard Theological Library. For early studies, see Barkley, *Ride through Asia Minor*; Childs, *Across Asia Minor*; Clement, *Constantinople*; Dwight, *Constantinople and Its Problems*; Elder, *Vindicating a Vision*; Hornblow, *Private Life*; Prime, *Forty Years*; Tracy, *Silkenbraid*; and Walsh, *Residence at Constantinople*. One interesting, well-sold monograph promoted the credentials of its author, noting that he "had wide experience in the mission field." Beaver, *Ecumenical Beginnings*, cover page.

7 Fairbank, "Assignment for the '70's." Revisionist studies include Stevens, ed., *United States*; DeNovo, *American Interests and Policies*; Field, *America and the Mediterranean World*; and Pakin, "American Studies."

8 Oren, *Power, Faith, and Fantasy*, 172, 603–4; Makdisi, *Artillery of Heaven*, 3, 171–2; Erhan, "Ottoman Official Attitudes"; Kocabaşoğlu,

Kendi Belgeleriyle. See also Murre-van den Berg, ed., *New Faith*; Çakır, *Anadolumuz*; Şafak, *Osmanlı-Amerikan İlişkileri*; Wilson, "In the Name of God"; Howard, "Bicentennial"; and Salt, "Trouble Wherever They Went." On nation, narration, and identity, see Bhabha, ed., *Nation and Narration*, 1–16; and McQuillan, *Culture, Religion*, 8–12. The field's prominent works include Deringil, *Well-Protected Domains*; and Suny, Göçek, and Naimark, eds, *Question of Genocide*.

9 For a literature review, see Şahin, "American-Turkish Relations." Fairbank's call registered little impact, as American Board collections continued to fashion the historical inquiry. Ironically, John DeNovo's criticism of James Field's perspective as "sympathetic" to the missionaries applied to his own perspective as well as to the dominant scholarly views. DeNovo, "Review of America," 932; DeNovo, *American Interests and Policies*, 88–127.

10 Bruce DeSilva, "Modern Man's Encroachment in Quebec Forever Alters Cree Way of Life," *Hartford Courant*, 15 January 1989. The Cree hunter is quoted in Clifford and Marcus, eds, *Writing Culture*, 8. For an inspiring presentation of interpretive thinking, see Yanow and Schwartz-Shea, eds, *Interpretation and Method*, 5–26.

11 Katzenstein and Okawara, "Japan," 154; on analytical eclecticism applied, Uzer, *Identity and Foreign Policy*, 2, 55–87. On multiplex methodology, see Druckman, *Doing Research*, 13; and Boudreau, "Intergroup Conflict Reduction." The cited works are Dittes, "Christian Mission"; Grabill, *Protestant Diplomacy*, 155–90, 250–85; Kocabaşoğlu, *Kendi Belgeleriyle*; Lewis, *Faith and Power*; Makdisi, *Artillery of Heaven*, 180–220 (for a critical review of Makdisi's views, see Kieser, "U. Makdisi"); and Makdisi, "Ottoman Orientalism"; as well as Ortaylı, *Osmanlı Mirası*; Provence, "Ottoman Modernity," 206–8; Akarlı, "Tangled Ends"; Findley, *Bureaucratic Reform*, 239–387; and Roberts and Şahin, "Construction of National Identities," 507–8.

12 On Ottoman periodization paradigms, see Dağlı, "Limits of Ottoman Pragmatism"; Darling, "Another Look"; Karateke, "Challenge of Periodization"; İnalcık, *Essays in Ottoman History*, 15–28; and Kafadar, "Question of Ottoman Decline." Alternative studies include Costantini and Koller, eds, *Living in the Ottoman Ecumenical Community*; Fortna, *Learning to Read*; Tezcan, *Second Ottoman Empire*; Özdalga, *Late Ottoman Society*; Salzmann, *Tocqueville in the Ottoman Empire*; and Yurdusev, *Ottoman Diplomacy*, 5–35.

13 Deringil, *Well-Protected Domains*, 112–34. On Ottoman politics, economy, and society, see Fortna, *Imperial Classroom*, 1–40; Hanioğlu, *Brief*

History, 110–49; Pamuk, "Ottoman Empire"; and Göçek, "Ethnic Segmentation."

14 On edicts and other messages, see Gök, "Introduction of the Berat." On Carol Gluck's comparable analysis of Meiji, Japan, see Deringil, *Well-Protected Domains*, 18–20. The oft-cited terms are included in *A. Mkt. Mhm.* 615/9, nos 1–5, 29 Safer 1324 (24 April 1906); *A. Mkt. Mhm.* 658/25, nos 1–3, 19 Şaban 1313 (4 February 1896); *A. Mkt. Mhm.* 702/19, nos 1–24, 23 Ramazan 1313 (8 March 1896); *Dh. Mkt.* 2091/127, no. 1, 28 Rabiulevvel 1316 (16 August 1898); *Hr. Sys.* 2742/4, nos 1–2, 14 May 1898; *Y. Prk. Hr.* 25/51, 12 Zilhicce 1315 (4 May 1898); *Y. Prk. Mf.* 5/20, nos 1–4, 2 Recep 1325 (11 August 1907); and *Ya. Hus.* 326/102, nos 1–9, 9 Zilhicce 1312 (9 April 1895).

15 *A. Mkt. Mhm.* 763/28, no. 1, 9 Rabiulahir 1307 (3 December 1889).

16 Erhan, "Ottoman Official Attitudes"; and Dinçer, *Yabancı Özel Okullar*, 79–81.

17 On Ottoman Turkish sources, see Sertoğlu, *Muhteva Bakımından*; Shaw, "Ottoman Archives"; *Guide on the General Directorate*; and Binark, *Short History*. Turkey's General Directorate of State Archives also published the papers presented in Montreal at the 1992 International Archives Congress in *XII. Milletlerarası Arşiv Kongresi*. Stanford Shaw notes that Turkey's research facilities improved after the 1960s. The archival documents, "catalogued and made available," have thus enabled scholars to examine a wide array of documents unavailable to "earlier research." Shaw, "Ottoman Archival Materials," 94. Since 2010 the archives administration has also catalogued and digitalized the imperial decrees and some other collections.

18 The mentioned record is *Bb. Ek. Od.* For the records of the Sublime Porte, see *A. Mkt. Mhm.*, classified incoming correspondence, dossier 647, file 39, 59 documents, 105 sheets, dated 1313, C. 20. I cite this record as *A. Mkt. Mhm.* 647/39, nos 1–105, 20 Cemaziyelevvel 1313 (8 November 1895), 1–105.

CHAPTER TWO

1 "The Unscrupulous Turk," *New York Times*, 17 April 1892, 17. Signed by Sultan Mahmud II and President Andrew Jackson, the 1830 Commerce and Navigation Treaty stood for a century. The original treaty is printed in *Treaties, Conventions, International Acts*, vol. 2, 1318–21; and in *Muahedat Mecmuası*, vol. 2, 2–6. See also Thayer, "Capitulations of the Ottoman Empire."

2 "Scores on the Turk," *Meridian Weekly Republican*, 26 April 1900, 4; "Turks as Violators," *Los Angeles Times*, 2 June 1896, 9. For James Ross's reaction to George Knapp's 21 March 1899 editorial, see *Washington Post*, 24 March 1899, 6. On massacres, see Suny, Göçek, and Naimark, eds, *Question of Genocide*, 221–43, 276–84. On Ahmet Emin Yalman and Turks in the United States, see Yalman, *Turkey in My Time*, 28–31; and Grabowski, "Prospects and Challenges," 85–9.

3 "Terrible Turk Beaten," *Hartford Courant*, 8 March 1899, 1; "Champion Frank Gotch Downs Terrified Turk," *Chicago Tribune*, 15 April 1909, 9. For Ahmet Tevfik's discussion of Turkish and American perspectives, see *Y. Ee.* 136/96, nos 1–3, 25 Cemaziyelevvel 1316 (11 October 1898). On US perceptions of the Turks, see Madi-Şişman and Şişman, "From 'Heathen Turks'"; and McCarthy, *Turk in America*, 9–18.

4 Hogan, "Stories, Wars, and Emotions," 49. See also Hogan, *Mind and Its Stories*, 76–151. On Orientalism and manifest destiny, see Said, *Orientalism*; O'Sullivan, "Annexation"; and Merk and Merk, eds, *Manifest Destiny*. President Theodore Roosevelt (1901–1909) likewise narrated American ideals and expansions in his remarkable six-volume *The Winning of the West*.

5 Davison, "Turkish Attitudes"; Makdisi, "Ottoman Orientalism"; Akarlı, "Tangled Ends of an Empire"; Erhan, "Ottoman Official Attitudes." See also Finkel, *Osman's Dream*, 500; Murphey, "Continuity and Discontinuity"; and Faroqhi, *Ottoman Empire*, 27–73.

6 The 1885 figures identified 147 missionaries in Anatolia, 52 in the Balkans, 50 in Syria, and 150 in other regions. *American Board Charts*, 2, Andover-Harvard Theological Library; *Guide to the Microfilm Collection*, 228–66; *Annual Report* (1909), 52–80, 111–27; *Annual Report* (1917), 62–95, 145–91. The 1867 Boston meeting is quoted in Doğan, "American Board," 136.

7 Deringil, *Well-Protected Domains*, 39–42. For Ottoman perspectives, see *Hr. Sys.* 45/15, nos 5–7, 17 February 1875; *Hr. Sys.* 54/4, nos 1–8, 13 August 1896; *Hr. Sys.* 67/38, nos 1–2, 1 May 1908; and *Dh. Eum. Ayş.* 1/53, nos 1–4, 17 Cemaziyelahir 1337 (20 March 1919). See also Ortaylı, "Some Observations"; Grabill, *Protestant Diplomacy*, 17; Findley, *Ottoman Civil Officialdom*, 87–130; and Akgün, "Turkish Image."

8 Peirce, *Morality Tales*, 36; Smyth, *Year with the Turks*, 238; "The Unscrupulous Turk," *New York Times*, 17 April 1892, 17. The Sublime Porte came to be seen as the late Ottoman government, and it became "the effective centre both of authority and of government" when "the real power of the Sultan decreased." Lewis, *Middle East*, 303. See also İpşirli, "Bâb-ı Âli." In the late nineteenth century, legislative powers were transferred from the sultan to the imperial bureaucrats. Where the sultan, grand

vizier, and ministers remained the decision makers, local intelligence agents also affected the cases involving the missionaries and minorities. On Ottoman imperial statecraft, see Shaw and Shaw, *Osmanlı İmparatorluğu*, vol. 2, 270–2; Özdemir, *Osmanlı Devletinde Bürokrasi*; Findley, *Bureaucratic Reform*, 298–337; İnalcık, "Decision Making"; and Neumann, "Integrity and Integration."

9 Henry Barkley's works include *Between the Danube and Black Sea*, *Bulgaria before the War*, and *Ride through Asia Minor*. On travellers and customs protocols, see *Dh. Mkt.* 1728/79, no. 1, 14 Şevval 1307 (3 June 1890); Üçel-Aybet, *Avrupalı Seyyahların Gözünden*; Yerasimos, *Les voyageurs*; Faroqhi, *Ottoman Empire*, 213–14; and Faroqhi, *Approaching Ottoman History*, 110–43.

10 *Dh. Mkt.* 1728/79, no. 1, 14 Şevval 1307 (3 June 1890); *İ. Hus.* 128/1323 S 052, no. 1, 15 Safer 1323 (21 April 1905).

11 Akgün, *Kendi Kaynaklarından*, sec. 2123. For reports on missionary activities, see *Dh. Eum. 5Şb.* 19/11, nos 1–2, 14 Muharrem 1334 (22 November 1915); *Ya. Res.* 78/54, no. 1, 6 Şevval 1313 (21 March 1896); *Y. Prk. Myd.* 20/87, nos 1–2, 9 Ramazan 1315 (1 February 1898). For further reports from Adana, Aydın, Afyonkarahisar, Aleppo, Ankara, Bursa, Diyarbakır, Erzincan, Erzurum, Istanbul, Kastamonu, Muğla, and Urfa, see *Dh. Eum. 5Şb.* 76/10, nos 1–14, 25 Safer 1337 (30 November 1918); and *Y. Prk. Myd.* 21/42, nos 1–2, 29 Rabiulevvel 1316 (17 August 1898). On local insurgents being sheltered in Merzifon Anatolia College, see Maksudyan, "Amerikan Kaynaklarında," 142–7. The Treaty of Lausanne (1923) abrogated the existing arrangements. In Richard Horowitz's view, the Turkish authority had become weak and thus granted capitulations to foreigners. This view relates to the issue of "extraterritoriality," an international problem further exacerbated by "protégés-Ottoman nationals" who sought external protection by way of purchasing "family connection." Yet it largely overlooks the complex development of Ottoman economic dynamics that traditionally aimed to maximize affordable market supplies. Horowitz, "International Law," 461. See also "Attempt of Turkey"; Şahin, "Capitulations"; and Angell, "Turkish Capitulations."

12 On imperial surveys and the 1917 order of the Ministry of the Interior, see *Dh. Eum. 3Şb.* 23/43, nos 1–97, 8 Zilhicce 1335 (25 September 1918). Fearlessly ambitious men like Mehmet Talat used public sentiments to achieve power. In April 1909 the anti-unionists even "organized the [Armenian] massacre" in Adana, hoping the British government would interfere and oust the Union and Progress Cabinet in Istanbul, which was pro-German. Ahmad, *Making of Modern Turkey*, 36.

13 The 1883 survey order is in *Y. Prk. Hr.* 7/36, nos 1–9, 18 Safer 1301 (19 December 1883). See also Shaw, "Ottoman Census System"; and Karpat, "Ottoman Population Records." The US consul received the Syria registry as a draft submitted by Asım Efendi to Istanbul. The original registry might be in Syria, but it was not available in the archives in Istanbul. An archival source also indicates that the authorities reprinted the registry in French after the consulates "did not respond to the [original] decree" in Turkish. *Y. Prk. Hr.* 7/36, no. 2, 18 Safer 1301 (19 December 1883).

14 *Y. Prk. Hr.* 7/36, no. 9, 18 Safer 1301 (19 December 1883). For consecutive warnings to the consulates, see *Y. Prk. Hr.* 7/36, nos 3–5, 18 Safer 1301 (19 December 1883).

15 *Y. Prk. Hr.* 7/36, no. 5, 18 Safer 1301 (19 December 1883).

16 *Y. Prk. Hr.* 7/36, nos 1, 5–6, 18 Safer 1301 (19 December 1883). The next chapter discusses diplomacy at length.

17 *Y. Prk. Hr.* 7/36, nos 2–8, 18 Safer 1301 (19 December 1883); Shaw, "Ottoman Census System."

18 Minister Tevfik to Sultan Abdulhamid, in *Y. Prk. Hr.* 25/51, no. 1, 12 Zilhicce 1315 (4 May 1898). Tevfik kept himself abreast of missionary-minority interactions through field reports, including *Ya. Res.* 92/51, nos 1–2, 28 Zilkade 1315 (20 April 1898); and *Y. Prk. Hr.* 25/51, no. 1, 12 Zilhicce 1315 (4 May 1898).

19 Minister Tevfik to Sultan Abdulhamid, in *Y. Prk. Hr.* 25/51, no. 1, 12 Zilhicce 1315 (4 May 1898).

20 *Y. Prk. Mf.* 5/20, no. 3, 2 Recep 1325 (15 May 1907); on American Board institutions, *Y. Prk. Mf.* 4/66, no. 1, 27 Zilhicce 1320 (27 March 1903); for Ministry of Education records, *Y. Prk. Mf.* 4/80, nos 1–3, 12 Cemaziyelahir 1321 (5 September 1903). The US Department of Foreign Affairs requested that the Ottoman government acknowledge missionary establishments, as recorded in *Y. Mrz. D.* 14516, edict 2544. The database regarding the missionary enterprise is incomplete but available in *Dh. Eum. 5Şb.* 19/11, nos 1–2, 14 Muharrem 1334 (22 November 1915); *Y. Mtv.* 183/10, no. 12, 3 Cemaziyelahir 1316 (19 October 1898); and *Y. Prk. Eşa.* 42/57, nos 1–6, 29 Zilhicce 1320 (29 March 1903). Provincial reports – variously transmitted from Aleppo, Ankara, Bursa, Diyarbakır, Erzincan, Erzurum, Harput, Istanbul, Izmir, Kastamonu, Muğla, Trabzon, Urfa, and Yemen – are in *Dh. Eum. 5Şb.* 76/10, nos 1–14, 25 Safer 1337 (30 November 1918); *Y. Mrz. D.* 11576, edict 5782; *Y. Mrz. D.* 11662, edict 7210; *Y. Mrz. D.* 11681, edict 7479, *Y. Mrz. D.* 11694, edict 7605, *Y. Mrz. D.* 12525, edict 4660, *Y. Mrz. D.* 14527, edict 2759; *Y. Prk. Mf.* 4/36, no. 1, 28 Zilkade 1317 (30 March 1900); *Y. Prk. Myd.* 20/87, nos 1–2,

9 Ramazan 1315 (1 February 1898); *Y. Prk. Myd.* 21/42, nos 1–2, 29 Rabiulevvel 1316 (17 August 1898); *Y. Prk. Um.* 67/30, nos 1–10, 12 Şaban 1321 (3 November 1903); *Y. Prk. Zb.* 25/32, no. 1, 20 Zilhicce 1317 (20 April 1900); *Ya. Res.* 105/5, nos 1–2, 6 Ramazan 1317 (8 January 1900); *Ya. Res.* 78/54, nos 1–2, 6 Şevval 1313 (21 March 1896); and *Ya. Res.* 106/43, no. 1, 2 Zilhicce 1317 (3 April 1900). More general reports are in *Ya. Res.* 119/50, nos 1–10, 20 Zilkade 1320 (18 February 1903); *Y. Prk. Eşa.* 17/19, no. 1, 3 Ramazan 1310 (21 March 1893); and *Y. Prk. Eşa.* 23/6, no. 1, 7 Cemaziyelevvel 1313 (26 October 1895). My wish is to examine regional population movements in a future research paper based on these documents.

21 Halit Efendi, in *Y. Prk. Mf.* 5/20, no. 7, 2 Recep 1325 (11 August 1907). See also *Y. Prk. Mf.* 4/80 nos 1–3, 12 Cemaziyelahir 1321 (5 September 1903).

22 Halit Efendi, in *Y. Prk. Mf.* 5/20, nos 1–7, 2 Recep 1325 (11 August 1907); and *Y. Prk. Mf.* 4/80, nos 1–2, 12 Cemaziyelahir 1321 (5 September 1903). Ottoman elites strived "to uphold the state's autonomy and supremacy in the polity." Heper, "Center and Periphery," 85.

23 "Diplomatic Posts, Turkey," National Archives, Records of Foreign Service Posts, vol. 112, no. 2, February 1903, quoted in Evered, *Empire and Education*, 127–9; on the making of Beirut, Fortna, *Imperial Classroom*, 50–8; Issawi, "British Trade"; Strohmeier, "Muslim Education"; Labaki, "Commercial Network." Beirut officials created surprisingly detailed reports on hyperactive missionaries in their region. For example, on American Board institutions, see *Dh. İd.* 117/44, no. 2, 12 Ramazan 1329 (6 September 1911); and *Y. Prk. Mf.* 2/22, 22 Safer 1309 (27 September 1891); on Muslim-minority settlements, see *Hr. Sys.* 67/38, no. 2, 1 May 1908; and on the American University of Beirut, see *Hr. Sys.* 67/34, nos 1–2, 17 November 1907.

24 Halil Efendi, in *Y. Prk. Mf.* 5/20, no. 5, 11–12, 2 Recep 1325 (11 August 1907). Halil Efendi read the Tripoli telegraph several days later and reported that "since 1883, one primary school has enrolled male and female students, including Muslim children, and thus the number of American missionary schools therein has increased from 29 to 30." In his study of Beirut, Jen Hanssen explains that "local interest groups not only depended on, but also sought, the presence of Ottoman imperial power in Beirut." This dependence was a "public construction – literally as well as figuratively," and it cemented Ottomanism as a state ideology." Hanssen, *Fin de Siècle Beirut*, 73, 266.

25 Imperial debates over evangelical enterprise, in *Ya. Hus.* 477/43, nos 1–3, 6 Cemaziyelevvel 1322 (19 July 1904); on political exiles as a state

practice to punish intellectuals and officials, Daşçıoğlu, *Osmanlı'da Sürgün*; on Ottoman competition with American colleges, *Y. Mtv.* 32/45, nos 1–2, 19 Şaban 1305 (1 May 1888), discussed further in Fortna, *Imperial Classroom*, 51–8.

26 *H.H.* 512/25086, no. 1, 18 Zilhicce 1254 (4 March 1839); early directives to the Armenian Patriarchate, in *H.H.* 794/36842, no. 1, 3 Zilhicce 1254 (17 February 1839); on Armenian reactions to American missionaries as discussed in the Bithynia Union's Annual Meeting of May 1885 in Istanbul, *Controversy between the Missionaries*. See also İnalcık, "Status of the Greek"; Ortaylı, "Ottoman Millet System"; Ortaylı, *Osmanlı Barışı*, 124–6; and Küçük, "Osmanlı İmparatorluğu'nda."

27 *Hr. Sys.* 2429/59, no. 1, 28 December 1916. The 1896 report revealed that the officials and residents of Harput had complained that the missionaries were "indoctrinating" their children. *A. Mkt. Mhm.* 702/19, nos 1–24, 23 Ramazan 1313 (8 March 1896). The 1897 census recorded that the local communities consisted of 74.07 per cent Muslims, 13.49 per cent Greeks, 5.47 per cent Armenians, 1.13 per cent Jews, and 0.24 per cent Protestants. On the census statistics and the legal conditions of Armenians, Greeks, and Jews, see Shaw and Shaw, *Osmanlı İmparatorluğu*, vol. 2, 163–6, 293.

28 *Hr. Mkt.* 25/49, nos 1–3, 13 Cemaziyelahir 1265 (6 May 1849). For an insightful analysis of conversions, see Deringil, *Conversion and Apostasy*, 1–27, 197–239.

29 *Zb.* 351/37, no. 1, 9 Şaban 1323 (9 October 1905); on the case of Reşit, *Y. Prk. Eşa.* 29/9, no. 1, 18 Şevval 1315 (12 March 1898). See also, on the notable Mahmud Pasha's son who married a US citizen, *Y. Prk. Mk.* 9/108, nos 1–4, 17 Cemaziyelahir 1318 (12 September 1900).

30 Jessup, *Kamil*, 6; Makdisi, *Artillery of Heaven*, 144–79; *Dh. Mkt.* 2395/6, no. 1, 29 Rabiulahir 1318 (26 August 1900). The Malatya officials investigated Mehmet's mental state so that staff of the Ministry of the Interior could evaluate his petition. Mehmet stayed in Malatya for another year. *Dh. Mkt.* 2418/81, nos 1–2, 28 Cemaziyelahir 1318 (23 October 1900); *Dh. Mkt.* 2462/135, no. 1, 27 Zilkade 1318 (18 March 1901). Ottoman authorities resorted to diplomatic requests and duty rotations. In one case, the Ministry of the Interior demanded that "M.O. Heckman," the agent of the American Hamburg's, be discharged from the company branch in Istanbul because he had illegally boarded on his ship Hüseyin Efendi, a professor of Turkish at Robert College of Istanbul. Although unmentioned, the reason for this interesting request related to the possibility that locals affiliated with the American Board might be fooled into treason. *Dh. Mkt.* 1207/8, no. 1, 16 Ramazan 1325 (23 October 1907).

31 White, *Adventuring with Anatolia College*, part 2, no. 22. The Quran calls the flesh of swine "impure" (2:173, 5:3, 6:145, and 16:115). For an excellent regional study of the consumption and prohibition of pigs, see Redding, "Pig and the Chicken," 350–8.

32 *Hr. Sys.* 2741/50, nos 1–2, 12 June 1896. When authorities forbade missionaries to distribute certain donations collected by *the Christian Herald*, US secretary of state Richard Olney wanted to discuss this issue. *A. Mkt. Mhm.* 688/6, nos 1–7, 19 Ramazan 1313 (4 March 1896); *A. Mkt. Mhm.* 688/11, nos 1–2, 11 Şevval 1313 (26 March 1896).

33 *Dh. Mkt.* 534/65, nos 1–12, 29 Rabiulevvel 1320 (6 July 1902); *Hr. Sys.* 67/31, nos 1–4, 3 April 1906; on Istanbul patriarchs, Cobham, *Patriarchs*, 89–106. See also *A. Mkt. Mhm.* 657/45, nos 1–3, 12 Cemaziyelahir 1313 (30 November 1895); and for later reactions, *Dh. İd.* 154/18, no. 1, 10 Safer 1341 (2 October 1922). Imperial authorities deported and relocated several missionaries based on field reports. *A. Mkt. Mhm.* 637/42, nos 1–13, 3 Zilhicce 1316 (14 April 1899).

34 Kalpakçıoğlu, in *Dh. İd.* 154/7, nos 1–10, 3 Recep 1331 (8 June 1913).

35 For surprisingly rich documents on Nestorian girls, see *A. Mkt. Mhm.* 700/5, nos 1–65, 8 Şevval 1312 (4 April 1895). On various other cases, see *Hr. Sys.* 71/32, nos 1–5, 24 March 1891; *Hr. Sys.* 45/15, nos 1–7, 17 February 1875; and *Dh. İd.* 117/27, nos 1–2, 3 Rabiulevvel 1329 (4 March 1911). For the phrases "save Muslim children" and "deport the missionaries," which state officials used on various occasions, see *A. Mkt. Mhm.* 700/5, no. 3, 4-65, 3 Cemaziyelahir 1311 (12 December 1893). In another case, missionaries in Bursa took four Muslim girls to a smuggler named Rupen. If the officers had not caught him, the smuggler would have delivered the girls to the United States. *Dh. Eum. 5Şb.* 37/59, no. 1, 16 Şevval 1337 (15 July 1919).

36 Informed studies of the late Ottoman Empire include Hanioğlu, *Brief History*; Clay, *Gold for the Sultan*; İnalcık and Quataert, eds, *Economic and Social History*; Göçek, "Ethnic Segmentation"; and Pamuk, "Ottoman Empire."

37 Fortna, *Imperial Classroom*, 1–40.

38 *Hr. Mkt.* 29/16, nos 1–2, 21 Muharrem 1266 (7 December 1849).

39 On Diyarbakır, *Hr. Mkt.* 59/36, no. 1, 28 Recep 1269 (7 May 1853). See also *Hr. Mkt.* 91/15, nos 1–2, 29 Muharrem 1271 (22 October 1854); on Merzifon, *Hr. Mkt.* 47/78, nos 1–2, 3 Zilkade 1268 (12 August 1852); and *Hr. Mkt.* 61/21, no. 1, 7 Şevval 1269 (14 July 1853).

40 *Y. Prk. Mf.* 5/20, no. 10, 13–15, 17, 18–20, 24–9, 34–5, 39–42, 2 Recep 1325 (11 August 1907); *Hr. Sys.* 81/59, nos 1–2, 30 December 1871;

Hr. Sys. 2742/80, nos 1–2, 12 September 1905; *Hr. Sys.* 2860/51, no. 1, 3 October 1896. On Ottoman Islamism, see Karpat, *Politicization of Islam*, 20–67, 117–35, 155–82. Some scholars take provincial agency for granted and claim that the missionaries caused the Armenians to replace Turkish with Armenian in their rituals. Sevinç, *Ajan Okulları*, 51, quoted in Şafak, *Osmanlı-Amerikan*, 198. H.N. Barnum, the American Board's dedicated missionary to east Anatolia from 1859 to 1910, reported from Harput that a petite caucus had provoked the Armenians, who otherwise would not have revolted against the Istanbul government. In New York the Armenian ultra-nationalists protested such views and noted that "the imperial yoke" had always exploited and frustrated their people. Strikingly, however, many Armenians in Anatolia and the United States agreed that their own leaders had inspired them more than evangelical missionaries. On Ottoman Ambassador Alexander Mavroyeni's remarks about this subject, on H.N. Barnum, and for a nuanced study of Barnum's life and times, see *Hr. Sys.* 2735/28, nos 1–2, 22 December 1890; *Memorial Records for Herman N. Barnum, 1826–1910*, American Research Institute in Turkey; and Sipahi, "At Arm's Length," esp. 213–331.

41 *Hatt-ı Hümâyûn* 512/25086, no. 1, 18 Zilhicce 1254 (4 March 1839); *Dh. Mkt.* 1769/57, no. 1, 25 Safer 1308 (10 October 1890); *Hr. Sys.* 81/59, nos 1–2, 30 December 1871; *Ya. Res.* 122/88, nos 1–14, 7 Cemaziyelahir 1321 (31 August 1903).

42 *Dh. Mkt.* 1769/57, no. 1, 25 Safer 1308 (10 October 1890); *Dh. Mkt.* 1914/36, no. 1, 20 Cemaziyelahir 1309 (21 January 1892); *Ya. Res.* 122/88, nos 2–5, 7 Cemaziyelahir 1321 (31 August 1903); on early development of state communications, Matuz, "Transmission of Directives."

43 *Dh. Mkt.* 1794/18, no. 1, 9 Cemaziyelevvel 1308 (20 December 1890). On the anti-Ottoman agitator Abkarian and his consular protection, see *Dh. Mkt.* 1789/19, no. 1, 23 Rabiulahir 1308 (6 December 1890); and *Dh. Mkt.* 1809/5, nos 1–5, 5 Recep 1308 (14 February 1891). Other locals under state surveillance included the photographer Gabrian and the scribe Batakjian the son of Tandirian. *Dh. Mkt.* 1786/32, no. 1, 16 Rabiulahir 1308 (29 November 1890).

44 *Dh. Mkt.* 1800/141, no. 1, 8 Cemaziyelahir 1308 (19 January 1891). For other cases, including the priest Mesaros's "provocative" anti-state speech before the Armenian Unity Committee and the serious accusation that the bestial Turks had attacked the Greek community, see *Dh. Eum. Ayş.* 13/47, no. 1, 24 Ramazan 1337 (23 June 1919); and *Hr. Sys.* 61/16, nos 1–10, 31 March 1892.

45 *Dh. Mkt.* 1802/3, no. 1, 13 Cemaziyelahir 1308 (24 January 1891); *Dh. Mkt.* 1827/17, no. 1, 29 Şaban 1308 (9 April 1891). On female missionaries using home as an educational space, see Ellington, *Domestic Frontiers*, 17–49. In a February 1895 case, authorities ordered local agents that Bogos, the translator for American citizens in Adana, be "treated fairly" in the court case. *İ. Hus.* 34/1312 Ş 019, no. 1, 6 Şaban 1312 (2 February 1895). Intriguingly, in these troubled times, several locals appreciated that imperial authorities had preserved peace and order in their regions. For instance, see Mikalem, in *A. Mkt. Mhm.* 652/1, nos 1–2, 8 Safer 1314 (17 July 1896).

46 *A. Mkt. Mhm.* 694/13, nos 1–4, 23 Safer 1314 (3 August 1896).

47 The murdered preachers were Nazaret Heghinian of the Marash Third Church, Hagop Albarian of Geben, Hovagim Kayaian of Albustan, Sdepan Hovhannessian of Kharne, and Takvor Hagopian of Baghche. *Annual Report* (1909), 63. My analysis also derives from other documents, including *Hr. Sys.* 73/18, no. 1, 22 January 1895; *Hr. Sys.* 73/20, nos 1–3, 27 January 1895; *İ. Hus.* 34/1312 Ş 19, no. 1, 6 Şaban 1312 (2 February 1895); and *Y. Prk. Tkm.* 10/23, no. 1, 26 Cemaziyelahir 1304 (10 February 1887). See also newspaper comments in *A. Mkt. Mhm.* 657/34, nos 1–3, 3 Cemaziyelahir 1313 (21 November 1895); and *Y. Prk. Tkm.* 10/32, no. 1, 14 Recep 1304 (8 April 1887). In a June 1880 incident in Haifa, Christian and Muslim residents suddenly began fighting at a wedding. American missionaries were absent on site but were still cited as potential "instigators." Authorities failed to unravel this case. *A. Mkt. Mhm.* 657/53, nos 1–4, 9 Recep 1313 (27 December 1895); see also *Hr. Sys.* 64/17, nos 1–18, 8 November 1895. On the US government's claim that Ottoman officials "could but did not avert unfortunate incidents," see *A. Mkt. Mhm.* 657/36, nos 1–2, 6–17, 3 Cemaziyelahir 1313 (21 November 1895). In Beirut the US ambassador requested interviews with some residents of Mersin to identify who had led the assault against Tarsus American College. *A. Mkt. Mhm.* 616/5, nos 1–4, 26 Rabiulahir 1313 (16 October 1895). For micro-level studies of massacres in Sasun and Diyarbakır, see Miller, "Sasun 1894"; and Verheij, "Diyarbekir," 124–38.

48 On Kabadaian and some other incidents, see *Hr. Sys.* 64/17, nos 1–18, 8 November 1895.

49 On ethno-religious conflicts, see *Hr. Sys.* 73/18, no. 1, 22 January 1895; and *Hr. Sys.* 73/20, nos 1–3, 22 January 1895. On the "burning of missionary institutions" and the imperial assignment of guards and tasks to protect and relocate missionaries, see *A. Mkt. Mhm.* 694/3, nos 1–3,

11 Cemaziyelevvel 1313 (30 October 1895); *Hr. Sys.* 73/21, nos 1–2, 28 January 1895; *Hr. Sys.* 73/44, no. 1, 5 December 1895; and *Hr. Sys.* 73/53, no. 1, 16 January 1896. The US secretary of state appreciated Ottoman authorities for their concerns about the safety of their citizens. *Hr. Sys.* 73/54, nos 1–2, 20 January 1896. On US-Canadian debates over Ottoman massacres, see *Hr. Sys.* 73/51, nos 1–8, 9 January 1896; and *Hr. Sys.* 2741/43, nos 1–2, 25 April 1896.

50 *Y. Prk. Mf.* 5/20, no. 3, 2 Recep 1325 (11 August 1907).

51 *Dh. Mkt.* 2185/83, no. 1, 23 Zilkade 1316 (4 April 1899); on Yannakis's replacement by Abdulhalim, *Dh. Mkt.* 1259/41, nos 1–3, 10 Cemaziyelevvel 1326 (10 June 1908).

52 *Hr. Sys.* 132/31, nos 1–4, 24 August 1909; *Hr. Sys.* 132/32, nos 1–3, 30 August 1909; *Hr. Sys.* 132/33, nos 1–5, 18 September 1909. Erickson's later legacy inspired the Albanian nation during the post-reconstruction period. Tellingly, at an elegant 2012 reception in the presence of US diplomats and eastern European ambassadors, Mal Berisha, Albania's chargé d'affaires to the United Kingdom, launched his book *Jeta e jashtëzakonshme e amerikanit Charles Telford Erickson kushtuar Shqipërisë* [Charles Telford Erickson: The extraordinary life of an American dedicated to Albania]. Future research can examine a substantial collection of Erickson's correspondence and writings in the *Charles Telford Erickson Papers*, RG 26, Yale University Divinity School Library.

53 On missionaries, minorities, and imperial debates over "Christianization of the Muslim millet," see *Dh. Eum. Ayş.* 1/53, nos 2–4, 17 Cemaziyelahir 1337 (20 March 1919); and *Dh. Eum. 5Şb.* 68/21, nos 1–2, 2 Zilhicce 1336 (8 September 1918).

54 *Hr. Sys.* 54/4, nos 1–8, 13 August 1896; on Bitola, *Y. Prk. Eşa.* 24/58, no. 1, 27 Zilhicce 1313 (9 June 1896).

55 Hafızi Efendi, in *Y. Prk. Mf.* 5/20, no. 9, 2 Recep 1325 (11 August 1907).

56 Seyfullah Efendi, in *Y. Prk. Mf.* 5/20, no. 4, 38, 2 Recep 1325 (11 August 1907).

57 *Y. Prk. Mf.* 5/20, nos 4–5, 2 Recep 1325 (11 August 1907).

58 *A. Mkt. Mhm.* 701/02, no. 1, 29 Safer 1312 (1 September 1894); for instructions to governors, *Dh. Mkt.* 2351/130, no. 1, 29 Muharrem 1318 (29 May 1900); for Izmir report, *Y. Prk. Mf.* 5/20, no. 41, 2 Recep 1325 (11 August 1907); for the 1915 imperial address to the American University of Beirut, *Hr. Sys.* 2266/54, no. 1, 13 September 1915.

59 *Hr. Sys.* 68/10, nos 1–4, 24 February 1873; *A. Mkt. Mhm.* 495/32, nos 1–2, 7 Rabiulevvel 1305 (23 November 1887). See also *Hr. Sys.* 2429/59, nos 1–3, 28 December 1916; and *Hr. Sys.* 2427/16, nos 1–4,

17 October 1916. For discussion on Mormon missionaries in Aleppo, see *Y. Mtv.* 242/43, nos 1–4, 9 Muharrem 1321 (7 April 1903). In Antep, Birecik, and Maraş, several officials claimed that the Mormon missionaries would sow the seeds of discord in their region. *Dh. Mkt.* 1855/29, no. 1, 26 Zilhicce 1308 (2 August 1891); *Dh. Mkt.* 1875/55, no. 1, 3 Rabiulevvel 1309 (7 October 1891). In a September 1891 report, local officials informed imperial authorities that an unnamed Mormon progenitor had invited some of his fellows to address people in Antep. *Dh. Mkt.* 1871/11, no. 1, 18 Safer 1309 (23 September 1891). Strikingly, the authorities announced that the US government alone would be responsible if something happened to these Mormons. *Dh. Mkt.* 455/15, no. 1, 17 Zilhicce 1319 (27 March 1902); see also Akgün, "Mormon Missionaries."

60 "The Unscrupulous Turk," *New York Times*, 17 April 1892, 17; report by Muncî Bey, the imperial consul-general in New York, in *Ya. Hus.* 376/68, no. 1, 15 Rabiulahir 1315 (13 September 1897); Milaslı Durmuş Zade, *Alem-i İslam'da Cihad-ı Ekber* [The greater jihad in the Islamic world], 25, quoted in Deringil, *Well-Protected Domains*, 126–7, 133–4.

61 Sultan Abdulhamid II's letter, in *İ. Dh.* 100258, no. 6975, 27 Şevval 1309 (25 May 1892), translated and analyzed in Deringil, *Well-Protected Domains*, 114–15; on imperial-provincial dialectics regarding American missionaries, Fortna, *Imperial Classroom*, 75–6.

62 *Y. Prk. Mf.* 5/20, no. 3, 2 Recep 1325 (11 August 1907).

CHAPTER THREE

1 On Ellen Maria Stone (1846–1927), see Howe and Graves, eds, *Sketches of Representative Women*, 459–63.

2 "Captured by Brigands," *Houston Daily Post*, 7 September 1901, 3; on the Internal Macedonian Revolutionary Organization's tactics, Duncan, *Politics of Terror*, 31–142. The Stone memorandum, sent by Robert College president George Washburn to US diplomatic agent Charles Dickinson, is in *Papers Relating to the Foreign Relations* (1903), esp. 1017. For some other interpretations, see Carpenter, *Miss Stone Affair*, 16–42; Curtis, *Turk and His Lost Provinces*, 217–42; and Oren, *Power, Faith, and Fantasy*, 311–12. In a later 1979 incident, Islamist radicals caused political terror with a comparable effect by capturing sixty-six Americans in Iran. Farber, *Taken Hostage*, 102–36.

3 "American Woman," *Houston Daily Post*, 29 September 1901, 1; "Why the Stone Case Worries Europe," *Bisbee Daily Review*, 19 January 1902, 2; "Russian Authorities," *San Francisco Call*, 22 October 1901, 5; "To

Secure Miss Stone's Release," *Salt Lake Herald*, 4 October 1901, 1; Carpenter, *Miss Stone Affair*, 165–86. For Ottoman views of US opinions and vessels, see *Ya. Hus.* 323/128, nos 1–5, 12 Şevval 1312 (8 April 1895); *Ya. Hus.* 324/95, no. 2, 21 Şevval 1312 (17 April 1895); *Ya. Hus.* 326/62, nos 1–2, 5 Zilkade 1312 (30 April 1895); *Ya. Hus.* 326/83, nos 1–2, 6 Zilkade 1312 (1 May 1895); and *Ya. Hus.* 389/57, nos 1–2, 11 Cemaziyelevvel 1316 (27 September 1898). On American battleships in the Ottoman Mediterranean, see Hourihan, "Roosevelt and the Sultans," v–23.

4 "Roosevelt Hopes," *The World*, 7 October 1901, 1. For an excellent study of Roosevelt, see Kohn, *Heir to the Empire City*, 208–16.

5 "Large Donations," *New York Times*, 6 October 1901 (special issue), 1; "17.808 dollars," *The World*, 5 October 1901, 1; "Roosevelt Hopes," *The World*, 7 October 1901, 1; "Brigands Give Up," *Suburban Citizen*, 22 February 1902, 1.

6 *Treaties, Conventions, International Acts*, vol. 2, 1318–20; for Mehmet Sait's letter to Abdulhamid II and the three-page summary of US letters regarding the case, *Ya. Hus.* 424/41, nos 1–4, 14 Şevval 1319 (24 January 1902); for substantial records regarding Ellen Stone, *Hr. Sys.* 56/2, nos 1–126, 28 June 1903. Sait served as grand vizier for nine years and nine terms intermittently from 1879 to 1912.

7 *Ya. Hus.* 424/41, nos 1, 3–4, 14 Şevval 1319 (24 January 1902); Şakir Bey to Sultan Abdulhamid II, in *Y. Prk. Mk.* 11/6, no. 2, 25 Cemaziyelahir 1319 (9 October 1901). For more Stone-related directives, see *Dh. Mkt.* 458/21, no. 1, 17 Zilhicce 1319 (27 March 1902); *Dh. Mkt.* 441/21, nos 1–19, 5 Zilhicce 1319 (15 March 1902); *Dh. Mkt.* 460/56, nos 1–4, 17 Zilhicce 1319 (27 March 1902); *Y. Mtv.* 231/147, no. 1, 24 Rabiulevvel 1320 (1 July 1902); and *Y. Prk. Tşf.* 6/70, no. 1, 7 Zilkade 1319 (15 February 1902).

8 DeNovo, *American Interests and Policies*, 33–4. Major studies on Ottoman-US relations include Aydın and Erhan, eds, *Turkish-American Relations*; Doğan and Sharkey, eds, *American Missionaries*; Fendoğlu, *Modernleşme Bağlamında*; Field, *America and the Mediterranean World*; Grabill, *Protestant Diplomacy*; and Makdisi, *Faith Misplaced*.

9 Shaw and Shaw, *Osmanlı İmparatorluğu*, vol. 2, 125–6, 267; Okçabol, *Türk Zabıta Tarihi*; Lévy, "La police ottomane."

10 Ergut, "Policing the Poor," 151–2; Swanson, "Ottoman Police." My research on Ottoman security derives from archival documents, including *Dh. Eum. 5Şb.* 2/59, nos 1–2, 9 Zilhicce 1332 (29 October 1914); *Dh. Eum. 5Şb.* 72/12, no. 1, 11 Muharrem 1337 (17 October 1918); *Dh. Eum.*

5Şb. 75/4, nos 1–11, 1 Safer 1337 (6 November 1918); *Dh. Eum. Emn.* 52/19, nos 1–11, 16 Rabiulevvel 1332 (12 February 1914); *Dh. Mkt.* 2355/32, no. 1, 6 Safer 1318 (5 June 1900); *Dh. Mui.* 11/2-16, nos 1–2, 3 Ramazan 1327 (18 September 1909); *Hr. Sys.* 73/14, no. 1, 15 January 1895; *İ. Hus.* 84/1318 Ca 48, no. 1, 22 Cemaziyelevvel 1318 (17 September 1900); *Y. Mtv.* 110/51, no. 1, 6 Cemaziyelahir 1312 (5 December 1894); *Y. Mtv.* 183/10, 3 Cemaziyelahir 1316 (19 October 1898); *Y. Mtv.* 242/43, nos 1–4, 9 Muharrem 1321 (7 April 1903); *Y. Prk. Eşa.* 24/58, no. 1, 27 Zilhicce 1313 (9 June 1896); *Y. Prk. Eşa.* 52/2, no. 1, 2 Muharrem 1326 (5 February 1908). For several reports on American missionaries, see *Y. Prk. Um.* 67/30, nos 1–10, 12 Şaban 1321 (3 November 1903); and *Ya. Hus.* 409/84, nos 1–3, 22 Rabiulahir 1318 (19 August 1900). For the January 1854 Ministers Council decree, which established the Investigation Assembly for handling public crimes involving foreign subjects, see *A. Dvn.* 95/67, no. 1, 1 Cemaziyelevvel 1270 (30 January 1854). On the case of Maria Gerber, see *Zb.* 46/13, nos 1–24, 28 Teşrinievvel 1323 (10 November 1907).

11 Ahmet Tevfik to Alexander Terrell, 24 February 1896, in *Papers Relating to the Foreign Relations* (1896), 880–1; Mehmet Sait's memorandum, in *Ya. Hus.* 424/41, nos 1–2, 14 Şevval 1319 (24 January 1902).

12 For more on Ottoman-US relations, see DeNovo, *American Interests and Policies*, 3–166; Howard, "Bicentennial"; Oren, *Power, Faith, and Fantasy*, 305–46; Şafak, *Osmanlı-Amerikan İlişkileri*, 36–155; Şahin, ed., *Bir Zamanlar Amerika ve Türkler*; and Yılmaz, *Turkish-American Relations*, 9–39.

13 Colton, ed., *Speeches of Henry Clay*, vol. 1, 251.

14 Ibid.; Field, *America and the Mediterranean World*, 125–6.

15 Aydın and Erhan, eds, *Turkish-American Relations*, 3–25; DeNovo, *American Interests and Policies*, 18–25; Gordon, *American Relations*, 3–56. For an interesting narrative of the Barbary Wars of 1801–15, see Kilmeade and Yaeger, *Thomas Jefferson and the Tripoli Pirates*.

16 *Treaties, Conventions, International Acts*, vol. 2, 1318–20; for the Ottoman version of the 1830 treaty, *Muahedat Mecmuası*, vol. 2, 2–6. On capitulations, treaties, and US foreign policy, see Şahin, "Capitulations"; Köprülü, "Tarihte Türk Amerikan Münasebetleri"; and Mead, *Special Providence*, 3–29.

17 On trade balances, regulations, and consular reports, see Turgay, "Ottoman-American Trade," esp. appendix 4; Pamuk, "Ottoman Empire"; and Eldem, "Ottoman Financial Integration."

18 *Treaties, Conventions, International Acts*, vol. 2, 1319; Kuneralp, "Ottoman Diplomacy and Controversy."

19 *Treaties, Conventions, International Acts*, vol. 2, 1318–41.

20 Ibid., vol. 2, 1341–8.

21 Ibid., vol. 2, 1318; DeNovo, *American Interests and Policies*, 22. On court cases worth over 500 piasters, see *A. Mkt. Mhm.* 702/12, nos 1–15, 8 Rabiulevvel 1313 (29 August 1895); *Hr. Sys.* 74/44, nos 1–6, 28 November 1896; *Mv.* 218/16, no. 1, 23 Rabiulahir 1338 (15 January 1920); *Ya. Res.* 96/44, nos 1–4, 9 Recep 1316 (23 November 1898); *Y. Prk. Eşa.* 42/57, nos 1–6, 29 Zilhicce 1320 (29 March 1903); and *Y. Prk. Eşa.* 49/70, nos 2–3. On US concerns over Ottoman agreements, see *Hr. Sys.* 51/15, nos 1–2, 19 July 1860; and *Hr. Sys.* 69/34, nos 1–6, 7 December 1896. For Ottoman-US debates (in French), see *Y. Prk. Tkm.* 11/44, nos 1–25, 20 Rabiulevvel 1305 (6 December 1887). For an inspiring study of plausible deniability as a concept, see Walton, "Plausible Deniability," 50–3.

22 Dwight, *Treaty Rights*, 2, 20, also available in the ABCFM pamphlet box at Andover-Harvard Theological Library.

23 Ibid., 20; Gordon, "Turkish-American Treaty Relations," 714; on the Ministers Council's July 1893 meeting on evangelical institutions, *Ya. Hus.* 278/29, nos 1–2, 3 Muharrem 1311 (17 July 1893).

24 Şahin, "Capitulations"; Thayer, "Capitulations of the Ottoman Empire."

25 For Ambassador Alexander Mavroyeni's note to Istanbul, *Ya. Hus.* 317/89, nos 1–3, 28 September 1894; on diplomatic debates involving US demands, *Y. Prk. Eşa.* 42/57, nos 1–6, 29 Zilhicce 1320 (29 March 1903); for Ottoman views on US citizens in Ottoman courts, *Mv.* 218/16, no. 1, 23 Rabiulahir 1338 (15 January 1920). See also the imperial memorandum in *Hr. Sys.* 69/27, nos 1–2, 11 January 1896.

26 Ahmet Tevfik to Alexander W. Terrell, 22 February 1896, in *Papers Relating to the Foreign Relations* (1896), 852. See also the note of Ali Ferruh, the Ottoman ambassador to Washington (1898–1901), in *Y. Ee.* 136/96, no. 1, 25 Cemaziyelevvel 1316 (11 September 1898).

27 For Ahmet Tevfik's note to Alexander Terrell, dated 24 February 1896, and on the American Board's losses in Harput and Maraş, *Papers Relating to the Foreign Relations* (1896), 879–90, esp. 880–1; on the post-1894 ethno-religious conflicts and for a balanced micro-study of rebellions and massacres in Diyarbakır, Verheij, "Diyarbekir," 97–117; for competing narratives on the 1893–1894 violence in the province of Bitlis, Miller, "Sasun 1894," 157–231; for an informed socio-study of collective violence against the Armenian millet, Göçek, *Transformation of Turkey*, 211–40.

For a nuanced study of rumours, violence, and collective senses regarding the 1895 Harput massacres, see also Sipahi, "At Arm's Length," esp. 298–331.

28 Ali Ferruh's address to Tahsin Pasha, 11 October 1898, in *Y. Ee.* 136/96, no. 1, 25 Cemaziyelevvel 1316 (11 October 1898). For various Ottoman views, see *Ya. Hus.* 357/87, nos 1–6, 11 Rabiulevvel 1314 (20 August 1896); *Ya. Res.* 96/44, nos 1–4, 9 Recep 1316 (23 November 1898); and *Y. Ee.* 94/43, nos 1–3, 5 Cemaziyelevvel 1320 (10 August 1902).

29 *Y. Ee.* 136/96, nos 1–2, 25 Cemaziyelevvel 1316 (11 October 1898). For self-criticisms of state officials, see *İ. Hr.* 437/58, no. 1, 22 Rabiulevvel 1322 (6 June 1904).

30 Ahmet Tevfik's note to John G.A. Leishman, 12 August 1904; and Leishman to Tevfik, 12–13 August 1904, both in *Papers Relating to the Foreign Relations* (1904), 828–9.

31 On American battleships, see Hourihan, "Roosevelt and the Sultans," 63–183; *Ya. Hus.* 457/77, nos 1–3, 25 Cemaziyelahir 1321 (18 September 1903); *Ya. Hus.* 473/123, no. 2, 22 Rabiulevvel 1322 (6 June 1904); *A. Mkt. Mhm.* 702/12, nos 1–15, 8 Rabiulevvel 1313 (29 August 1895); and *Y. Prk. Tkm.* 10/32, no. 1, 14 Recep 1304 (8 April 1887). On the Canadian Parliament debates, see *Hr. Sys.* 73/51, nos 1–8, 9 January 1896. For Secretary of State John M. Hay's note of 5 August 1904, which informed Ambassador John Leishman of three American ships on their way to Izmir, see *Papers Relating to the Foreign Relations* (1904), 824.

32 John Leishman's letter to Secretary of State John Hay, 7 December 1903, in *Papers Relating to the Foreign Relations* (1904), 833; "American Consul Attacked," *New York Times*, 8 December 1903; on Ottoman-US treaties and citizenship matters, Karpat, "Ottoman Emigration to America," 190.

33 John Leishman to John Hay, 7 December 1903; Mr Loomis from the Department of State to John Leishman, 14 December 1903; John Leishman to John Hay, 15 December 1903; and John Hay to John Leishman, 16 December 1903, all in *Papers Relating to the Foreign Relations* (1904), 833–5.

34 John Leishman to John Hay, 1 April 1904; John Leishman to Ahmet Tevfik, 20 April 1904; and John Hay to John Leishman, 9 June 1904, all in *Papers Relating to the Foreign Relations* (1904), 819–21.

35 Ahmet Tevfik to John Leishman, 12 August 1904; John Leishman to Ahmet Tevfik, 12–13 August 1904; and John Leishman to John Hay, 16 August and 15 September 1904, all in *Papers Relating to the Foreign Relations* (1904), 828–32.

36 Ottoman documents regarding evangelical missionaries include *Hr. Sys.* 2803/1, nos 1–131, 26 June 1890. On local tensions and the suffering of missionaries, see *A. Mkt. Mhm.* 538/27, nos 1–6, 3 Recep 1314 (8 December 1896). For local petitions against the missionaries, see *Hr. Sys.* 51/16, nos 1–2, 1 November 1860; *İ. Hus.* 21/1311 Ş 60, no. 1, 18 Şaban 1311 (24 February 1894); *Ya. Hus.* 278/29, nos 1–2; *Ya. Hus.* 319/2, nos 1–3, 10 Şaban 1312 (6 February 1895); and *Y. Mtv.* 144/135, no. 1, 24 Safer 1314 (4 August 1896). On the Washington meeting, see *Hr. Sys.* 74/47, nos 1–4, 4 December 1896. On other debates, see *Ya. Hus.* 357/87, nos 1–6, 11 Rabiulevvel 1314 (20 August 1896). On numerous cases of American suspects in Ottoman courts, see *Hr. Sys.* 2803/1, nos 1–131, 26 June 1890. See also *Y. Prk. Eşa.* 30/49, nos 1–2, 10 Safer 1316 (30 June 1898).

37 The government analysis here is drawn from various sources, including *A. Mkt. Mhm.* 1/14, nos 1–2, 17 Muharrem 1260 (7 February 1844); *A. Mkt. Mvl.* 147/29, no. 1, 5 Zilhicce 1278 (3 June 1862); *A. Mkt. Nzd.* 318/17, nos 1–2, 27 Zilhicce 1276 (16 July 1860); *A. Mkt. Um.* 566/67, no. 1, 20 Zilkade 1278 (9 May 1862); and *A. Mkt. Um.* 574/50, no. 1, 26 Zilhicce 1278 (24 June 1862). For an inspiring study of state power, see Currie, "Distribution of Powers," 19–40. On Ottoman state modernization, see Findley, *Bureaucratic Reform*; Faroqhi, *Ottoman Empire*, 2–73; Barkey, "Islam and Toleration"; Weiker, "Ottoman Bureaucracy"; Ergene, "On Ottoman Justice"; and Horowitz, "International Law," 445–55.

38 For examples of "sedition" in the Ottoman lexicon, see *A. Mkt. Mhm.* 609/5, nos 1–4, 13 Cemaziyelevvel 1315 (10 October 1897); *A. Mkt. Mhm.* 609/31, nos 1–4, 5 Cemaziyelahir 1313 (23 November 1895); *A. Mkt. Mhm.* 612/4, nos 1–3, 21 Rabiulevvel 1314 (30 August 1896); *Y. Prk. Eşa.* 26/100, no. 1, 23 Şevval 1314 (27 March 1897); and *Y. Prk. Mf.* 3/11, nos 1–3, 2 Recep 1311 (9 January 1894). Additionally, see the incident reports in *İ. Hus.* 128/1323 S 052, no. 1, 15 Safer 1323 (21 April 1905); *Y. Mtv.* 183/10, nos 1–12, 3 Cemaziyelahir 1316 (19 October 1898); *Y. Prk. Hr.* 7/36, nos 1–8, 18 Safer 1301 (19 December 1883); *Y. Prk. Myd.* 20/87, nos 1–2, 9 Ramazan 1315 (1 February 1898); *Y. Prk. Myd.* 21/42, nos 1–2, 29 Rabiulevvel 1316 (17 August 1898); *Ya. Hus.* 409/84, nos 1–3, 22 Rabiulahir 1318 (19 August 1900); *Ya. Res.* 78/54, nos 1–2, 6 Şevval 1313 (21 March 1896); and *Ya. Res.* 122/88, nos 1–14, 7 Cemaziyelahir 1321 (31 August 1903). For an imperial memorandum regarding local incidents of sedition, see *Y. Ee.* 43/103, nos 1–2, 6 Rabiulahir 1327 (30 April 1909). For imperial surveys on US and Greek

citizens, see *Dh. Eum. 3Şb.* 23/43, nos 1–97, 8 Zilhicce 1335 (25 September 1917). See also Karpat, "Ottoman Population Records."

39 On Harput, *Dh. Mkt.* 2185/83, no. 1, 23 Zilkade 1316 (4 April 1899); on Hasan, *A. Mkt. Mhm.* 701/5, 23 Zilkade 1312 (18 May 1895); on Zekeriya, *Dh. Eum. Ayş.* 23/1, nos 1–16, 1 Muharrem 1338 (26 September 1919); on Varjabedian, *Zb.* 93/64, nos 1–3, 29 Teşrinievvel 1323 (11 November 1907). On other cases and local misconduct, see *Hr. Mkt.* 88/8, nos 1–4, 10 Muharrem 1271 (3 September 1854); *A. Mkt. Um.* 521/47, no. 1, 27 Cemaziyelevvel 1278 (10 November 1861); and *Zb.* 351/37, no. 1. See also *Ya. Hus.* 318/97, nos 1–3, 9 Şaban 1312 (5 February 1895).

40 *A. Mkt. Um.* 566/67, no. 1, 20 Zilkade 1278 (9 May 1862); on Abdino, *Dh. Mui.* 7/3-36, nos 1–19, 9 Şevval 1327 (24 October 1909).

41 On Kayseri, *A. Mkt. Mhm.* 724/4, nos 1–5, 19 Şaban 1311 (25 February 1894); on Rakım, *Zb.* 351/37, no. 1, 9 Şaban 1323 (9 October 1905); for the 1897 memorandum, *Y. Ee.* 132/40, nos 1–6, 10 Safer 1315 (11 July 1897). On incompetent agents, see *Y. Prk. Mf.* 3/11, nos 1–3, 2 Recep 1311 (9 January 1894); and *Ya. Hus.* 269/129, nos 1–6, 24 Recep 1310 (11 February 1893).

42 For specific directives, see *Y. Prk. Eşa.* 26/100, no. 1, 23 Şevval 1314 (27 March 1897); and *A. Mkt. Mhm.* 648/13, 20 Recep 1313 (6 January 1896). On missionary safety, see *A. Mkt. Mhm.* 609/5, nos 1–4, 13 Cemaziyelevvel 1315 (10 October 1897); *A. Mkt. Mhm.* 609/31, nos 2–3, 5 Cemaziyelahir 1313 (23 November 1895); and *A. Mkt. Mhm.* 612/4, nos 1–3, 21 Rabiulevvel 1314 (30 August 1896). For the quotations on guards and missionaries, see *A. Dvn.* 104/64, no. 1, 15 Şevval 1271 (1 July 1855); *A. Mkt. Mhm.* 651/4, nos 1–5, 1 Zilkade 1313 (14 April 1896); *A. Mkt. Mhm.* 660/73, nos 1–2, 16 Cemaziyelahir 1313 (4 December 1895); *A. Mkt. Mhm.* 662/5, nos 1–4, 21 Şevval 1314 (25 March 1897); and *Y. Prk. Ask.* 10/60, 30 Cemaziyelevvel 1313 (18 November 1895). For general orders, see *A. Mkt. Mhm.* 616/11, nos 1–6, 24 Cemaziyelevvel 1313 (12 November 1895); *A. Mkt. Mhm.* 617/21, nos 1–3, 3 Zilkade 1314 (5 April 1897); and *A. Mkt. Mhm.* 657/23, no. 1, 24 Cemaziyelevvel 1313 (12 November 1895).

43 Karpat, *Ottoman Population*, 156–61; *Salnâme-i Vilayet-i Bitlis*; Nazım, *Ermeni Olayları Tarihi*, vol. 1, 166–7. On the Armenian versus Kurdish hostilities, see Mayewski, *Les Massacres d'Arménie*, 15–66.

44 Nazım, *Ermeni Olayları Tarihi*, vol. 1, 166–7; Verheij, "Diyarbekir," 120–36.

45 Nazım, *Ermeni Olayları Tarihi*, vol. 1, 166–7; Knapp, *Tragedy of Bitlis*, 17; Hogan, "Stories, Wars, and Emotions," 47–58. Recent studies of the

Armenian genocide include Göçek, *Transformation of Turkey*, 211–40; Jongerden and Verheij, eds, *Social Relations in Ottoman Diyarbekir*; Miller, "Sasun 1894"; Sipahi, "At Arm's Length," 298–331; and Suny, Göçek, and Naimark, eds, *Question of Genocide*, 221–84.

46 White, *Adventuring with Anatolia College*, part 1, no. 6; on "sedition" and "revolutionary" students, *Papers Relating to the Foreign Relations* (1896), 849. For personal anecdotes and stories of Anatolia College, see *Report and Catalogue of Anatolia College*, 6–45; White, *Charles Chapin Tracy*, 9–75; Compton, *Morning Cometh*, 63–98; and McGrew, *Educating across Cultures*, esp. 1–177. On Tomaian and Kayaian, seditious activities, and the engagement of Tracy and Terrell with the trial and for some post-exile letters to Ernest Riggs, the later president of Anatolia College (1933–50), see *A. Mkt. Mhm.* 733/35, nos 1–4, 26 Ramazan 1310 (13 April 1893); *Bb. Ek. Od.* 179/13409, nos 1–2, 16 Ramazan 1310 (3 April 1893); and *Y. Prk. Um.* 28/60, nos 1–2, 19 Recep 1311 (24 September 1893). For Ottoman views on Anatolia College and a report submitted by Ottoman ambassador Alexander Mavrogenis, see *Hr. Sys.* 2735/10, nos 1–8, 10 November 1889.

47 The story about the fire incident is drawn from various sources, including *Dh. Mkt.* 2053/39, nos 1–3, 1 Şaban 1310 (18 February 1893); White, *Adventuring with Anatolia College*, part 1, no. 6; and *Hr. Sys.* 2825/15, nos 1–4, 10 April 1893. On local claims and other investigations, see *Y. Prk. Um.* 26/67, nos 1–21, 26 Şaban 1310 (15 March 1893); *İ. Ml.* 5/1310, no. 1, 30 Ramazan 1310 (17 April 1893); *A. Mkt. Mhm.* 37/733, 16 Şevval 1310 (3 May 1893); and *Y. Prk. Bşk.* 34/13, no. 1, 25 Cemaziyelevvel 1311 (4 December 1893). On another Anatolia College incident, see *Ya. Res.* 75/21, nos 1–2, 19 Şevval 1312 (15 April 1895). Interestingly, US consul Henry M. Jewett was a diplomat born and raised in Anatolia. In the 1850s his parents, Fayette Jewett and Mary Ann Jewett, had settled in Tokat as evangelical missionaries to serve the Armenians. *Annual Report* (1852), 69; *Annual Report* (1854), 78.

48 White, *Adventuring with Anatolia College*, part 1, no. 7; part 2, no. 26. On Ottoman patrols guarding the college premises and the police station, just built to guard the college but to be closed soon, see *Y. Prk. Ask.* 109/33, no. 1, 8 Recep 1313 (25 December 1895); *Hr. Sys.* 2792/65, nos 1–2, 25 October 1897; and *A. Mkt. Mhm.* 662/34, no. 1, 20 Cemaziyelahir 1315 (16 November 1897). On the American Board's view of the complex 1876–96 period, see Salt, *Imperialism*, 71–135.

49 White, *Adventuring with Anatolia College*, part 1, no. 12. US ambassador John Leishman noted that the Armenian peasants were facing "three sources of constant danger": "being caught in a mélée," "harboring

refugees," and the "damage which might be inflicted upon them by the revolutionists themselves, with the hope of causing foreign interference." On these conditions and the suffering of the "innocent" Armenians at the hands of insurgent fellows, see *Papers Relating to the Foreign Relations* (1904), esp. 839.

50 White, *Adventuring with Anatolia College*, part 2, no. 24. US accounts of the 1895–96 Merzifon deportations and massacres include *Papers Relating to the Foreign Relations* (1896), 849–50; and White, *Charles Chapin Tracy*, 74–5. For a notable story of the college's cook during this time, see Piranyan, *Aşçının Kitabı*; and Maksudyan, "Amerikan Kaynaklarında," 133–78. At the Modern Greek Studies Association Symposium in November 2015, I presented the political challenges that caused the 1924 relocation of Anatolia College from Merzifon to Thessaloniki. In a future article, I wish to explain how the 1915 deportations affected American missionaries and their activities in Merzifon. Previously untapped sources include what the Ottoman ministries wrote as cipher telegrams during this time. Along with American Board and Ottoman public security records, the telegrams can help to unpack significant information on Anatolia College's administration, Muslim students, Armenian staff, and eventual confiscation by state officials during the First World War. The sources of these telegrams include *Dh. Şfr.* 454/148, 9 Kanun-ı Evvel 1330 (22 December 1914); *Dh. Şfr.* 479/62, 27 Haziran 1331 (10 July 1915); *Dh. Şfr.* 484/23, 2 Ağustos 1331 (15 August 1915); *Dh. Şfr.* 484/30, 3 Ağustos 1331 (16 August 1915); *Dh. Şfr.* 522/89, 28 Mayıs 1332 (10 June 1916); *Dh. Şfr.* 546/102, 14 Ağustos 1332 (26 August 1916); and *Dh. Şfr.* 633/133, 9 Ağustos 1335 (9 August 1919).

51 *Memorial Records for George P. Knapp, 1863–1915*, American Research Institute in Turkey. On accusations against Knapp, see *A. Mkt. Mhm.* 694/2, nos 1–7, 13 Rabiulahir 1313 (3 October 1895); "Accusations against Rev. George P. Knapp," *Sacramento Daily Union*, 26 June 1896, 1; and "Terrell Insists," *New York Times*, 11 February 1896, 5. Knapp's own narrative, received on 29 May 1896 by Richard Olney, US secretary of state (1895–97), is in *Papers Relating to the Foreign Relations* (1896), 907–12. See also Knapp, *Tragedy of Bitlis*, 96–111; Knapp, *Mission at Van*; and other documents in *Grace Knapp Papers, 1893–1953*, LD 7096.6, 1893, Mount Holyoke College Manuscript Collections, Massachusetts. On the progression of the Knapp Case, see *Papers Relating to the Foreign Relations* (1896), 905–13; and Salt, *Imperialism*, 115–17.

52 Alexander Terrell to Ahmet Tevfik, 11 February 1896; and Ahmet Tevfik to Alexander Terrell, 9 April 1896, both in *Papers Relating to the Foreign Relations* (1896), 901–2, 905.

53 On Knapp's relocation, see *A. Mkt. Mhm.* 619/17, nos 1–4, 27 Cemaziyelevvel 1313 (15 November 1895); *A. Mkt. Mhm.* 662/5, nos 2–3, 21 Şevval 1314 (25 March 1897); *A. Mkt. Mhm.* 694/1, nos 1–6, 5 Zilhicce 1312 (30 May 1895); and *A. Mkt. Mhm.* 694/4, nos 1–3, 1 Cemaziyelahir 1313 (19 November 1895). For other directives, see *A. Mkt. Mhm.* 612/4, nos 1–3, 21 Rabiulevvel 1314 (30 August 1896); and *Hr. Sys.* 73/15, no. 1, 17 January 1895. On the Üsküdar American Academy for Girls, see *A. Mkt. Mhm.* 742/20, nos 1–2, 24 Zilkade 1330 (4 November 1912).

54 Ahmet Tevfik's memorandum and his letter of 6 June 1896 to John W. Riddle, in *Papers Relating to the Foreign Relations* (1896), 913–14. Grand Vizier Rıfat's views are quoted in Salt, *Imperialism*, 116.

55 On the British consul's "quiet investigation," see Salt, *Imperialism*, 116. Knapp's defence and his letter of 12 May 1896, received on 29 May 1896 by John W. Riddle at the Department of State, are in *Papers Relating to the Foreign Relations* (1896), 907–12. See also *Memorial Records for George P. Knapp, 1863–1915*, American Research Institute in Turkey.

56 *Memorial Records for George P. Knapp, 1863–1915*, American Research Institute in Turkey.

57 Ibid.

58 Alexander Terrell to missionaries, 5 August 1896; and Alexander Terrell to Richard Olney, 10 August 1896, both in *Papers Relating to the Foreign Relations* (1896), 859, 860.

59 Telegrams sent between 6 and 8 August 1896 by American Board missionaries Barnum in Harput, Fuller in Antep, Riggs in Merzifon, Christie in Mersin, and Fowle (misspelled "Fowell" in the original telegram) in Kayseri, in *Papers Relating to the Foreign Relations* (1896), 860.

60 Alexander Terrell to missionaries, 11 August 1896, in *Papers Relating to the Foreign Relations* (1896), 859–60.

61 *Dh. Mui.* 11/2-16, nos 1–2, 3 Ramazan 1327 (18 September 1909).

62 Moustapha Bey to Richard Olney (translation of Mustafa Tahsin's note), 16 November 1896, in *Papers Relating to the Foreign Relations* (1896), 894.

63 The investigation began with the April 1907 directive from the Ministry of the Interior to search Gerber's residence based on a circular letter from a local notable named Hasan Hazım. For imperial records and local reports on Gerber, *Zb.* 46/13, esp. no. 15, 28 Teşrinievvel 1323 (10 November 1907); for Gerber's passionate and gripping autobiography, Gerber, *Passed Experiences*, 143–57. See also Cosmades, *Maria, God's Angel*; and Cosmades, "At Zion Orphanage."

64 *Zb.* 46/13, nos 2–15, 28 Teşrinievvel 1323 (10 November 1907).

65 *Zb.* 46/13, nos 4–15, 28 Teşrinievvel 1323 (10 November 1907). For imperial comments on local interactions, see *Ya. Hus.* 409/84, nos 1–2, 22 Rabiulahir 1318 (19 August 1900); *Y. Mtv.* 183/10, nos 1–2, 3 Cemaziyelahir 1316 (19 October 1898); *Y. Mtv.* 242/43, nos 2–3, 9 Muharrem 1321 (7 April 1903); and *Y. Prk. Eşa.* 24/58, no. 1, 27 Zilhicce 1313 (9 June 1896).

66 This analysis derives from the Ottoman records, including *Dh. Kms.* 52/2-79, nos 1–10, 30 Ramazan 1337 (29 June 1919); *Dh. Mkt.* 458/21, no. 1, 17 Zilhicce 1319 (27 March 1902); *Dh. Mkt.* 460/56, nos 1–4, 17 Zilhicce 1319 (27 March 1902); *Hr. Sys.* 56/2, nos 1–18, 28 June 1903; *Ya. Hus.* 424/41, no. 2, 14 Şevval 1319 (24 January 1902); *Y. Mtv.* 56/51, no. 1, 21 Recep 1309 (20 February 1892); *Y. Mtv.* 107/8, no. 1, 22 Recep 1312 (19 January 1895); *Y. Mtv.* 110/51, no. 1, 6 Cemaziyelahir 1312 (5 December 1894); *Y. Mtv.* 231/147, no. 1, 24 Rabiulevvel 1320 (1 July 1902); *Zb.* 46/13, nos 1–24, 28 Teşrinievvel 1323 (10 November 1907); *Zb.* 309/29, no. 1, 8 Nisan 1322 (21 April 1906); *Zb.* 311/44, no. 1, 3 Mayıs 1324 (16 May 1908); *Zb.* 321/78, no. 1, 8 Kanunuevvel 1323 (21 December 1907). On officers and officials, see *Y. Ee.* 132/40, nos 1–6, 10 Safer 1315 (11 July 1897); and *Y. Prk. Um.* 74/122, no. 1, 7 Muharrem 1323 (14 March 1905). On Şevket, see *Zb.* 351/19, no. 1, 19 Teşrinisani 1323 (2 December 1907); and *Zb.* 351/25, no. 1, 1 Eylül 1323 (14 September 1907). See also Shaw and Shaw, *Osmanlı İmparatorluğu*, vol. 2, 120; and Bektaş, "Sultan's Messenger."

67 *Zb.* 46/13, nos 3–4, 15, 20, 28 Teşrinievvel 1323 (10 November 1907). On public crimes, see *A. Mkt. Mhm.* 649/14, no. 1, 21 Şaban 1313 (6 February 1896); *Dh. Mkt.* 33/42, nos 1–3, 22 Şevval 1310 (9 May 1893); *Dh. Mkt.* 911/14, nos 1–4, 24 Şaban 1322 (3 November 1904); *Dh. Mkt.* 948/42, nos 1–29, 15 Safer 1323 (21 April 1905); *Dh. Mkt.* 1947/47, no. 1, 13 Şevval 1309 (11 May 1892); *İ. Hus.* 73/1316 L 46, 17 Şevval 1316 (28 February 1899); and *Zb.* 309/102, 9 Teşrinisani 1322 (22 November 1906).

68 For examples, see *Dh. Eum. 5Şb.* 2/59, nos 1–2, 9 Zilhicce 1332 (29 October 1914); *Y. Prk. Mk.* 11/6, no. 2, 25 Cemaziyelahir 1319 (9 October 1901); *Ya. Hus.* 424/41, no. 2, 14 Şevval 1319 (24 January 1902); and *Zb.* 309/102, no. 1, 9 Teşrinisani 1322 (22 Novemeber 1906). On the arrest of a chief superintendent, see *Dh. Kms.* 61/2-3, nos 1–3, 18 Zilhicce 1339 (23 August 1921).

69 *Dh. Eum. Emn.* 52/19, no. 1, 6–11, 16 Rabiulevvel 1332 (12 February 1914); Earle, "Early American Policy."

70 *Zb.* 319/29, no. 2, 17 Teşrinievvel 1322 (30 October 1906). Ashjian contacted US diplomats in Alexandretta possibly through his American colleagues.

71 *Zb.* 319/29, no. 2, 17 Teşrinievvel 1322 (30 October 1906).

72 *A. Mkt. Mhm.* 609/5, nos 1–4, 13 Cemaziyelevvel 1315 (10 October 1897); *A. Mkt. Mhm.* 694/4, nos 1–4, 1 Cemaziyelahir 1313 (19 November 1895); *Y. Prk. Ask.* 10/60, no. 1, 30 Cemaziyelevvel 1313 (18 November 1895).

73 *Ya. Hus.* 477/43, no. 4, 6 Cemaziyelahir 1322 (18 August 1904).

74 *Dh. Eum. 5Şb.* 75/4, no. 2, 1 Safer 1337 (6 November 1918); *Dh. Mkt.* 2355/32, no. 1, 6 Safer 1318 (5 June 1900); *Dh. Mui.* 11/2-16, nos 1–2, 3 Ramazan 1327 (18 September 1909); *Hr. Sys.* 73/14, no. 1, 15 January 1895; *İ. Hus.* 84/1318 Ca 48, no. 1, 22 Cemaziyelevvel 1318 (17 September 1900); *Y. Mtv.* 183/10, nos 1–2, 3 Cemaziyelahir 1316 (19 October 1898); *Y. Prk. Bşk.* 35/78, nos 1–7, 28 Ramazan 1311 (4 April 1894); *Y. Prk. Eşa.* 24/58, no. 1, 27 Zilhicce 1313 (9 June 1896); *Y. Prk. Um.* 67/30, nos 1–10, 12 Şaban 1321 (3 November 1903); *Zb.* 46/13, nos 1–24, 28 Teşrinievvel 1323 (10 November 1907); *Zb.* 319/29, nos 1–2, 17 Teşrinievvel 1322 (30 October 1906). On imperial justice, see *Dh. Mui.* 7/3-36, nos 1–19, 9 Şevval 1327 (24 October 1909); and *Hr. Mkt.* 88/8, nos 1–4, 10 Muharrem 1271 (3 September 1854). On guarding missionaries, see *Y. Prk. Eşa.* 26/100, no. 1, 23 Şevval 1314 (27 March 1897). For further examples, see *A. Mkt. Um.* 521/47, no. 1, 27 Cemaziyelevvel 1278 (10 November 1861); and *Ya. Hus.* 322/5, nos 1–2, 19 Ramazan 1312 (16 March 1895).

75 The embassy note is in *Ya. Hus.* 317–89, nos 1–6, 27 Recep 1312 (24 January 1895). On mischief-makers and sedition committees, see *Y. Prk. Eşa.* 52/2, no. 1, 2 Muharrem 1326 (5 February 1908); *Y. Prk. Eşa.* 52/99, no. 1, 20 Zilhicce 1326 (13 January 1909); and *Zb.* 317/144, no. 1, 14 Ağustos 1322 (27 August 1906). On anti-Ottoman literature, see *Zb.* 339/51, no. 1, 1 Teşrinisani 1324 (14 November 1908).

76 *Y. Mrz. D.* 11662, edict 7210; *Y. Mrz. D.* 11681, edict 7479; *Y. Mrz. D.* 14527, edict 2759; *Y. Prk. Myd.* 20/87, 9 Ramazan 1315 (1 February 1898); *Y. Prk. Um.* 67/30, 12 Şaban 1321 (3 November 1903); *Y. Prk. Tşf.* 4/1, 10 Safer 1312 (13 August 1894); on missionaries protected, *Y. Prk. Eşa.* 26/100, no. 1, 23 Şevval 1314 (27 March 1897); on an American Board's orphanage working to proselytize children, *Ya. Hus.* 409/84, nos 1–2, 22 Rabiulahir 1318 (19 August 1900); on illegal seminaries, *Y. Prk. Um.* 23/69, no. 1, 27 Cemaziyelevvel 1309 (29 December 1891); on an early murder case, *A. Mkt. Um.* 521/47, no. 1, 27 Cemaziyelevvel 1278 (10 November 1861); on cases of robbery, *Ya. Hus.* 322/5, no. 1, 19 Ramazan 1312 (16 March 1895); and *Y. Mtv.* 110/51, no. 1, 6 Cemaziyelahir 1312 (5 December 1894).

77 On the burning of colleges, *Y. Prk. Ask.* 8/66, no. 1, 30 Zilhicce 1310 (19 August 1900); on Hasan, *A. Mkt. Mhm.* 701/5, nos 1–17, 23 Zilkade

1312 (18 May 1895); on local attacks in Aleppo, *Hr. Sys.* 71/28, nos 1–3, 21 February 1891; on other attacks, *A. Mkt. Um.* 521/47, no. 1, 27 Cemaziyelevvel 1278 (10 November 1861); *A. Mkt. Um.* 567/9, no. 1, 21 Zilkade 1278 (20 May 1862); and *A. Mkt. Um.* 568/54, no. 1, 26 Zilkade 1278 (25 May 1862); on an unnamed priest murdered, *A. Mkt. Um.* 554/74, nos 1–2, 15 Şevval 1278 (15 April 1862); on a Muslim thief mugging a female missionary, *Ya. Hus.* 322/5, no. 1–2, 19 Ramazan 1312 (16 March 1895). For various other examples and local petitions, see *A. Mkt. Mhm.* 647/39, nos 1–59, 20 Cemaziyelahir 1313 (8 December 1895); *Hr. Sys.* 73/18, no. 1, 22–23 January 1895; *Hr. Sys.* 73/20, nos 1–3, 27 January 1895; *Hr. Sys.* 73/53, no. 1, 16 January 1896; *Hr. Sys.* 74/46, no. 1, 3 December 1896; *Ya. Hus.* 318/97, no. 1, 9 Şaban 1312 (5 February 1895); *Ya. Hus.* 357/87, nos 1–6, 11 Rabiulevvel 1314 (20 August 1896); *Ya. Res.* 96/44, nos 1–4, 9 Recep 1316 (23 November 1898); *Y. Prk. Eşa.* 49/70, nos 1–3, 26 Şaban 1324 (15 October 1906); and *Y. Prk. Bşk.* 36/107, no. 1, 30 Zilhicce 1311 (4 July 1894). For debates on public crimes and missionaries, see *Ya. Hus.* 335/67, no. 1, 11 Rabiulahir 1313 (1 October 1895).

78 *Hr. Mkt.* 56/3, nos 1–2, 20 Recep 1269 (29 April 1853); for examples, *Y. Prk. Ask.* 10/60, no. 1, 30 Cemaziyelevvel 1313 (18 November 1895); on houses, *Y. Prk. Eşa.* 26/100, no. 1, 23 Şevval 1314 (27 March 1897); on the suffering of missionaries, *A. Mkt. Mhm.* 609/5, nos 3–4, 13 Cemaziyelevvel 1315 (10 October 1897). On missionaries under protection, see *A. Mkt. Mhm.* 616/11, nos 1–6, 24 Cemaziyelevvel 1313 (12 November 1895); *A. Mkt. Mhm.* 617/21, nos 1–3, 3 Zilkade 1314 (5 April 1897); *A. Mkt. Mhm.* 651/4, no. 1–5, 1 Zilkade 1313 (14 April 1896); *A. Mkt. Mhm.* 657/23, no. 1, 24 Cemaziyelevvel 1313 (12 November 1895); *A. Mkt. Mhm.* 660/73, nos 1–2, 16 Cemaziyelahir 1313 (4 December 1895); and *A. Mkt. Mhm.* 662/5, nos 1–4, 21 Şevval 1314 (25 March 1897).

79 On the Bartlett incident, *Dh. Mkt.* 1916/93, no. 1, 28 Cemaziyelevvel 1309 (30 December 1891); *Dh. Mkt.* 1991/71, no. 1, 30 Muharrem 1310 (24 August 1892); *Dh. Mkt.* 1996/63, no. 1, 11 Safer 1310 (4 September 1892); *Dh. Mui.* 72/11, nos 1–2, 25 Safer 1328 (8 March 1910); *Hr. Sys.* 71/59, nos 1–2, 8 November 1891; and *Ya. Hus.* 264/183, no. 1, 24 Rabiulahir 1310 (15 November 1892). See also Bartlett, *Biographies and Letters*, Houghton Library.

80 *Ya. Hus.* 264/183, no. 1, 24 Rabiulahir 1310 (15 November 1892). The document cites the original legal statement: "duçar olduğu zarar ve ziyan mukabili."

81 *Ya. Hus.* 264/183, no. 1, 24 Rabiulahir 1310 (15 November 1892).

82 *Ya. Hus.* 264/183, no. 1, 24 Rabiulahir 1310 (15 November 1892); on compensation claims in Adana, *A. Mkt. Mhm.* 647/39, nos 1–59, 20 Cemaziyelevvel 1313 (8 November 1895); on compensation protocol, *Dh. Eum. 5Şb.* 2/59, nos 1–2, 9 Zilhicce 1332 (29 October 1914).

83 *Hr. Sys.* 70/19, nos 1–5, 5 July 1905.

CHAPTER FOUR

1 "Dodd, Edward Mills (1824–65)"; *Memorial Records for William S. Dodd*, American Research Institute in Turkey. The published works of Edward Jr (1887–1967) include Dodd, *Our Medical Task Overseas*, *How Far to the Nearest Doctor?* and *Why Medical Missions?*

2 Dodd, *Beloved Physician*, n.p.; John 13:34–5; *Memorial Records for William S. Dodd*, 1, American Research Institute in Turkey.

3 *Personnel Records for William S. Dodd*, 1; and *Memorial Records for William S. Dodd*, 1–2, both in American Research Institute in Turkey.

4 *Memorial Records for William S. Dodd*, 2, American Research Institute in Turkey; on the Near East Foundation, Barton, *Story of Near East Relief*, 58–78; for an informative pamphlet published by the New York Near East Relief, *Oldest Christian Nation.*

5 Dodd, *Beloved Physician*, n.p.; *Memorial Records for William S. Dodd*, 1, American Research Institute in Turkey; Romans 5:8. William's memorial information, given by his grandchild Dennis Dodd, includes the coordinates of his grave in New Jersey, which is no. 16931752 in the Babbitt Plot's first old section, Hilltop Cemetery, Mendham.

6 *Letter from William S. Dodd to Friends,* Talas, 10 April 1905, 827–9, Bilkent Library. Ottoman records on William's medical missions include *Dh. Mkt.* 161/17, nos 1–9, 26 Cemaziyelahir 1311 (4 January 1894); *Dh. Mkt.* 550/52, nos 1–2, 1 Rabiulahir 1320 (8 July 1902); *Dh. Mkt.* 551/21, 24 Rabiulahir 1320 (31 July 1902); and *Dh. Mkt.* 2130/43, no. 1, 23 Cemaziyelahir 1316 (8 November 1898). For an interesting comparison between "witch doctors" and "Christian doctors," see Dodd, *How Far to the Nearest Doctor?* 41–59.

7 Makdisi, *Artillery of Heaven*, 5, 35; Akgün, "Turkish Image"; Erhan, "Ottoman Official Attitudes."

8 On Christian and Muslim propaganda, see Fortna, *Imperial Classroom*, 50–78; Deringil, *Well-Protected Domains*, 115–19; Şahin, "Sultan's America"; and Birol, "XIX. Yüzyıl Sonlarında."

9 On Ottoman state reforms, see İnalcık and Seyitdanoğlu, eds, *Tanzimat*, 83–124; Karpat, *Studies*, 27–74; Barkey, *Empire of Difference*, 266–9; Köksal, "Rethinking Nationalism," 1502; Polk and Chambers, eds, *Beginnings of Modernization*, 29–90; and Levy, "Military Reform."

10 For debates over philanthropy, *Dh. Mkt.* 183/48, nos 1–19, 10 Cemaziyelahir 1311 (19 December 1893).

11 The Ottoman economy deserves further attention. The existing works include Darling, *Revenue-Raising and Legitimacy*, 246–306; Genç, "Principle"; Shaw, "Nineteenth-Century Ottoman"; and Coşgel, "Efficiency and Continuity."

12 On foreign educational institutions in Beirut and Istanbul, including the termination of a missionary school project because its construction site faced the military barracks in Adana, see Kortepeter, "American Liberalism"; Şahin, *Errand into the East*, 59–92; and *İ. Hus.* 165/1326 Ra 13, no. 1, 4 Rabiulevvel 1326 (6 April 1908).

13 The 1858 Land Code, "Acquisition of Property by Foreigners," in Ongley, *Ottoman Land Code*, 168–71. For Stéphane Yerasimos's conclusion that the post-Tanzimat reforms complicated urban deed transactions rather than facilitating them, see İnalcık and Seyitdanoğlu, eds, *Tanzimat*, 365–80.

14 On the Regulations for General Education, see Özalp and Ataünal, *Türk Milli Eğitim Sisteminde*, 549–69.

15 On Ottoman socio-political developments, see Blumi, "Teaching Loyalty"; Fuhrmann and Kechriotis, "Late Ottoman Port-Cities"; and Özdalga, *Late Ottoman Society*, 14–224.

16 White, *Adventuring with Anatolia College*, part 2, no. 35.

17 Ibid.

18 *Dh. Mkt.* 2038/76, no. 1, 14 Cemaziyelahir 1310 (3 January 1893). See also *Dh. Mkt.* 1844/82, no. 1, 20 Zilkade 1308 (27 June 1891).

19 For diplomatic discussion regarding "charitable organizations," see *Dh. Mkt.* 183/48, nos 1–19, 10 Cemaziyelahir 1311 (19 December 1893); and *Dh. İd.* 43/2-27, nos 1–4, 16 Şevval 1329 (10 October 1911).

20 *Dh. Mkt.* 123/26, nos 1–4, 20 Rabiulevvel 1311 (1 October 1893). For substantial records on Üsküdar American Academy for Girls, see *American College for Girls Records, 1880s–1979*, no. 6799283, 58 boxes, Columbia University Archives, New York. As popular literature, see the accounts of Etta Doane Marden, including *Gedik Pasha* and *American School*. The sanjaks and judgeships were the smaller administrative units, but the agents therein made limited contact with the missionaries. For informed studies of the post-1840 administrative transformation, see

Ortaylı, *Tanzimat Devrinde*, 119–232; and Findley, *Bureaucratic Reform*, 41–68.

21 *Dh. Mkt.* 149/14, nos 1–2, 2 Rabiulahir 1311 (13 October 1893).

22 On Aleppo, *Dh. Mkt.* 2489/123, nos 1–2, 8 Safer 1319 (27 May 1901); on Mersin, *Dh. Mkt.* 469/69, no. 1, 26 Zilhicce 1319 (5 April 1902). See also *Dh. Mkt.* 1765/118, 15 Safer 1308 (30 September 1890); *A. Mkt. Mhm.* 701/24, nos 1–2, 22 Şevval 1312 (18 April 1895); and *Dh. İd.* 163/8, nos 1–6, 6 Safer 1331 (12 January 1913).

23 *Dh. Mkt.* 1131/82, nos 1–2, 16 Şevval 1324 (3 December 1906); on the Sivas case in April 1908, *İ. Hus.* 165/1326 Ra 13, no. 1, 4 Rabiulevvel 1326 (6 April 1908). Tarsus American College signifies the evangelical Christian legacy in Turkey, as its graduates had risen to pre-eminence since 1888, including several generations of the Sabancı family, Turkey's industrial business tycoons. Affiliated today with Turkey's Ministry of Education, this college ranks in the top ten Turkish colleges.

24 For instance, see the case of an archaeologist named Edgar in *İ. Hr.* 385/1321 Ca 27, nos 1–2, 30 Cemaziyelevvel 1321 (24 August 1903). On religious architecture and cultural landscapes, see Ousterhout, "Ethnic Identity"; Çelik, *Empire, Architecture*, 24–70; and Kuran, "Spatial Study."

25 For the 1911 instructions, see *Dh. İd.* 43/2-27, nos 1–4, 16 Şevval 1329 (10 October 1911). These instructions forbade all "foreigners" to "establish schools in absence of an imperial decree." For examples related to such instructions, see *Dh. Mkt.* 249/5, nos 1–2, 16 Zilhicce 1311 (20 June 1894); *Dh. Mkt.* 2061/70, no. 1, 22 Şaban 1310 (11 March 1893); and *Dh. Mkt.* 2183/97, no. 1, 17 Zilkade 1316 (29 March 1899). For an excellent quantitative analysis of Ottoman imperial laws and their local irrelevance, see Kuran and Lustig, "Judicial Biases."

26 *Dh. Mkt.* 1033/11, nos 1–5, 20 Şevval 1323 (18 December 1905); on Dodd's case, *Dh. İd.* 43/2-27, nos 1–2, 16 Şevval 1329 (10 October 1911). George Post, a New Yorker and a graduate of Union Theological Seminary, led the Surgery Department at the American University of Beirut until his death in 1909. He also published on his medical practices and religious views. "Dr. George E. Post Dead," *New York Times*, 1 October 1909, 9.

27 For the cited directives, see *Dh. Mui.* 54/1–58, nos 1–8, 25 Muharrem 1328 (6 February 1910).

28 Founded in 1863 as an Istanbul-based theological seminary, Anatolia College obtained the status of a liberal-arts college following its relocation to Merzifon. For substantial accounts of its origins and students, see Compton, *Morning Cometh*, 153–203; and White, *Charles Chapin Tracy*,

11–33. On the monitorial method and its application by evangelical missionaries, see Rayman, "Joseph Lancaster's Monitorial System," 400–5; and Sedra, "Exposure to the Eyes of God," 267–79. The educational philosophies of Ottoman madrasas and American colleges are worth a comparison. Even though the madrasas offered no self-help workshops, their faculty required senior students to help others learn to recite the Quran.

29 The figures are drawn from several sources, including *Annual Report* (1909), 59–60; and ABCFM *Higher Education Statistics*, 26 May 1910 and 7 July 1910, Bilkent Library, quoted in Maksudyan, "Amerikan Kaynaklarında," 136–8.

30 *İ. Mms.* 78/3413, nos 1–5, 3 Şaban 1301 (29 May 1884).

31 *A. Mkt. Mhm.* 701/24, nos 1–7, 22 Şevval 1312 (18 April 1895); on the 1899 permission for the Sungurlu Church to "turn into a Protestant college" after thirty-six years of service, *Dh. Mkt.* 2171/52, no. 1, 16 Şevval 1316 (27 February 1899); on Euphrates College, *A. Mkt. Mhm.* 701/4, nos 1–3, 10 Rabiulahir 1312 (11 October 1894). Many evangelical institutions operated in buildings previously owned by minorities and other foreigners, thus retaining tax exemptions after obtaining new licences for them. On unlicensed colleges and their tax matters, see *A. Mkt. Mhm.* 700/12, nos 1–15, 28 Zilkade 1311 (2 June 1894); and *Dh. Mkt.* 249/5, no. 1–2, 16 Zilhicce 1311 (20 June 1894).

32 Karpat, *Politicization of Islam*, 10–19; Deringil, *Well-Protected Domains*, 44–67.

33 On various cases related to flags, donations, schools, and students, see *A. Mkt. Mhm.* 536/14, nos 1–9, 14 Şaban 1313 (30 January 1896); *A. Mkt. Mhm.* 613/14, nos 1–9, 29 Cemaziyelevvel 1313 (17 November 1895); *A. Mkt. Mhm.* 615/9, nos 1–5, 30 Safer 1324 (24–25 April 1906); *Dh. İd.* 43/2-27, nos 1–4, 16 Şevval 1329 (10 October 1911); and *Dh. Mkt.* 2183/97, no. 1, 17 Zilkade 1316 (29 March 1899). See also Şişman, "Egyptian and Armenian Schools."

34 This analysis is drawn from various reports in *Dh. Mkt.* 267/58, no. 1, 29 Muharrem 1312 (2 August 1894); *Dh. Mkt.* 291/62, no. 1, 6 Rabiulahir 1312 (7 October 1894); *Dh. Mkt.* 2004/29, no. 1, 27 Safer 1310 (20 September 1892); *Dh. Mkt.* 2093/60, no. 1, 2 Rabiulahir 1316 (20 August 1898); and *Dh. Mkt.* 2112/79, no. 1, 17 Cemaziyelevvel 1316 (3 October 1898).

35 On instructions and exemptions, *Dh. Mui.* 26/3-17, nos 1–47, 28 Şevval 1328 (2 November 1910); on taxation policy, *Dh. Mui.* 54/1-58, nos 1–8, 25 Muharrem 1328 (6 February 1910).

36 On Parsen and Ateşli, see *Dh. Mkt.* 1964/45, no. 1, 26 Zilkade 1309 (22 June 1892); and *Dh. Mkt.* 394/19, 14 Muharrem 1313 (7 July 1895).

37 On schooling and legal violations in the municipality of Beylan, Aleppo, see *Dh. Mkt.* 267/58, no. 1; and *Dh. Mkt.* 291/62, no. 1.

38 *Dh. Mkt.* 914/46, nos 1–4, 8 Şevval 1322 (16 December 1904).

39 On the 1896 Elazığ case, see *A. Mkt. Mhm.* 659/9, nos 1–4, 24 Cemaziyelevvel 1314 (31 October 1896). See also *Y. Prk. Um.* 23/69, no. 1, 27 Cemaziyelevvel 1309 (29 December 1891); and the excellent 2013 narrative of home missions by Reeves-Ellington, *Domestic Frontiers.*

40 *A. Mkt. Mhm.* 659/9, nos 1–4, 24 Cemaziyelevvel 1314 (31 October 1896).

41 On Haskell's house and school, see *Dh. Mkt.* 2093/60, no. 1, 2 Rabiulahir 1316 (20 August 1898); *Dh. Mkt.* 2112/79, no. 1, 17 Cemaziyelevvel 1316 (3 October 1898); and *İ. Hus.* 142/1324 R 01, no. 1, 2 Recep 1324 (22 August 1906). See also Haskell, *Haskell Papers, 1853–1935*, Houghton Library; and Haskell, "Plan for Social Work," quoted in Kieser, *Nearest East*, 74–5. During this time, imperial authorities also received letters from college students such as Seragi Cürüboğlu and Prodermas Teolisi. As graduates of the American University of Beirut, these two students requested the Ministry of the Interior's reapproval of their degrees, which they had lost during the Adana massacre. *Dh. İd.* 48/2-7, nos 1–2, 22 Ramazan 1329 (16 September 1911).

42 On Dodd, see *Dh. Mkt.* 2130/43, no. 1, 23 Cemaziyelahir 1316 (8 November 1898); and *Letter from William S. Dodd to Friends*, Talas, 10 April 1905, 827–9, Bilkent Library. On Mary Garbis, see *A. Mkt. Mhm.* 549/36, nos 1–19, 22 Şaban 1323 (22 October 1905); Mahjoubian, *Garbis to America*; and John G.A. Leishman to John Hay, US Secretary of State, 16 August and 15 September 1904, in *Papers Relating to the Foreign Relations* (1904), 828–32.

43 For the Ohio Missionary Society's address to the Maraş district governor, see *Hr. Sys.* 72/37, no. 1, 2 February 1893.

44 Washburn, *Fifty Years*, 168–78, 293–304; "From George to His Wife Henrietta," New York, 28 January 1890, in *Papers of Cyrus Hamlin and George Washburn, 1863–1910*, Houghton Library. On the history of Robert College, see Greenwood, *Robert College*, 72–122; Freely, *History of Robert College*; and Şahin, *Errand into the East*, 66–8. On the emergence of colleges in Istanbul and Beirut, see Kortepeter, "American Liberalism."

45 *Y. Prk. Mf.* 4/66, nos 1–2, 27 Zilhicce 1320 (27 March 1903).

46 *Dh. Mkt.* 1602/18, no. 1, 4 Recep 1306 (6 March 1889). For the Robert College application by President Caleb Frank Gates and for the request of the board of Euphrates College in Harput to reconstruct the buildings burned down by the local mobs, see *Dh. Mui.* 26-1/1, nos 1–33, 13 Cemaziyelahir 1324 (4 August 1906). For numerous post-1889 documents addressing Robert College, see *Dh. Mkt.* 1586/71, no. 1, 20 Cemaziyelevvel 1306 (22 January 1889); *Dh. Mkt.* 1627/117, no. 1, 12 Şevval 1306 (11 June 1889); *Dh. Mkt.* 1679/48, nos 1–2, 11 Rabiulahir 1307 (5 December 1889); *Dh. Mkt.* 1699/73, nos 1–2, 25 Cemaziyelahir 1307 (16 February 1890); *Dh. Mkt.* 31/57, no. 1, 28 Cemaziyelevvel 1318 (23 September 1900); *Dh. Mkt.* 2313/116, nos 1–2, 3 Zilkade 1317 (5 March 1900); and *Dh. Mkt.* 2343/42, no. 1, 10 Muharrem 1318 (10 May 1900).

47 *Mv.* 98/2-80, no. 1, 3 Şaban 1317 (7 December 1899). See also *Dh. Mui.* 26-1/1, nos 1–33, 13 Cemaziyelahir 1324 (4 August 1906).

48 *Dh. Mui.* 73-2/19, nos 1–5, 10 Cemaziyelahir 1328 (19 June 1910); and *Dh. Mui.* 26-1/1, nos 1–33, 10 Cemaziyelahir 1328 (19 June 1910).

49 On Robert College and the construction law, *Dh. Um. Vm.* 106/7, nos 1–11, 6 Şevval 1333 (17 August 1915); on Robert College's new campus, *Dh. Mkt.* 2390/17, no. 1, 19 Rabiulahir 1318 (16 August 1900).

50 From the Governorate of Beirut to Istanbul, in *Y. Mtv.* 32/45, no. 1, 19 Şaban 1305 (1 May 1888), quoted in Fortna, *Imperial Classroom*, 51–2; on the American University of Beirut, *Dh. Mkt.* 895/18, nos 1–6, 22 Recep 1322 (2 October 1904); for an informative study of Beirut-based intellectuals, officials, and missionaries, Hanssen, *Fin de Siècle Beirut*, 163–90.

51 On Syrian Protestant College's hospital, see *Dh. Mkt.* 895/18, nos 1–6; and Hamdan and Hitti, "Glimpses into Student Life." For further examples, see *Dh. Mui.* 9/2-6, nos 1–2, 28 Şaban 1327 (14 September 1909); *Dh. Mui.* 127/16, nos 1–2, 29 Şaban 1328 (5 September 1910); *Dh. Mkt.* 964/9, no. 1, 27 Rabiulevvel 1323 (1 June 1905); *Dh. İd.* 117/2, nos 1–2, 2 Ramazan 1328 (7 September 1910); *Dh. İd.* 117/5, nos 1–7, 24 Ramazan 1328 (29 September 1910); and *İ. Hr.* 418/1327 B 17, nos 1–4, 20 Recep 1327 (7 August 1907).

52 On Halide's life and times (1884–1964) and American schools in Istanbul, see Adıvar, *Memoirs of Halide Edip*; and Lewis and Micklewright, eds, *Gender, Modernity, and Liberty*, 188–208.

53 *İ. Dh.* 1309/1311 Ca 40, no. 1, 20 Cemaziyelevvel 1311 (29 November 1893).

54 *Dh. Mkt.* 1924/59, no. 1, 21 Recep 1309 (20 February 1892); on the old imperial college in Beirut, Fortna, *Imperial Classroom*, 51–8; on Ottoman

educational planning, the containment strategy, and missionary schools, *A. Mkt. Mhm.* 700/12, nos 1–15, 28 Zilkade 1311 (2 June 1894).

55 On the second orphanage to be constructed in Everek, *Dh. İd.* 117/8, nos 1–2, 8 Şevval 1328 (13 October 1910); on the 1915 orphanage case in Maraş, *Dh. Eum. 5Şb.* 12/31, nos 1–3, 26 Cemaziyelahir 1333 (11 May 1915); on other cases, *A. Mkt. Mhm.* 702/24, no. 1, 5–14, 20 Cemaziyelahir 1315 (17 October 1897); on the Parker family, *Parker Family Collection*, Houghton Library; on the orphanage project of the German missionaries, *Dh. İd.* 123/5, nos 1–11, 11 Recep 1329 (8 July 1911).

56 Examples of property transactions, or "title corrections" in Ottoman legal terms, include the Tripoli case, in *İ. Hr.* 431/1331 B 23, nos 1–4, 21 Recep 1331 (26 June 1913); Adana, in *İ. Hr.* 422/1328 R 19, nos 1–4, 10 Recep 1328 (18 July 1910); Basra, in *İ. Mf.* 15/1328 S 2, no. 1, 10 Safer 1328 (21 February 1910); Beirut, in *İ. Hr.* 430/1331 M 08, nos 1–10, 9 Muharrem 1331 (19 December 1912); Konya, in *İ. Hr.* 421/1328 S 15, nos 1–16, 10 Safer 1328 (21 February 1910); Lebanon, in *Dh. Mui.* 76/2-11, nos 1–2, 5 Şaban 1328 (12 August 1910); and *Dh. Mui.* 6/1-13, nos 1–2, 23 Şaban 1328 (30 August 1910); Mersin, in *İ. Mf.* 16/1328 Ş 12, no. 1, 23 Şaban 1328 (30 August 1910); Urfa, in *Dh. Mui.* 6/1-12, nos 1–2, 23 Şaban 1328 (30 August 1910); and *İ. Hr.* 419/1327 N 06, nos 1–7, 7 Ramazan 1327 (22 September 1909); and some other transactions, in *İ. Duit.* 36/37, nos 1–3, 30 Zilhicce 1334 (27–28 October 1916). For US complaints about the slow bureaucracy in Istanbul, see *Papers Relating to the Foreign Relations* (1904), 828–32. On the inner dynamics of the Ottoman state, see Karpat, "Transformation of the Ottoman State."

57 On the respective cases in Adana, Beirut, Kayseri, and Mardin, see *İ. Mf.* 16/1328 Ş 11, no. 1, 15 Şaban 1328 (22 August 1910); *Dh. İd.* 117/45, nos 1–2, 10 Şevval 1329 (4 October 1911); *İ. Mf.* 17/1329 R 4, no. 1, 11 Recep 1329 (8 July 1911); *İ. Mf.* 16/1328 N 2, no. 1, 16 Ramazan 1328 (21 September 1910); and *Dh. İd.* 117/2, nos 1–2, 3 Rabiulevvel 1329 (4 March 1911). On the International College's ownership of "state land," *Dh. İd.* 154/15, nos 1–43, 2 Zilhicce 1332 (22 October 1914); on "compulsory taxes," *Dh. İd.* 117/40, nos 1–5, 17 Cemaziyelahir 1329 (15 June 1911). In an example of wartime policy, the governor of Kayseri advised Istanbul to rent Talas American College. *Dh. Eum. 5Şb.* 21/13, no. 1, 27 Rabiulevvel 1334 (2 January 1916). For an informed analysis of imperial conversations with local agencies, see Heper, "Center and Periphery."

58 Şafak, *Osmanlı-Amerikan*, 172, 188. See also, Makdisi, *Artillery of Heaven*, 5, 35; and Murre-van den berg, "Middle East."

59 *Dh. İd.* 117/41, nos 1–3, 8 Recep 1329 (5 July 1911); *Dh. İd.* 160/2-4, nos 1–3, 13 Cemaziyelevvel 1331 (23 April 1913); on the Tripoli case, *Dh. İd.* 123/18, nos 1–13, 18 Muharrem 1332 (17 December 1913).

60 *Dh. Mkt.* 1765/118, no. 1, 15 Safer 1308 (30 September 1890).

61 On Bartlett's case and his licence being granted and then revoked, see *Hr. Sys.* 71/59, nos 1–2, 8 November 1891; *Dh. Mkt.* 1916/93, no. 1, 28 Cemaziyelahir 1309 (29 January 1892); and *Dh. Mkt.* 1991/71, no. 1, 30 Muharrem 1310 (24 August 1892).

62 *Dh. Mkt.* 1996/63, no. 1, 11 Safer 1310 (4 September 1892); *Dh. Mui.* 72/11, nos 1–2, 25 Safer 1328 (8 March 1910).

63 On cases from Adana and other provinces and on US officials' involvement, see *Dh. Mkt.* 267/58, no. 1, 29 Muharrem 1312 (2 August 1894); and *Dh. Mkt.* 291/62, no. 1, 6 Rabiulahir 1312 (7 October 1894). For further examples, see *Dh. Kms.* 28/26, nos 1–6, 30 Zilkade 1332 (20 October 1914); and *Dh. Mkt.* 1131/82, nos 1–2.

64 Deringil, *Well-Protected Domains*, 26–35. For an inspiring and pathbreaking story of what sound meant in *fin de siècle* France, see Corbin, *Village Bells*. Carla Shapreau's current research project tells about 175,000 bells confiscated in Europe during the First World War by Nazi Germany. Sections of her interesting analysis are available in Gretchen Kell, "Nazis' Silence of the Bells: Campus Researcher Speaks Out," *BerkeleyNews*,23February2015,http://news.berkeley.edu/2015/02/23/nazis-silence-of-the-bells-campus-researcher-speaks-out.

65 A future study of Ottoman identity symbols should engage with the existing literature, including Costantini and Koller, eds, *Living in the Ottoman Ecumenical Community*; Ortaylı, *Osmanlı Barışı*; and Aral, "Idea of Human Rights."

66 *Dh. Mkt.* 2051/3, no. 1, 23 Recep 1310 (10 February 1893); and the following cases.

67 *Dh. İd.* 117/52, nos 1–2, 21 Zilkade 1329 (13 November 1911); *Dh. İd.* 154/17, no. 1, 20 Şevval 1333 (31 August 1915); on the flag case, *Dh. Eum. Ayş.* 23/1, nos 1–16, 1 Muharrem 1338 (26 September 1919).

68 *Dh. İd.* 117/52, nos 1–2, 21 Zilkade 1329 (13 November 1911); *Dh. İd.* 154/17, no. 1, 20 Şevval 1333 (31 August 1915); *Dh. İd.* 123/18, nos 1–13, 18 Muharrem 1332 (17 December 1913).

69 Dodd, *Beloved Physician*; Dodd, *Our Medical Task Overseas*; *Dh. Mkt.* 161/17, nos 1–9, 26 Cemaziyelahir 1311 (4 January 1894). On the local reactions against Metini, another American Board physician, see *Dh. Mkt.* 1467/61, no. 1, 18 Rabiulevvel 1305 (4 December 1887); and *Dh. Mkt.* 1517/56, 20 Şevval 1305 (30 June 1888).

70 *Dh. Mkt.* 161/17, nos 1–2, 26 Cemaziyelahir 1311 (4 January 1894).

71 *Dh. Mkt.* 161/17, no. 4, 26 Cemaziyelahir 1311 (4 January 1894).

72 *Dh. Mkt.* 161/17, nos 5–7, 26 Cemaziyelahir 1311 (4 January 1894). See also *Dh. Mkt.* 550/52, nos 1–2, 1 Rabiulahir 1320 (8 July 1902).

73 *Dh. Mkt.* 536/39, nos 1–6, 9 Rabiulahir 1320 (16 July 1902); *Dh. Mkt.* 551/21, no. 1, 24 Rabiulahir 1320 (31 July 1902).

74 Wilfred Post reached Istanbul after the closure of the hospital. *Dh. Eum. 5Şb.* 35/45, nos 1–37, 24 Cemaziyelahir 1335 (17 April 1917).

75 *Dh. Mkt.* 1765/118, no. 1, 15 Safer 1308 (30 September 1890); on the US consul's involvement, *A. Mkt. Mhm.* 701/24, nos 1–7, 22 Şevval 1312 (18 April 1895); and *Dh. İd.* 163/8, nos. 1–4, 6 Safer 1331 (12 January 1913); on Tarsus, *Dh. Mkt.* 469/69. no. 1, 26 Zilhicce 1319 (5 April 1902).

76 *Dh. Mkt.* 1517/56, no. 1, 20 Şevval 1305 (30 June 1888); *Dh. Mkt.* 1467/61, no. 1, 18 Rabiulevvel 1305 (4 December 1887).

CHAPTER FIVE

1 The 1880 publications totalled 3,536,000 pages in Armenian, 21,000 in Greek, and 4,762,200 pages in Turkish variously written in Arabic, Armenian, and Greek scripts. The cited figures are in *Annual Report* (1909), 53; *Papers of the ABCFM*, 10/103, 16.9.3, Bilkent Library; and *American Board Charts*, Andover-Harvard Theological Library. See also the American Board's publications inventory compiled by Dwight's colleague John Vinton, in Anderson, *History of the Missions*, 503–18. As an author, Henry Otis Dwight (1843–1917) contributed to the *Missionary Herald* and the *New York Tribune*, and he wrote and edited several works, including *Turkish Life in War Time* and *The Centennial History of the American Bible Society*.

2 Dwight, *Constantinople and Its Problems*, 42–3; Hebrews 13:2. In this book, Dwight attributed the Ottoman Empire's early success to Christianity and its later downfall to Islam, concluding that the American Board's missionaries might well liberate Ottoman locals. New Englanders read it in multiple editions, and it was reviewed in *Outlook*, 26 October 1901, 511; *Literary Digest*, 9 November 1901, 581; and *The Nation*, 12 December 1901, 460. Additionally, the local congregants of the Bible House's chapel founded the Emmanuel Church in November 1908. *Annual Report* (1909), 54.

3 Dwight, *Constantinople and Its Problems*, 37; *American Board Charts*, Andover-Harvard Theological Library; for the 1902 Bible House book

titles, *Catalogue and Price List of Publications*, 1–45, American Research Institute in Turkey.

4 Tanör, *Osmanlı-Türk*, 162; on forbidden words and censored items, İskit, *Türkiye'de Neşriyat*, 65, quoted in, Güçtürk, "Comparative Study," 30–1.

5 Inspection and Examination Committee, in *Y. Prk. Dh.* 10/58, no. 2, 29 Zilhicce 1315 (21 May 1898); on print media censorship, Güçtürk, "Comparative Study," 29–31.

6 For Ottoman reactions to missionary publications, see *A. Mkt. Mhm.* 615/9, nos 1–5, 30 Safer 1324 (24–25 April 1906); *A. Mkt. Mhm.* 658/25, nos 1–3, 19 Şaban 1313 (4 February 1896); *A. Mkt. Mhm.* 763/28, no. 1, 9 Rabiulahir 1307 (3 December 1889); *Hr. Sys.* 2740/48, no. 1, 21 November 1895; *Hr. Sys.* 2742/4, nos 1–2, 14 May 1898; *Dh. Mkt.* 1509/67, no. 1, 14 Ramazan 1305 (25 May 1888); *Dh. Mkt.* 1540/31, 1 Muharrem 1306 (7 September 1888); and *Y. Prk. Dh.* 10/58, 29 Zilhicce 1315 (21 May 1898). See also the January 1896 missionary publication report by the Ministry of Foreign Affairs, in *Hr. Sys.* 73/56, no. 1, 25 January 1896. On the Güvener case (no. 2002/788) and public debates, see "Kilise Davasında Beraat" [Acquittal at the church trial], *NTV Güncel*, 12 May 2004; and Yıldırım, "Tarihten Bugüne," 73–83.

7 *Washington Post*, 21 December 1894, 7; for the Ottoman translation, *Ya. Hus.* 396/104, nos 1–5, 19 Muharrem 1317 (30 May 1889).

8 Dwight, *Constantinople and Its Problems*, 37, 246.

9 Erhan, "Ottoman Official Attitudes"; Kocabaşoğlu, "Osmanlı İmparatorluğu'nda." The leading works in the field include Field, *America and the Mediterranean World*; and Oren, *Power, Faith, and Fantasy*, 123–48, 290–6. See also the intriguing story of Ahmad Shidyaq (1805–87), a Maronite scholar who converted to Protestantism and then to Islam, in Makdisi, *Artillery of Heaven*.

10 Strauss, "'Kütüp ve Resail-i Mevkute,'" 225; Strauss, "Les livres"; Strauss, "Zum Istanbuler Buchwesen," 307–38. On the unusual career of Mehmet Murat, nicknamed Mizancı Murat (1853–1912), see Zürcher, *Unionist Factor*, 15–21.

11 On the Ottoman press laws of 1864, 1877, and 1888, see Güçtürk, "Comparative Study," 22–9. On *Mirat-ı alem* and other periodicals (43 in Turkish, 11 in Armenian and Greek, 8 in Arabic, Hebrew, and Persian, and 5 in English and French), see Tokgöz, *Matbuat Hatıralarım*, vol. 1, 32–3; and Şehremaneti İstatistik Şubesi, *1330 Senesi İstanbul*, 112, quoted in Strauss, "'Kütüp ve Resail-i Mevkute,'" 245, 227–8. For the 1893 book titles published in the Ottoman Empire, see Strauss, "Zum Istanbuler Buchwesen," 307–17, 332–5.

12 In the southeastern Anatolian town of Halfeti, "80 of 100 Muslim families" read the Bible published and distributed by American Board presses. Akgün, *Kendi Kaynaklarından*, sec. 2134. On Ottoman state offices, see İnalcık, "Decision Making"; Karpat, *Politicization of Islam*, 223–40; Findley, *Ottoman Civil Officialdom*; and Swanson, "Ottoman Police."

13 *Y. Prk. Dh.* 10/58, no. 2, 29 Zilhicce 1315 (21 May 1898). See also *A. Mkt. Mhm.* 763/28, no. 1, 9 Rabiulahir 1307 (3 December 1889); and *A. Mkt. Mhm.* 615/9, nos 1–5, 29 Safer 1324 (24 April 1906).

14 *Y. Prk. Dh.* 10/58, no. 2, 29 Zilhicce 1315 (21 May 1898). On intellectuals, bureaucrats, and ideologies, see Karpat, *Politicization of Islam*, 117–35; and Faroqhi, *Ottoman Empire*, 13.

15 *Dh. Mkt.* 1509/67, no. 1, 14 Ramazan 1305 (25 May 1888); *Dh. Mkt.* 1540/31, no. 1, 1 Muharrem 1306 (7 September 1888); on George White's encounter with ignorant officials, White, *Adventuring with Anatolia College*, part 2, no. 35.

16 *Y. Prk. Mf.* 5/20, nos 3–4, 2 Recep 1325 (11 August 1907). For Ioannina yearbooks and memorandums, see *1319 Yanya Salnamesi*; and *1321 Maarif Salnamesi*. See also Blumi, "Teaching Loyalty"; and Nizamoğlu, "Yanya Vilayetinin Durumuna Dair."

17 *Y. Prk. Dh.* 10/58, no. 2, 29 Zilhicce 1315 (21 May 1898); Mardin, *Religion, Society, and Modernity*, 1–19; Hanioğlu, *Osmanlı'dan Cumhuriyet'e*, 36–9, 129–32; Göçek, *Rise of the Bourgeoisie*, 3–43. In Charles Tracy's words, "the Scriptures, in tongues familiar to the common people, the religious treatise or tract, the book of spiritual songs," and "the family newspaper" could better deliver the message. Tracy, "Salient Points," in *Services at the Seventy-Fifth Anniversary*, 67, Andover-Harvard Theological Library. Strikingly, any kind of undocumented literature imported from the United States raised critical concern among Ottoman authorities. In May 1892 local officers arrested two Armenian merchants, Krigor Gasparian and Baghdasarian. They had imported various books that could provoke an anti-state "rebellion." In June 1893 Minister of the Interior Halil Rıfat likewise declared that state agents had to "inspect and approve" all "missionary papers and letters being shipped to the Empire." The agents would deliver missionary publications to Istanbul for registry in the Ministry of Education's publication index, and only then would Rıfat permit their circulation. *Dh. Mkt.* 61/33, nos 1–2, 22 Zilkade 1310 (7 June 1893). The Ministers Council eventually outlawed "importing and distributing" foreign literature without official permission. *Dh. Mkt.* 1948/97, no. 1, 15 Şevval 1329 (9 October 1911).

18 *American Board Charts*, 2, Andover-Harvard Theological Library; Tracy, "Salient Points," in *Services at the Seventy-Fifth Anniversary*, 67, Andover-Harvard Theological Library. See also Anderson, *History of the Missions*, 503–18; and Kocabaşoğlu, *Kendi Belgeleriyle*, 48–9.

19 *Hr. Sys.* 73/56, no. 1, 25 January 1896. For examples, see Tracy, *Silken-braid*; Hamlin, *Among the Turks*; Prime, *Forty Years*; and Dwight, *Constantinople and Its Problems*. The American Board's publications vilified Islam and the Turks. In a symbolic case, the Ottoman ambassador to Washington sent George Hepworth's articles to Istanbul for an imperial discussion over their content. *Hr. Sys.* 66/62, no. 1, 14 November 1892; George Hepworth, "America's Big Interests in Turkey," *Boston Daily Globe*, 4 September 1904, 2A4. Hepworth also wrote on Ottoman atrocities in the *Atlantic Monthly*, *Chicago Tribune*, *Hartford Courant*, and *The Sun*. For Ottoman counter-propaganda, see *Dh. Mkt.* 61/33, nos 1–2, 22 Zilkade 1310 (7 June 1893); *Dh. Mkt.* 412/50, 23 Safer 1313 (15 August 1895); *Dh. Mkt.* 785/3, 10 Şaban 1321 (1 November 1903); and *Dh. Mkt.* 999/75, 20 Cemaziyelahir 1323 (23 July 1905). See also Şahin, "Sultan's America."

20 On imperial state conservatism, see *İ. Mms.* 95/4054, 8 Cemaziyelahir 1325 (19 July 1907); and *Dh. Um. Mvm.* 26/33, 4 Rabiulevvel 1305 (20 November 1887).

21 *Y. Prk. Hr.* 7/36, nos 1–9, 18 Safer 1301 (19 December 1883); *Dh. Mkt.* 1540/31, no. 1, 1 Muharrem 1306 (7 September 1888). On later bureaucratic developments, see *Dh. Mkt.* 412/50, nos 1–3, 23 Safer 1313 (15 August 1895); Deringil, *Well-Protected Domains*, 16–43, 125–34; Deringil, "Legitimacy Structures"; Özbek, "Philanthropic Activity"; and Weiker, "Ottoman Bureaucracy," 458–62. The Directorate of the Foreign and International Press steered the business of monitoring in non-Ottoman languages. Established in 1821 by Sultan Mahmud II, the Translation Bureau functioned for personnel as a training unit in foreign languages, but it had become largely understaffed by the 1890s. The Inspection and Examination Committee also failed to translate missionary publications around this time. Quataert, *Ottoman Empire*, 81; Deringil, *Well-Protected Domains*, 136.

22 *Dh. Mkt.* 412/50, nos 1–3, 23 Safer 1313 (15 August 1895).

23 *Dh. Mkt.* 2091/127, no. 1, 28 Rabiulevvel 1316 (16 August 1898). See also *İ. Hus.* 73/1316 L 46, 17 Şevval 1316 (28 February 1899).

24 *Dh. Mkt.* 999/75, nos 1–11, 20 Cemaziyelahir 1323 (23 July 1905). Local incidents were correlated with the missionary propaganda and implicated citizenship issues. A February 1899 edict cited the case of Hambar, an Ottoman native of Maraş who had departed south-central Anatolia for the

United States. Five years after "the escape," the US consul welcomed him aboard a ship and showed him the way to his hometown. Imperial authorities charged Hambar with violating citizenship agreements and defending missionaries against Ottoman laws. *İ. Hus.* 73/1316 L 46, 17 Şevval 1316 (28 February 1899).

25 *Dh. Mkt.* 999/75, nos 1–11, 20 Cemaziyelahir 1323 (23 July 1905).

26 On American Board presses printing pamphlets and Biblical translations in Ottoman languages, see *Hr. Sys.* 65/34, no. 1, 13 March 1896; *Hr. Sys.* 66/82, nos 1–2, 12 May 1900; *Dh. Mb. Hps.* 154/27, 25 Recep 1333 (8 June 1915); *Dh. Mkt.* 1540/31, 1 Muharrem 1306 (7 September 1888); *Dh. Mkt.* 16/28, 26 Zilhicce 1310 (11 July 1893); and *Dh. Mkt.* 2309/49, no. 1, 21 Şevval 1317 (22 February 1900). Ottoman officials interpreted "public order" broadly, and "state interests" subsumed social and political developments within imperial traditions. Cjivanović, "Modus Vivendi"; Karpat, *Studies*, 655; Davison, "Turkish Attitudes."

27 On Neşet and the censors respectively, see *Dh. Mkt.* 412/50, nos 1–3, 23 Safer 1313 (15 August 1895); and *Dh. Mkt.* 460/40, nos 1–2, 17 Zilhicce 1319 (27 March 1902).

28 On official tardiness, *Dh. Mkt.* 509/39, nos 1–2, 13 Safer 1320 (22 May 1902); on difficulties with occidental languages, Koloğlu, "Penetration and Effects"; on the hiring of polyglot agents, *Dh. Mkt.* 460/40, nos 1–2, 17 Zilhicce 1319 (27 March 1902). On telegraphy, see Shaw and Shaw, *History of the Ottoman Empire*, vol. 2, 120; and Bektaş, "Sultan's Messenger."

29 *Dh. Mkt.* 779/71, nos 1–5, 28 Recep 1321 (20 October 1903); on Ottoman centralization, Duguid, "Centralization and Localism," 205–323. See also Finkel, *Osman's Dream*, 500; and Karaman and Pamuk, "Ottoman State Finances."

30 *Dh. Mkt.* 779/71, nos 1–5, 28 Recep 1321 (20 October 1903). On Kayseri and the evangelical institutions there, see Jennings, *Studies on Ottoman Social History*; and *Dh. Mui.* 9/2-6, 28 Şaban 1327 (14 September 1909).

31 *Dh. Mkt.* 742/8, nos 1–2, 29 Rabiulevvel 1321 (25 June 1903); *İ. Hus.* 73/1316 L 46, 17 Şevval 1316 (28 February 1899).

32 Jessup, *Fifty-Three Years*, vol. 2, 504, 694; Moody, *To the Work!*; Hoskins, "Press." In 1866 Jessup and his colleagues founded Syrian Protestant College, today's American University of Beirut. Stuart, *History of Arabic Literature*, 439; Hays, "Henry Jessup"; Kidd, *American Christians and Islam*, 37–57.

33 Jessup, *Fifty-Three Years*, vol. 2, 694.

34 Ibid. Jessup authored several monographs, including *The Women of the Arabs*, *Syrian Home Life*, *The Mohammedan Missionary Problem*, and *Kamil*. See also Makdisi, *Artillery of Heaven*, 166–76.

35 *Dh. Mkt.* 1732/30, no. 1, 27 Şevval 1307 (16 June 1890); *Dh. Mkt.* 2001/10, 21 Safer 1310 (14 September 1892). See also Jessup, *Fifty-Three Years*, vol. 2, 505; Moody, *To the Work!*; and Womack and Lindner, "'Pick Up the Pearls.'"

36 *Dh. Mkt.* 821/6, nos 1–6, 27 Zilkade 1321 (14 February 1904); *Dh. Mkt.* 2001/10, no. 1, 21 Safer 1310 (14 September 1892); Jessup, *Fifty-Three Years*, vol. 2, 505.

37 *Dh. Mkt.* 742/8, nos 1–2, 29 Rabiulevvel 1321 (25 June 1903); Dwight, *Constantinople and Its Problems*, 37.

38 Jessup was not the journal's editor by then, but the Ministry of the Interior's Inspection and Examination Committee treated him as though he were. *Dh. Mkt.* 742/8, no. 2, 29 Rabiulevvel 1321 (25 June 1903); *Dh. Mkt.* 821/6, no. 1, 3–4, 27 Zilkade 1321 (14 February 1904).

39 *Dh. Mkt.* 16/28, nos 1–3, 26 Zilhicce 1310 (11 July 1893).

40 *Dh. Mkt.* 86/42, nos 1–2, 15 Safer 1311 (28 August 1893).

41 For debates over publishers and publishing devices, see *Dh. Mkt.* 86/42, nos 1–2, 15 Safer 1311 (28 August 1893); *Dh. Mkt.* 2309/49, no. 1, 21 Şevval 1317 (22 February 1900); and *Dh. Mkt.* 1020/19, nos 1–5, 26 Şaban 1323 (26 October 1905). Even before non-Muslim merchants and American missionaries dominated the Ottoman printing landscape, Europe-linked merchants – including the Spanish-born brothers Daniel and Samuel ben Nahmias, the British-educated Nicodemus Metaxas, and the travelling entrepreneur Eremia Kömürjian – transferred early technologies to Beirut, Istanbul, and Izmir. However, the publishing houses thrived with the American Board's investment and leadership. On the understudied topic of the Ottoman publishing industry, see Beydilli, "Matbaa"; Kut, "Matbaa Hurufatı"; and Koloğlu, "Penetration and Effects," 241–3. See also the Kömürjian entry in Bardakjian, *Reference Guide*, 59–63; and the literature review in Güçtürk, "Comparative Study," 4–18.

42 *İ. Hus.* 73/1316 L-46, no. 1, 17 Şevval 1316 (28 February 1899). See also *Dh. Mkt.* 2050/92, no. 1, 21 Recep 1310 (8 February 1893); "Missionaries Not Molested," *New York Times*, 29 November 1914, 2; and Ahmet Tevfik's letter to Sultan Abdulhamid II, in *Y. Prk. Hr.* 25/51, 12 Zilhicce 1315 (4 May 1898).

43 The notoriety of publishers prompted the confiscation of their equipment. For examples, see *Dh. Mkt.* 86/42, nos 1–2, 15 Safer 1311 (28 August 1893); and *Dh. Mkt.* 2309/49, no. 1, 21 Şevval 1317 (22 February 1900).

I wish to examine in a future article the issue of imperial tax collection and foreign-owned institutions.

44 *Dh. Mkt.* 2164/89, no. 1, 21 Ramazan 1316 (2 February 1899). See also *Dh. Mkt.* 2113/54, no. 1, 19 Cemaziyelevvel 1316 (5 October 1898); and *Dh. Mkt.* 2184/31, no. 1, 19 Zilkade 1316 (31 March 1899).

45 *Dh. Mkt.* 2309/49, no. 1, 21 Şevval 1317 (22 February 1900). Khalil Sarkis edited the newspaper *Lisan al-hal* (*Mouthpiece*) and the magazine *Miskhah* (*Niche*); and Khalil Badawi published the newspaper *Al-Ahwal* (*Conditions*). On Khalil Sarkis, Khalil Badawi, and the print media in Syria, see Meisami and Starkey, *Encyclopedia of Arabic Literature*, vol. 2, 692. See also Cioeta, "Ottoman Censorship"; Ayalon, "Private Publishing"; and Ayalon, *Press*, 63, 107–242.

46 *Dh. Mkt.* 2309/49, no. 1, 21 Şevval 1317 (22 February 1900).

47 *Dh. Mkt.* 997/3, nos 1–4, 11 Cemaziyelahir 1323 (13 August 1905).

48 *Dh. Mkt.* 1043/73, nos 1–2, 29 Zilkade 1323 (25 January 1906); *Dh. Mkt* 1049/33, 19 Zilhicce 1323 (14 February 1906). On the printing devices imported by the American Plaza publishers, see *Dh. Mkt.* 870/93, nos 1–3, 3 Cemaziyelevvel 1322 (16 July 1904); *Dh. Mkt.* 1054/64, nos 1–2, 7 Muharrem 1324 (3 March 1906); and *Dh. Mkt.* 1081/31, 25 Rabiulevvel 1324 (19 May 1906). For permissions, see *Dh. Mkt.* 2235/47, no. 1, 10 Rabiulahir 1317 (18 August 1899). On Liverpool and Marseilles, see *Dh. Mkt.* 1049/33, nos 1–2, 19 Zilhicce 1323 (14 February 1906); *Dh. Mkt.* 595/24, nos 1–4, 11 Recep 1320 (14 October 1902); and *Dh. Mkt.* 529/53, no. 3, 19 Rabiulevvel 1320 (26 June 1902). For a series of imperial orders for extra vigilance, see *Dh. Mkt.* 2309/49, no. 1, 21 Şevval 1317 (22 February 1900); and *Dh. Mkt.* 86/42, no. 2, 15 Safer 1311 (28 August 1893). See also *Papers of the* ABCFM, 10/103, 16.9.3, Bilkent Library, quoted in Kocabaşoğlu, *Kendi Belgeleriyle*, 145.

49 *Dh. Mkt.* 642/37, nos 1–2, 28 Şevval 1320 (28 January 1903).

50 For other examples, see *Dh. Mkt.* 1043/73, nos 1–2, 29 Zilkade 1323 (25 January 1906); *Dh. Mkt.* 1081/31, nos 1–2, 25 Rabiulevvel 1324 (19 May 1906); *Dh. Mkt.* 1054/64, nos 1–2, 7 Muharrem 1324 (3 March 1906); and *Dh. Mkt.* 1040/27, nos 1–3, 14 Zilkade 1323 (10 January 1906).

51 *Türkiye Büyük Millet Meclisi Tutanak Metinleri*, 16 December 1949, National Library of Turkey. For an excellent study of "abandoned property" in post-1921 Turkey, see Morack, *Dowry of the State?* 123–210.

52 *Dh. Mkt.* 785/3, nos 1–3, 10 Şaban 1321 (1 November 1903). For an alternative perspective on Ottoman reactions to missionary publishers that claims the authorities in Istanbul overlooked the publishers' demands, see

Erhan, "Ottoman Official Attitudes." On several cases involving on-site inspections, debates, and the problems caused by the customs officials, see *Dh. Mkt.* 1049/33, nos 1–2, 19 Zilhicce 1323 (14 February 1906); *Dh. Mkt.* 918/25, nos. 1–2, 22 Şevval 1322 (30 December 1904); and *Dh. Mkt.* 529/53, nos 4, 8–9, 19 Rabiulevvel 1320. On Ottoman ports, see Eldem, Goffman, and Masters, eds, *Ottoman City*, 79–206; Kolluoğlu and Toksöz, *Cities of the Mediterranean*; Fuhrmann and Kechriotis, "Late Ottoman Port-Cities"; Driessen, "Mediterranean Port Cities"; and Küçükkalay, "Imports to Smyrna."

53 *Dh. Mkt.* 529/53, no. 2, 19 Rabiulevvel 1320 (26 June 1902).

54 *Dh. Mkt.* 529/53, nos 2–3, 19 Rabiulevvel 1320 (26 June 1902).

55 *Dh. Mkt.* 529/53, nos 5, 7, 10, 19 Rabiulevvel 1320 (26 June 1902).

56 *Dh. Mkt.* 529/53, nos 7, 3–4, 19 Rabiulevvel 1320 (26 June 1902); on the official inspection of American-made printing type imported by the *Levant Herald* (Istanbul), *Dh. Mkt.* 894/9, nos 1–2, 19 Recep 1322 (29 September 1904); for an excellent review of the Ottoman bureaucracy, Weiker, "Ottoman Bureaucracy," esp. 452, 455–62. See also İnalcık, "Nature of Traditional Society."

57 *Dh. Mkt.* 529/53, nos 6, 9–10, 19 Rabiulevvel 1320 (26 June 1902).

58 *Dh. Mkt.* 529/53, no. 6, 19 Rabiulevvel 1320 (26 June 1902).

59 *Dh. Mkt.* 785/3, nos 1–3, 10 Şaban 1321 (1 November 1903).

60 *Dh. Mkt.* 1081/31, nos 1–2, 25 Rabiulevvel 1324 (19 May 1906). Presidents of missionary colleges wrote to Minister of the Interior Mehmet Faik Memduh and pledged that the cast-steel type and printing machines, imported by Euphrates College in Harput and Anatolia College in Merzifon, would be used only within school libraries, not for printing books. *Dh. Mkt.* 918/25, nos 1–2, 22 Şevval 1322 (30 December 1904); *Dh. Mkt.* 882/78, nos 1–2, 10 Cemaziyelahir 1322 (22 August 1904); *Dh. Mkt.* 1119/53, nos 1–5, 6 Şaban 1324 (25 September 1906); *Dh. Mkt.* 1043/73, no. 2, 29 Zilkade 1323 (25 January 1906). For a similar case regarding the Jerusalem Orphanage, see *Dh. Mkt.* 1020/19, nos 1–5, 26 Şaban 1323 (26 October 1905).

61 George Herrick, "America's Big Interests in Turkey," *Boston Daily Globe*, 4 September 1904, 2A4. In Herrick's opinion, even though Ottoman authorities regarded evangelical institutions as a revenue source, "non-profit" institutions should retain tax-exempt status. On the Ottoman understanding of such a claim, see *Hr. Sys.* 2829/45, nos 1–3, 18 October 1893. Herrick argued that his claim was warranted by the common sense of his readers since New England communities had already developed the calculus of property taxes around this time. For an excellent study of early New England's economy and society, see Opal, *Beyond the Farm*, 44–68.

62 For instructions, *Dh. Mkt.* 1993/28, no. 1, 4 Safer 1310 (28 August 1892); on the imperial index, *Dh. Mkt.* 61/33, nos 1–2, 22 Zilkade 1310 (7 June 1893).

63 *Dh. Mkt.* 1709/7, no. 1, 26 Recep 1307 (18 March 1890); *Dh. Mkt.* 1544/26, no. 1, 11 Muharrem 1306 (17 September 1888). See also *Dh. Mkt.* 1765/117, 15 Safer 1308 (30 September 1890); *Dh. Mb. Hps.* 154/27, 25 Recep 1333 (8 June 1915); and *Hr. Sys.* 66/82, no. 2, 12 May 1900.

64 On the Beirut missionary press, for example, see *Dh. Mkt.* 1709/7, no. 1, 26 Recep 1307 (18 March 1890). For Leon Manukian's petition to take over his late father's publishing house, see *Dh. Mkt.* 2175/118, no. 1, 26 Şevval 1316 (9 March 1899). On the missionary proposal to hand out literature on city streets, see *Dh. Mkt.* 911/14, nos 1–4, 24 Şaban 1322 (3 November 1904); see also *Dh. Mkt.* 948/42, nos 1–5, 15 Safer 1323 (21 April 1905); and *Dh. Mkt.* 1056/25, nos 1–3, 15 Muharrem 1324 (11 March 1906). On imperial prohibition of anti-Islamic pamphlets in Anatolia, see *Dh. Mkt.* 1765/117, no. 1, 15 Safer 1308 (30 September 1890).

65 Provincial postures induced the formation of the Ottoman imperial policy regarding the American Board's printing agenda. *Hr. Sys.* 67/31, nos 1–4, 3 April 1906; *Hr. Sys.* 132/31, nos 1–4, 24 August 1909; *Hr. Sys.* 132/32, nos 1–3, 30 August 1909; *Hr. Sys.* 132/33, nos 1–5, 18 September 1909.

66 *Dh. Mkt.* 61/33, nos 1–2, 22 Zilkade 1310 (7 June 1893); *Dh. Mkt.* 1709/7, no. 1, 26 Recep 1307 (18 March 1890); *Dh. Mkt.* 1765/117, no. 1, 15 Safer 1308 (30 September 1890); *Dh. Mkt.* 1951/2, no. 1, 21 Şevval 1309 (19 May 1892); *Dh. Mkt.* 1993/28, no. 1, 4 Safer 1310 (28 August 1892); *Dh. Mkt.* 2006/61, no. 1, 8 Rabiulevvel 1310 (30 September 1892).

67 *Dh. Mkt.* 61/33, no. 1, 22 Zilkade 1310 (7 June 1893); *Dh. Mkt.* 1951/2, no. 1, 21 Şevval 1309 (19 May 1892); *Dh. Mkt.* 1993/28, no. 1, 4 Safer 1310 (28 August 1892).

68 *Dh. Mkt.* 61/33, nos 1–2, 22 Zilkade 1310 (7 June 1893); *Dh. Mkt.* 1993/28, no. 1, 4 Safer 1310 (28 August 1892). On the cases of 17 November 1903 and 11 March 1906, see *Dh. Mkt.* 795/5, nos 1–2, 26 Şaban 1321 (18 October 1903); and *Dh. Mkt.* 1056/25, nos 1–3, 15 Muharrem 1324 (11 March 1906).

69 Pendelton King, US chargé d'affaires, to Sait Halim Pasha, Ottoman Minister of Foreign Affairs, 13 January 1887; and King to Thomas Bayard, US secretary of state, 12 April 1887, both in *Papers Relating to the Foreign Relations* (1888), 1090–2.

70 The Sublime Porte to Pendelton King, 22 March 1887, in *Papers Relating to the Foreign Relations* (1888), 1092.

71 Pendelton King to the Sublime Porte, 6 April 1877, in *Papers Relating to the Foreign Relations* (1888), 1093.

72 Ibid.

73 *Dh. Mkt.* 911/14, nos 1–4; *Dh. Mkt.* 1056/25, no. 1, 15 Muharrem 1324 (11 March 1906). The imperial concept of the "malleable masses" originated in classical Islamic thought. Al-Ghazali, the eleventh-century jurist, philosopher, and theologian, premised that unauthorized religious interpretations "confuse the minds of the masses," and thus any such "unsanctioned innovation" must be punished. Jackson, ed., *On the Boundaries*, 109.

74 *Dh. Mkt.* 948/42, nos 1–29, 15 Safer 1323 (21 April 1905). Regarding the Bible trade, the Ministers Council extended conditional permission to local merchants such as Elias's son Nicholas as well as Ohannes, who was a licensed publisher and unlicensed street vendor working with the Bible House. *Dh. Mkt.* 1056/25, nos 1–3, 15 Muharrem 1324 (11 March 1906); *Dh. Mkt.* 502/53, nos 1–2, 4 Safer 1320 (13 May 1902); *Dh. Mkt.* 2427/82, no. 1, 19 Recep 1318 (12 November 1900); *Dh. Eum. Mkt.* 80/29, 14 Cemaziyelahir 1333 (29 April 1915); *Dh. Mb. Hps.* 154/27, 25 Recep 1333 (8 June 1915); George Herrick, "America's Big Interests in Turkey," *Boston Daily Globe*, 4 September 1904, 2A4.

75 *Dh. Mkt.* 1397/1, no. 1, 8 Cemaziyelevvel 1304 (2 February 1887); *Dh. Mkt.* 1509/67, no. 1, 14 Ramazan 1305 (25 May 1888). For imperial debates over the American Board's propaganda, see *Dh. Mkt.* 1540/31, no. 1, 1 Muharrem 1306 (7 September 1888), as well as the Garabet case below.

76 *Dh. Mkt.* 529/53, nos 2–10, 19 Rabiulevvel 1320 (26 June 1902); *A. Mkt. Mhm.* 657/45, nos 1–3, 13 Ramazan 1305 (24 May 1888); *Hr. Sys.* 64/17, nos 1–18, 8 November 1895.

77 *Dh. Mkt.* 1056/25, nos 1–3, 15 Muharrem 1324 (11 March 1906); *Dh. Mkt.* 1765/117, no. 1, 15 Safer 1308 (30 September 1890); Dwight, *Centennial History*; *Trustees' Minute Book*, Houghton Library. On anti-Islamic and anti-Ottoman literature, see *Hr. Sys.* 71/61, nos 1–3, 9 November 1891; *Hr. Sys.* 71/72, nos 1–5, 8 April 1892; *Hr. Sys.* 71/75, no. 1, 22 June 1892; and *Hr. Sys.* 71/76, no. 1, 29 August 1892. On the books certified by the Ministry of Education but confiscated by local agents, see *Dh. Mkt.* 1951/2, no. 1, 21 Şevval 1309 (19 May 1892). On the impulsive treatment of the missionary publisher H.N. Barnum, see *Dh. Mkt.* 1381/74, no. 1, 3 Rabiulevvel 1304 (30 November 1886); *Dh. Mkt.* 1449/78, no. 1, 3 Muharrem 1305 (21 September 1887); and *Dh. Mkt.* 1465/56, no. 1, 6 Rabiulevvel 1305 (22 November 1887). See also *Dh. Mkt.* 61/33, nos 1–2, 22 Zilkade 1310 (7 June 1893); *Dh. Mkt.* 795/5,

nos 1–2, 26 Şaban 1321 (18 October 1903); *Dh. Mkt.* 870/93, nos 1–3, 3 Cemaziyelevvel 1322 (16 July 1904); *Dh. Mkt.* 999/75, nos 1–11, 20 Cemaziyelahir 1323 (23 July 1905); *Dh. Mkt.* 732/30, no. 1; *Dh. Mkt.* 1951/2, no. 1, 21 Şevval 1309 (19 May 1892); and *Dh. Mkt.* 2164/89, no. 1, 21 Ramazan 1316 (2 February 1899).

78 For directives on these Arabic pamphlets, see *Dh. Mkt.* 2079/46, no. 1, 14 Şaban 1314 (18 January 1897); and *Dh. Eum. Mkt.* 80/29, 14 Cemaziyelahir 1333 (29 April 1915). On a pamphlet titled *Al-kavlu's sahih fi din'il Masih* [True word in the religion of Jesus], see *Hr. Sys.* 66/82, nos 1–2, 12 May 1900.

79 *Dh. Mb. Hps.* 154/27, 25 Recep 1333 (8 June 1915); *Dh. Eum. Mkt.* 80/29, 14 Cemaziyelahir 1333 (29 April 1915).

80 *Dh. Mkt.* 1925/27, no. 1, 23 Recep 1309 (22 February 1892); *A. Mkt. Mhm.* 649/14, no. 1, 21 Şaban 1313 (6 February 1896); *A. Mkt. Mhm.* 658/14, nos 1–6, 19 Şaban 1313 (4 February 1896). On the American Bible Society's challenge to the prohibition, see *Hr. Sys.* 71/61, nos 2–3, 9 November 1891. On the decree to shut the presses of Krigor Gasparian, Baghdasarian, and Baragh, see *Dh. Mkt.* 1544/26, no. 1, 11 Muharrem 1306 (17 September 1888); and *Dh. Mkt.* 1948/97, no. 1, 15 Şevval 1329 (9 October 1911). On the threat to civil order posed by local missionary communication, see *A. Mkt. Mhm.* 655/16, nos 1–14, 16 Cemaziyelevvel 1313 (4 November 1895). On missionary activities and demands, see *Hr. Sys.* 61/18, nos 1–31, 20 April 1892; *Hr. Sys.* 62/1, nos 1–2, 9 January 1893; and *Hr. Sys.* 65/63, no. 1, 18 August 1896. On missionary impact on local youth, see Somel, *Modernization of Public Education*, 202–41; and Karpat, *Studies*, 712–29.

81 Rauf Bey, the Governor of Mamuretülaziz, to Istanbul, in *A. Mkt. Mhm.* 658/14, nos 6–7, 19 Şaban 1313 (4 February 1896); on the detainment of a colleague of Antep American College's principal for "seditious leaflets," *A. Mkt. Mhm.* 649/14, no. 1, 21 Şaban 1313 (6 February 1896); on public security, Lévy and Toumarkine, eds, *Osmanlı'da Asayiş*; and Lévy, "La police ottomane."

82 For ministerial debate over the case of Garabet, *A. Mkt. Mhm.* 658/14, nos 1–2, 19 Şaban 1313 (4 February 1896). On the post-1894 massacres, for scholarly debates, and for competing narratives regarding local tragedies, see Verheij, "Diyarbekir," 89–138; Miller, "Sasun 1894," 157–231; Sipahi, "At Arm's Length," 298–331; Dyer, "Turkish 'Falsifiers'"; Quataert, "Massacre"; and Göçek, *Transformation of Turkey*, 1–240.

83 Garabet's letter, translated to Ottoman-Turkish as "true to the original," in *A. Mkt. Mhm.* 658/14, no. 4, 19 Şaban 1313 (4 February 1896).

84 Garabet's letter and defence, respectively, in *A. Mkt. Mhm.* 658/14, nos 5, 1–2, 19 Şaban 1313 (4 February 1896).

85 *A. Mkt. Mhm.* 658/14, nos 1–2, 5–6, 19 Şaban 1313 (4 February 1896). Interestingly, an anonymous *New York Times* reviewer recommended Will S. Monroe's book *Turkey and the Turks: An Account of the Lands, the Peoples, and the Institutions of the Ottoman Empire* (1907), arguing that the author had consulted no "native authority" for "reasons which should be obvious to those knowing anything of the empire" – namely the Ottoman authorities, already called "double-faced" in the same newspaper. "Boston Notes," *New York Times*, 1 June 1907, sec. 3, 355; "The Unscrupulous Turk," *New York Times*, 17 April 1892, 17.

86 White, *Adventuring with Anatolia College*, part 1, no. 6; Maksudyan, "Amerikan Kaynaklarında," 140–1. See also *Dh. Mkt.* 1947/47, no. 1, 13 Şevval 1309 (11 May 1892); and two anti-Ottoman incidents – one involving Kavaljian, a native professor at Adapazarı Protestant College, and another involving the American Board's school at Bahçecik (Izmit) and Bishop Robert Chambers – in *A. Mkt. Mhm.* 655/16, nos 1–14, 16 Cemaziyelevvel 1313 (4 November 1895).

87 Tracy, "Salient Points," in *Services at the Seventy-Fifth Anniversary*, 67, Andover-Harvard Theological Library. Charles C. Tracy's monographs include *A Cry to Heaven from a Housetop* (1893) and *Silkenbraid, or A Story of Mission Life in Turkey* (1893). For a list of approved books, see *Y. Prk. Mf.* 3/54, no. 2, 29 Zilhicce 1313 (11 June 1896). On numerous cases related to schoolbooks and religious propaganda, see *Dh. Mkt.* 412/50, nos 1–3, 23 Safer 1313 (15 August 1895); *Dh. Mkt.* 460/40, nos 1–2, 17 Zilhicce 1319 (27 March 1902); *Dh. Mkt.* 1540/31, 1 Muharrem 1306 (7 September 1888); *Dh. Mkt.* 1765/117, 15 Safer 1308 (30 September 1890); *Dh. Mkt.* 1925/27, 23 Recep 1309 (22 February 1892); *Dh. Mkt.* 2091/127, 28 Rabiulevvel 1316 (16 August 1898); and *Dh. Mkt.* 2309/49, 21 Şevval 1317 (22 February 1900). On the need to "prevent sedition" and "refund school expenses," see *İ. Hus.* 84/1318 Ca 48, 22 Cemaziyelevvel 1318 (17 September 1900). For the edict to facilitate the research trip of Carnegie professor Mr William, see *Dh. Mui.* 57/27, 12 Muharrem 1328 (24 January 1910); and *Dh. Mui.* 80/3-32, 30 Cemaziyelahir 1328 (8–9 July 1910). On the need to "protect Americans and their schools," see *Dh. Eum. 5Şb.* 72/12, 11 Muharrem 1337 (17 October 1918). See also Somel, *Modernization of Public Education*, 187, 271–7.

88 *Y. Prk. Mf.* 3/54, nos 2–3, 29 Zilhicce 1313 (11 June 1896). For various reports, see *Y. Prk. Hr.* 7/36, nos 2–8, 18 Safer 1301 (19 December 1883).

On missionary schools in Beirut, activities in Mersin, and books in the American library, see *Y. Prk. Mf.* 2/22, 22 Safer 1309 (27 September 1891); *Y. Prk. Mf.* 3/11, 2 Recep 1311 (9 January 1894); and *Y. Prk. Mf.* 4/44, 29 Zilhicce 1315 (21 May 1898). On Adana American College and Üsküdar American Academy for Girls, see *Hr. Sys.* 2415/53, nos 1–8, 16 December 1915. See also *Y. Prk. Tşf.* 4/13, 1 Recep 1312 (29 December 1894).

89 *Y. Prk. Mf.* 3/54, no. 2, 29 Zilhicce 1313 (11 June 1896); *Y. Prk. Mf.* 5/20, no. 41, 2 Recep 1325 (11 August 1907).

90 *Y. Prk. Mf.* 4/66, nos 1–18, 27 Zilhicce 1320 (27 March 1903). See also Maksudyan, "Amerikan Kaynaklarında," 133–78.

91 The figures are drawn from *Y. Prk. Mf.* 4/66, nos 1–18, 27 Zilhicce 1320 (27 March 1903); *American Board Charts*, Andover-Harvard Theological Library; and *List of American Educational, Religious, and Charitable Institutions*, American Research Institute in Turkey.

92 *Y. Prk. Mf.* 3/54, nos 2–3, 29 Zilhicce 1313 (11 June 1896). Recommended textbooks included *The History of Ancient Greek Cities and Monuments* (in Greek, 1879) and *Secrets of Being* (in Armenian, 1878).

93 *Y. Prk. Mf.* 3/54, nos 1–3, 29 Zilhicce 1313 (11 June 1896). The American Board exported numerous textbooks to the Ottoman Empire. Merzifon Anatolia College imported chemistry and logic textbooks from London, biology textbooks from Edinburgh, algebra and Greek-language textbooks from Athens, and French-language materials from Paris. Missionary and state schools taught the same curriculum on Ottoman history, language, and law, but their language courses assigned various materials. On imperial schoolbooks, see Somel, *Modernization of Public Education*, 187–202.

94 *Y. Prk. Mf.* 3/54, nos 1–3, 29 Zilhicce 1313 (11 June 1896).

95 In 1924 Merzifon Anatolia College was relocated from north-central Anatolia to Thessaloniki, Greece. See the memoirs of the college's president, George White, in *Adventuring with Anatolia College.*

96 Tracy, "Salient Points," in *Services at the Seventy-Fifth Anniversary*, 67, Andover-Harvard Theological Library.

97 Tracy, "Salient Points," in *Services at the Seventy-Fifth Anniversary*, 67, Andover-Harvard Theological Library. In March 1893 the police patrols arrested Professor Seyak Toumaian of Merzifon Anatolia College because he had "published provocative stuff." Istanbul authorities ensured that the prosecution would examine "solid proof," and they requested detailed explanations from the patrols. *A. Mkt. Mhm.* 73/10, nos 2–7, 27 Şaban 1310 (16 March 1893); *A. Mkt. Mhm* 733/35, nos 2–4, 26 Ramazan 1310 (13 April 1893).

98 Tracy, "Salient Points," in *Services at the Seventy-Fifth Anniversary*, 67, Andover-Harvard Theological Library; Anderson, *History of the Missions*, 503–18.

99 On the *Redhouse* publication committee, see Strauss, "'Kütüp ve Resail-i Mevkute,'" 241.

100 Ahmet Mithat's *Tercüman-ı Hakikat* editorials – "Müdafa" ("Defence"), "Müdafaya Mukabele ve Mukabeleye Müdafa" ("Response to the Defence and the Defence of the Response"), and "İslam ve Ulum" ("Islam and Worlds") – were republished in a four-volume pamphlet collection under their original titles by the Ottoman Imperial Press in Istanbul between 1882 and 1900. This press flourished under the leadership of Ahmet Mithat and Ahmet Vefik and with the help of Armenian senior publishers such as Boghos Arabian. Strauss, "'Kütüp ve Resail-i Mevkute,'" 227.

101 Dwight, *Constantinople and Its Problems*, 45–6. For the publication figures, see *Annual Report* (1909), 53; and *American Board Charts*, 3, Andover-Harvard Theological Library. The European Embassy's secretary, who was "Roman Catholic" and had travelled to "Asiatic Turkey some two or three years ago," is not mentioned, but he must be Jean Antoine Ernest Constans, the French ambassador to the Ottoman Empire from 1898 to 1909. Statistics on missionary publications that were imported or printed without permission are remarkable. In a June 1893 directive, Minister of the Interior Halil Rıfat proclaimed that "any text" would now receive fuller attention. If the publisher or sender, the receiver, and the content of a text passed inspection, the text made its way into the Ministry of Education's "publications index," and local officials allowed it to be copied and distributed. *Dh. Mkt.* 61/33, nos 1–2, 22 Zilkade 1310 (7 June 1893); *Dh. Mkt.* 1948/97, nos 1–3, 15 Şevval 1329 (9 October 1911).

EPILOGUE

1 Webster, "Cannibals and Kava," 185; Rothenberg, *Catalysis*. On the riddle's modern use, see Timberg, "Cannibals and Missionaries." For missionary accounts from the South Pacific nations, see Rowe, *Life of John Hunt*; Patterson, *Missionary Life*, 106–33; Dupeyrat, *Savage Papua*; and Brantlinger, *Taming Cannibals*, 27–85. For a safe end to the journey, the boat can make nine one-way trips. One missionary crosses with one cannibal and returns, two cannibals cross and one returns, two missionaries cross and one returns with one cannibal, two missionaries cross and one cannibal returns, and two cannibals cross, thus ending the traffic.

2 Wheatcroft, *Ottomans*, 234, 239. For some American perceptions of the Ottoman Empire, see McCarthy, *Turk in America*, 1–18, 105–57, 287–93; and Madi-Şişman and Şişman, "From 'Heathen Turks.'"

3 On metaphors as historical analytical tools, see Draaisma, *Metaphors of Memory*; and Burnham, "Changing Metaphors." For metaphorical examples, see Findley, *Turks in World History*, 224–38; Finkel, *Osman's Dream*; Branning, *Yes, I Would*; Worringer, "'Sick Man of Europe'"; and Gümüş, *American Missionaries*, 67–130.

4 Deringil, *Well-Protected Domains*, 150–65. See also Deringil, *Conversion and Apostasy*, 197–230.

5 For an informed study of the Jesuits in seventeenth-century Istanbul, see Ruiu, "Conflicting Visions," 262–72. See also Hanioğlu, *Young Turks*, 110–39; and Kurşun, "Mehmed Memduh Paşa."

6 On Turkish nationalism and post-Ottoman trauma, see Kieser, ed., *Turkey beyond Nationalism*, 37–82.

7 Samuel 1:19.

8 Aksekili, "Müslüman Kıyafetinde Gezen"; Enver, "Misyoner Tehlikesine Karşı." Strikingly, Ahmet Hamdi Aksekili had received the approval of Mustafa Kemal Atatürk, the founder of the Republic of Turkey, as a model republican scholar, and he later served as Turkey's director of religious affairs from 1947 to 1951. The *Sebilürreşad* journal, for which he often wrote, presented political developments from an Islamist perspective. Mehmet Akif, the prolific scholar, politician, and author of the Turkish national anthem, became the journal's editor-in-chief, and its contributors included modern Islamic pundits such as Ahmet Agayef, Farid Vajdi, Muhammad Abduh, and Yusuf Akçura. The journal's ethos of a united Muslim world addressed a transnational readership from the Ottoman Empire to Russia, China, India, and Japan. For an impressive study, published in German, that explains Turkish-Islamic thought through the lens of this journal, see Debus, *Sebilürreşad*. On Turkish-missionary encounters, see Dittes, "Christian Mission."

9 Karabekir, "Misyonerlerin Faaliyeti" [Activities of missionaries], *Yeni Sabah*, 12 February 1939, reprinted in Karabekir, "Müslümanların Karşılaştığı Tehlikeler: Misyonerlik" [Perils facing Muslims: Missionary work]," *İslam Türk Ansiklopedisi Mecmuası* 78 (n.d.), National Library of Turkey. For an account of the First World War, see Karabekir, *Birinci Cihan Harbine*. See also Zürcher, "Young Turk Memoirs."

10 Karabekir, "Müslümanların Karşılaştığı Tehlikeler: Misyonerlik" [Perils facing Muslims: Missionary work]," *İslam Türk Ansiklopedisi Mecmuası* 78 (n.d.), National Library of Turkey.

11 Haydaroğlu, *Osmanlı İmparatorluğu'nda*, 216–17; Morack, *Dowry of the State?* 211–46. On the impact of ethnic nationalism on Turkey's public education, see Çelik, "Unity vs. Uniformity."

12 On the impact of emotions on the narration of nations, see Hogan, "Stories, Wars, and Emotions," 47–58.

Bibliography

The American Board of Commissioners for Foreign Missions is often abbreviated herein as ABCFM.

MANUSCRIPT SOURCES

American Research Institute in Turkey, Istanbul

Catalogue and Price List of Publications of the Missions of the American Board, Bible House, Constantinople. By H. Matteosian, 1902. No. 11484.

List of American Educational, Religious, and Charitable Institutions in the Ottoman Empire. By H. Matteosian, 1903. No. 11159.

Memorial Records for George P. Knapp, 1863–1915. No. 17182.

Memorial Records for Herman N. Barnum, 1826–1910. No. 16686.

Memorial Records for William S. Dodd. No. 16837.

Personnel Records for William S. Dodd. No. 12070.

Bilkent Library and National Library of Turkey, Ankara

ABCFM Higher Education Statistics, 26 May 1910 and 7 July 1910. ABC 16, reel 629, Bilkent Library.

İslam Türk Ansiklopedisi Mecmuası [Journal of the Islamic Turkish encyclopedia] 78 (n.d.), National Library of Turkey.

Letter from William S. Dodd to Friends, Talas, 10 April 1905. Eastern Turkey Mission 18, ABC 16, reel 703, Bilkent Library.

Papers of the ABCFM. ABC 16, reel 583, Bilkent Library.

Türkiye Büyük Millet Meclisi Tutanak Metinleri [Turkey's grand national assembly minute books], 16 December 1949. B18, 240, National Library of Turkey.

Houghton Library and Andover-Harvard Theological Library, Cambridge, Massachusetts

American Board Charts: A Graphic Presentation of the Foreign Work of the Congregational Churches of America. Boston: ABCFM, 14 June 1916. ABCFM box 3, 3, Andover-Harvard Theological Library.

Bartlett, Lyman. *Biographies and Letters.* ABC 77-1, box 6, Houghton Library.

Catalogue of Missionary Publications. [ABCFM box 1, 817.81] Boston: ABCFM, n.d.

Dennis, James S. *Islam and Christian Missions.* New York: Funk and Wangalis, 1889 [The August 1889 issue of the *Missionary Review of the World*, Pamphlet D]

Duty of American Christians to the Heathen. [ABCFM box 3, 817.83] Boston: The Board, 1866

Eddy, David B. *Eddy Family Collection.* ABC 77-1, Houghton Library.

– *What Next in Turkey: Glimpses of the American Board's Work in the Near East.* Boston: ABCFM, 1913. Houghton Library.

Haskell, Edward B. *Haskell Papers, 1853–1935.* 21 boxes, Houghton Library.

Papers of Cyrus Hamlin and George Washburn, 1863–1910. Letters 69–73, Houghton Library.

Parker Family Collection. ABC 6, vol. 4, 161; vol. 11, 30–1; vol. 16, 183–4, Houghton Library.

The Problem of Turkey as the American Board Views It. Boston: ABCFM, 1923. Pamphlet BV 3160, Andover-Harvard Theological Library.

Services at the Seventy-Fifth Anniversary of the Establishment of the American Mission at Constantinople. ABCFM box 817.601, A512, Andover-Harvard Theological Library.

The Treaty Rights of the American Missionaries in Turkey. By Henry Otis Dwight. Boston: ABCFM, 8 April 1893. ABCFM pamphlet box, Andover-Harvard Theological Library.

Trustees' Minute Book. Bible House, Constantinople, Records, vol. 1, 1866–1923, ABC 26, Houghton Library.

Ottoman Archives Division, Prime Minister's Office, Istanbul

A. Dvn. (*Dîvân-ı Hümâyûn kalemi*). Imperial Ministers Council secretariat.

A. Mkt. Mhm. (*Amedî mektubî mühimme*). Classified incoming correspondence.

A. Mkt. Mvl. (*Amedî mektubî Meclis-i Vâlâ*). Supreme Ministers Council, incoming correspondence.

A. Mkt. Nzd. (*Amedî mektubî nezâret devâir*). Ministerial offices, incoming correspondence.

A. Mkt. Um. (*Amedî mektubî umum vilâyât*). Provinces general, incoming correspondence.

Bb. Ek. Od. (*Bâb-i âli evrak odası*). Sublime Porte records bureau.

Dh. Eum. (*Dâhiliye emniyet-i umûmiye*). Internal affairs, general security.

Dh. Eum. 3Şb. (*Dâhiliye emniyet-i umûmiye 3. Şube*). Internal affairs, general security, 3rd branch.

Dh. Eum. 5Şb. (*Dâhiliye emniyet-i umûmiye 5. Şube*). Internal affairs, general security, 5th branch.

Dh. Eum. Ayş. (*Dâhiliye emniyet-i umûmiye asayiş*). Internal affairs, police security.

Dh. Eum. Emn. (*Dâhiliye emniyet-i umûmiye emniyet*). Internal affairs, police safety.

Dh. Eum. Mkt. (*Dâhiliye emniyet-i umûmiye mektubî*). Internal affairs, police correspondence.

Dh. İd. (*Dâhiliye idâre*). Internal affairs, administration.

Dh. Kms. (*Dâhiliye kalem-i mahsûs*). Internal affairs, special secretariat.

Dh. Mb. Hps. (*Dâhiliye mebâni-i emîriye ve hapishaneler*). Internal affairs, state foundations and prisons.

Dh. Mkt. (*Dâhiliye mektubî*). Internal affairs, incoming.

Dh. Mui. (*Dâhiliye muhâberât-ı umûmiye idaresi*). Internal affairs general, communication bureau.

Dh. Şfr. (*Dâhiliye şifreli evrakı*). Internal affairs, cipher documents.

Dh. Um. Vm. (*Dâhiliye umûmiye meclis-i vukelâ mazbataları*). Internal affairs general, minutes of the Ministers Council.

H.H. (*Hatt-ı hümâyûn*). Imperial decree.

Hr. Mkt. (*Hâriciye mektubî*). Foreign affairs, correspondence.

Hr. Sys. (*Hâriciye siyâsî*). Foreign affairs, diplomatic.

İ. Dh. (*İrâde dâhiliye*). Imperial decrees, internal affairs.

İ. Duit. (*İrâde dâhiliye idâre-i umûmiye tasnifi*). Imperial decrees, general administration collection.

İ. Hr. (*İrâde hâriciye*). Imperial decrees, foreign affairs.

İ. Hus. (*İrâde husûsiye*). Imperial decrees, special.

İ. Mf. (*İrâde müteferrik*). Imperial decrees, assorted.

İ. Ml. (*İrâde maliye*). Imperial decrees, finance.

İ. Mms. (*İrâde meclis-i mahsûs*). Imperial decrees, special council.

Mv. (*Meclis-i vukelâ mazbataları*). Minutes of the Ministers Council.

Y. Ee. (*Yıldız esas evrâkı*). Yıldız Palace, principal documents.

Y. Mrz. D. (*Yıldız mâruzât defteri*). Yıldız Palace, register of petitions.

Y. Mtv. (*Yıldız mütenevvi mâruzât*). Yıldız Palace, particular petitions.

Y. Prk. Ask. (*Yıldız perâkende askerî*). Yıldız Palace, miscellaneous, military correspondence.

Y. Prk. Bşk. (*Yıldız perâkende başkitâbet*) Yıldız Palace, miscellaneous, chief secretariat.

Y. Prk. Dh. (*Yıldız perâkende dâhiliye*). Yıldız Palace, miscellaneous, internal affairs.

Y. Prk. Eşa. (*Yıldız perâkende elçilik, şehbenderlik ve ateşemiliterlik*). Yıldız Palace, miscellaneous, embassy, consul, and military attaché.

Y. Prk. Hr. (*Yıldız perâkende hariciye*). Yıldız Palace, miscellaneous, foreign affairs.

Y. Prk. Mf. (*Yıldız perâkende müteferrik*). Yıldız Palace, miscellaneous, assorted documents.

Y. Prk. Mk. (*Yıldız perâkende müfettişlikler ve komiserlikler tahrîrâtı*). Yıldız Palace, miscellaneous, registers of inspectors and police superintendents.

Y. Prk. Myd. (*Yıldız perâkende yâverân ve mâiyyet-i seniyye erkân-ı harbiye dâiresi*). Yıldız Palace, miscellaneous, the office of aides-de-camp, holy attendants, and general staff.

Y. Prk. Tkm. (*Yıldız perâkende tahrirât-ı ecnebiyye ve mabeyn mütercimliği*). Yıldız Palace, miscellaneous, the translation office of foreign papers and the palace.

Y. Prk. Tşf. (*Yıldız perâkende teşrifât-ı umûmiye dâiresi*). Yıldız Palace, miscellaneous, the office of protocol general.

Y. Prk. Um. (*Yıldız perâkende umûmî*). Yıldız Palace, miscellaneous, correspondence.

Y. Prk. Zb. (*Yıldız perâkende zabtiye*). Yıldız Palace, miscellaneous, public security.

Ya. Hus. (*Yıldız husûsî*). Yıldız Palace, special.

Ya. Res. (*Yıldız resmî mâruzât*). Yıldız Palace, chief petitions.

Zb. (*Zabtiye*). Public security.

NEWSPAPERS AND MAGAZINES

Al Jazeera (Doha, Qatar)

Atlantic Monthly (Boston)

BBC *World News* (London)

Berkeley News

Bisbee Daily Review

Boston Daily Globe
Chicago Tribune
CNN *Türk* (Istanbul)
Cumhuriyet (Istanbul)
Der Spiegel (Hamburg)
Florida Baptist Witness
Guardian (London)
Hartford Courant
Houston Daily Post
Hürriyet (Istanbul)
Hürriyet Daily (Istanbul)
International Christian Concern (Washington, DC)
Literary Digest (New York)
Los Angeles Times
L'Univers illustré (Paris)
Meridian Weekly Republican (Mississippi)
Milliyet (Istanbul)
Missionary Herald (Boston)
The Nation (New York)
New York Times
NTV *Güncel* (Istanbul)
Outlook (New York)
Posta (Istanbul)
Sabah (Istanbul)
Sacramento Daily Union
Salt Lake Herald
San Francisco Call
Suburban Citizen (Washington, DC)
The Sun (New York)
Tercüman-ı Hakikat (Istanbul)
Washington Post
The World (New York)
Yeni Sabah (Istanbul)

SECONDARY SOURCES

1319 Yanya Salnamesi [The 1902 almanac of the province of Ioannina]. Istanbul, 1902.

1321 Maarif Salnamesi [The 1904 almanac of the Ministry of Education]. Istanbul, 1904.

XII. Milletlerarası Arşiv Kongresi, 6–11 Eylül 1992, Montreal [12th International Archives Congress, 6–11 September 1992, Montreal]. Ankara: Başbakanlık Devlet Arşivleri Genel Müdürlüğü, 1992.

"The Attempt of Turkey to Abrogate the Capitulations." *American Journal of International Law* 8 (October 1914): 873–76.

Adıvar, Halide Edip. *Memoirs of Halide Edip*. New York: Century Co., 1928.

Ahmad, Feroz. *The Making of Modern Turkey*. London: Routledge, 1993.

Akarlı, Engin Deniz. "The Tangled Ends of an Empire: Ottoman Encounters with the West and Problems of Westernization, an Overview." *Comparative Studies of South Asia, Africa and the Middle East* 26, no. 3 (2006): 353–66.

Akçura, Yusuf. *Üç Tarz-ı Siyaset* [Three forms of politics]. Ankara: Türk Tarih Kurumu, 1998.

Akgün, Seçil Karal. *Kendi Kaynaklarından Amerikalı Misyonerlerin Türk Sosyal Yaşamına Etkisi, 1820–1914* [American missionaries' impact on Turkish social life, 1820–1914, a view from their own sources]. Ankara: TTK, 1994.

– "Mormon Missionaries in the Ottoman Empire." *Turcica* 28 (1996): 347–58.

– "The Turkish Image in the Reports of American Missionaries in the Ottoman Empire." *Turkish Studies Association Bulletin* 13, no. 2 (1991): 91–105.

Aksekili, Ahmet Hamdi. "Müslüman Kıyafetinde Gezen Bir Protestan Misyoneriyle Musahabe" [Rendezvous with a Protestant missionary travelling in the guise of a Muslim]. *Sebilürreşad* 11, no. 263 (November 1913): 43–4.

Akşin, Sina. *Turkey from Empire to Revolutionary Republic: The Emergence of the Turkish Nation from 1789 to the Present*. New York: New York University Press, 2007.

Akyıldız, Ali. "Misyonerliğe Karşı Yasal Tedbirler" [Legal measures against missionary work]. In Asife Ünsal, ed., *Dinler Tarihçileri Gözüyle Misyonerlik* [Missionary activity from the perspective of the historians of religion], 399–416. Ankara: Türkiye Dinler Tarihi Derneği Yayınları, 2005.

American College for Girls Records, 1880s-1979. No. 6799283, 58 boxes, Columbia University Archives, New York.

Anderson, Rufus. *History of the Missions of the American Board of Commissioners for Foreign Missions to the Oriental Churches*. Boston: Congregational Publishing Society, 1872.

Angell, James B. "The Turkish Capitulations." *American Historical Review* 6, no. 2 (January 1901): 254–9.

Annual Report of the American Board of Commissioners for Foreign Missions. Boston: Press of T.R. Marvin, 1852.

Annual Report of the American Board of Commissioners for Foreign Missions. Boston: Press of T.R. Marvin, 1854.

Annual Report of the American Board of Commissioners for Foreign Missions. Boston: American Board Congregational House, 1909.

Annual Report of the American Board of Commissioners for Foreign Missions. Boston: American Board Congregational House, 1917.

Aral, Berdal. "The Idea of Human Rights as Perceived in the Ottoman Empire." *Human Rights Quarterly* 26, no. 2 (May 2004): 454–82.

Aslantaş, Selim. "Bir Osmanlı Bürokratı: Mehmet Memduh Paşa" [Mehmet Memduh Pasha: An Ottoman bureaucrat]. KÖK *Araştırmalar* 3, no. 1 (Spring 2001): 185–202.

Atçıl, Abdurrahman. "The Route to the Top in the Ottoman İlmiye Hierarchy of the Sixteenth Century." *Bulletin of the School of Oriental and African Studies* 72, no. 3 (2009): 489–512.

– *Scholars and Sultans in the Early Modern Ottoman Empire*. Cambridge, UK: Cambridge University Press, 2017.

Ayalon, Ami. *The Press in the Arab Middle East: A History*. New York: Oxford University Press, 1995.

– "Private Publishing in the Nahda." *International Journal of Middle East Studies* 40, no. 4 (November 2008): 561–77.

Aydın, Cemil. *The Idea of the Muslim World: A Global Intellectual History*. Cambridge, MA: Harvard University Press, 2017.

– *The Politics of Anti-Westernism in Asia: Visions of World Order in Pan-Islamic and Pan-Asian Thought*. New York: Columbia University Press, 2007.

Aydın, Mustafa, and Çağrı Erhan, eds. *Turkish-American Relations: Past, Present and Future*. London and New York: Routledge.

Bardakjian, Kevork. *A Reference Guide to Modern Armenian Literature, 1500–1920: With an Introductory History*. Detroit: Wayne State University Press, 2000.

Barkan, Ömer Lütfi. "İstila Devirlerinin Kolonizatör Türk Dervişleri ve Zaviyeler" [Colonizing Turkish dervishes and dervish lodges in the ages of invasion]. *Vakıflar Dergisi* 2 (1942): 279–386.

Barkey, Karen. *Bandits and Bureaucrats: The Ottoman Route to State Centralization*. New York: Cornell University Press, 1994.

– *Empire of Difference: The Ottomans in Comparative Perspective*. Cambridge, UK: Cambridge University Press, 2008.

– "Islam and Toleration: Studying the Ottoman Imperial Model." *International Journal of Politics, Culture, and Society* 19, nos 1–2 (December 2005): 5–19.

Barkey, Karen, and George Gavrilis. "The Ottoman Millet System: Non-Territorial Autonomy and its Contemporary Legacy." *Ethnopolitics* 15, no. 1 (2016): 24–42.

Barkley, Henry C. *Between the Danube and Black Sea*. London: Murray, 1876.

– *Bulgaria before the War during Seven Years' Experience of European Turkey and Its Inhabitants*. London: Murray, 1877.

– *A Ride through Asia Minor and Armenia: Giving a Sketch of the Characters, Manners, and Customs of Both the Mussulman and Christian Inhabitants*. London: Murray, 1891.

Barton, James L. "American Educational and Philanthropic Interests in the Near East." *Muslim World* 23 (April 1933): 121–36.

– *Story of Near East Relief, 1915–1930: An Interpretation*. New York: Macmillan, 1930.

Beaver, R. Pierce. *Ecumenical Beginnings in Protestant World Mission: A History of Comity*. New York: Thomas Nelson and Sons, 1962.

Bektaş, Yakup. "The Sultan's Messenger: Cultural Constructions of Ottoman Telegraphy, 1847–1880." *Technology and Culture* 41, no. 4 (October 2000): 669–96.

Berisha, Mal. *Jeta e jashtëzakonshme e amerikanit Charles Telford Erickson kushtuar Shqipërisë* [Charles Telford Erickson: The extraordinary life of an American who dedicated his life to Albania]. Tiranë: Botime Edualba, 2012.

Berkes, Niyazi. *The Development of Secularism in Turkey*. New York: Routledge, 1998.

Beydilli, Kemal. "Matbaa" [Press]. In *Türkiye Diyanet Vakfı İslam Ansiklopedisi* [Turkiye Diyanet Foundation encyclopedia of Islam], vol. 28, 105–10. Istanbul: Türkiye Diyanet Vakfı, 2003.

Bhabha, Homi K., ed. *Nation and Narration*. New York: Routledge, 1990.

Binark, İsmet. *A Short History of the Turkish Archives and the Activities of the General Directorate of the State Archives*. Ankara: Başbakanlık Devlet Arşivleri Genel Müdürlüğü, 1994.

Birol, Nurettin. "XIX. Yüzyıl Sonlarında Sivas Vilayetinde Azınlık ve Yabancı Eğitim-Öğretim Kurumları ve Faaliyetleri" [Educational and instructional institutions owned by minorities and foreigners and their activities in the Sivas province by the end of the nineteenth century]. *Turkish Studies* 3, no. 4 (2008): 241–78.

Blumi, Isa. "Teaching Loyalty in the Late Ottoman Balkans: Educational Reform in the Vilayets of Manastir and Yanya, 1878–1912." *Comparative Studies of South Asia, Africa and the Middle East* 21, nos 1–2 (2001): 15–23.

Bobocel, D. Ramona, Aaron C. Kay, Mark P. Zanna, and James M. Olson, eds. *The Psychology of Justice and Legitimacy*. New York: Psychology, 2010.

Boudreau, Thomas. "Intergroup Conflict Reduction through Identity Affirmation: Overcoming the Image of the Ethnic or Enemy 'Other.'" *Peace and Conflict Studies* 10, no. 1 (2003): 87–107.

Bozarslan, Hamit. "Kurds and the Turkish State." In Reşat Kasaba, ed., *Turkey in the Modern World*, 349–54. Cambridge, UK: Cambridge University Press, 2008.

Branning, Katharine. *Yes, I Would Love Another Glass of Tea: An American Woman's Letters to Turkey*. New York: Bluedome, 2012.

Brantlinger, Patrick. *Taming Cannibals: Race and the Victorians*. Ithaca, NY: Cornell University Press, 2011.

Braudel, Fernand, and Immanuel Wallerstein. "History and the Social Sciences: The Long Durée." *Review* 32, no. 2 (2009): 171–203.

Burnham, John C. "Changing Metaphors in History of the Human Sciences." *History of the Human Sciences* 13, no. 4 (2000): 121–4.

Çakır, Musa. *Anadolumuz Asla Hristiyan Olmayacak: Misyonerler Memleketinize Geri Dönünüz* [Anatolia, our land, will not become Christian: You missionaries go back home]. Istanbul: M.S. Matbası, 1966.

Campos, Michelle. *Ottoman Brothers: Muslims, Christians, and Jews in Early Twentieth-Century Palestine*. Palo Alto, CA: Stanford University Press, 2011.

Carpenter, Teresa. *The Miss Stone Affair: America's First Modern Hostage Crisis*. New York: Simon and Schuster, 2003.

Casale, Giancarlo. "The Ottoman Administration of the Spice Trade in the Sixteenth-Century Red Sea and Persian Gulf." *Journal of the Economic and Social History of the Orient* 49, no. 2 (2006): 170–98.

Çelik, Rait. "Unity vs. Uniformity: The Influence of Ziya Gökalp and John Dewey on the Education System of the Republic of Turkey." *Education and Culture* 30, no. 1 (2014): 17–37.

Çelik, Zeynep. *Empire, Architecture, and the City: French-Ottoman Encounters, 1830–1914*. Seattle: University of Washington Press, 2008.

Chang, Derek. *Citizens of a Christian Nation: Evangelical Missions and the Problem of Race in the Nineteenth Century*. Philadelphia: University of Pennsylvania Press, 2010.

Charles Telford Erickson Papers. RG 26, Yale University Divinity School Library.

Childs, W.J. *Across Asia Minor on Foot*. New York: Blackwood, 1917.

Cioeta, Donald. "Ottoman Censorship in Lebanon and Syria, 1876–1908." *International Journal of Middle Eastern Studies* 10, no. 2 (1979): 167–86.

Cjivanović, Hrvoje. "Modus Vivendi: Concept of Coexistence in Pluralist Global Society." *Politička Misao* 43, no. 5 (2006): 29–44.

Clay, Christopher G.A. *Gold for the Sultan*. London: I.B. Tauris, 2000.

Clement, Clara. *Constantinople: The City of Sultans*. Boston: Estes and Company, 1895.

Clifford, James, and George E. Marcus, eds. *Writing Culture: The Poetics and Politics of Ethnography*. Berkeley: University of California Press, 1986.

Coakley, J.F. "The ABCFM Collection at Harvard." *Harvard Library Bulletin* 9, no. 1 (1998): 3–4.

Cobham, Claude. *The Patriarchs of Constantinople*. Cambridge, UK: Cambridge University Press, 1911.

Colton, Calvin, ed. *The Speeches of Henry Clay*. Vol. 1. New York: A.S. Barnes and Co., 1857.

Compton, Carl C. *The Morning Cometh: 45 Years with Anatolia College*. Athens, Greece: Anatolia College, 2008.

Controversy between the Missionaries of the American Board and the Evangelical Armenian Churches in Turkey. New York: Armenian Young Men's Christian Association, 1882.

Corbin, Alain. *Village Bells: Sound and Meaning in the Nineteenth-Century French Countryside*. New York: Columbia University Press, 1998.

Corke, Susan, Andrew Finkel, David J. Kramer, Carla Anne Robbins, and Nate Schenkkan. *Democracy in Crisis: Corruption, Media, and Power in Turkey*. Freedom House, February 2014. https://freedomhouse.org/sites/default/files/Turkey%20Report%20-%20Feb%203%2C%202014.pdf.

Coşgel, Metin M. "Efficiency and Continuity in Public Finance: The Ottoman System of Taxation." *International Journal of Middle East Studies* 37, no. 4 (2005): 567–86.

Cosmades, Thomas. "At Zion Orphanage." In *Anatolia, Anatolia!* Armenian Bible Church, n.d. http://armenianbiblechurch.org/food%20corner/anatolia/anatolia_index.htm.

– *Maria, God's Angel to Widows and Orphans in Anatolia*. 2009. http://www.cosmades.org/articles/Maria%20%20God's%20Angel%20to%20Widows%20and%20Orphans%20with%20pictures.pdf.

Costantini, Vera, and Markus Koller, eds. *Living in the Ottoman Ecumenical Community: Essays in Honour of Suraiya Faroqhi*. Leiden: Brill, 2008.

Criss, Nur Bilge, et al., eds. *American Turkish Encounters: Politics and Culture, 1830–1989*. New Castle upon Tyne, UK: Cambridge Scholars, 2011.

Currie, David P. "The Distribution of Powers after Bowsher." *Supreme Court Review* 1986 (1986): 19–40.

Curtis, William Eleroy. *The Turk and His Lost Provinces*. Chicago: Fleming H. Revell, 1903.

Dağlı, Murat. "The Limits of Ottoman Pragmatism." *History and Theory* 52 (May 2013): 194–213.

Dale, Stephen F. "Ibn Hhaldun: The Last Greek and the First *Annaliste* Historian." *International Journal of Middle Eastern Studies* 38, no. 3 (2006): 431–51.

Darling, Linda T. "Another Look at Periodization in Ottoman History." *Turkish Studies Association Journal* 26, no. 2 (Fall 2002): 9–28.

– *A History of Social Justice and Political Power in the Middle East: The Circle of Justice from Mesopotamia to Globalization*. New York: Routledge, 2013.

– *Revenue-Raising and Legitimacy: Tax Collection and Finance Administration in the Ottoman Empire, 1560–1660*. Leiden: Brill, 1996.

Daşçıoğlu, Kemal. *Osmanlı'da Sürgün: İskan, Suç ve Ceza* [Exiles in the Ottoman Empire: Settlement, crime, and punishment]. Istanbul: Yeditepe Yayınevi, 2007.

Davison, Roderick H. "Turkish Attitudes Concerning Christian-Muslim Equality in the Nineteenth Century." *American Historical Review* 59, no. 4 (1954): 844–64.

Debus, Esther. *Sebilürreşad: Eine vergleichende Untersuchung zur islamischen Opposition der vor- und nachkemalistischen Ära* [True path: A comparative study of the Islamic opposition in the pre-Kemalist and post-Kemalist eras]. Frankfurt am Main: Peter Lang, 1991.

DeNovo, John A. *American Interests and Policies in the Middle East, 1900–1939*. Minneapolis: University of Minnesota Press, 1963.

– "Review of America and the Mediterranean World." *Journal of American History* 56, no. 4 (1970): 932–3.

Deringil, Selim. *Conversion and Apostasy in the Late Ottoman Empire*. Cambridge, UK: Cambridge University Press, 2012.

– "Legitimacy Structures in the Ottoman State: The Reign of Abdulhamid II (1876–1909)." *International Journal of Middle East Studies* 23, no. 3 (1991): 345–59.

– "The Turks and 'Europe': The Argument from History." *Middle Eastern Studies* 43, no. 5 (2007): 709–23.
– *The Well-Protected Domains: Ideology and the Legitimation of Power in the Ottoman Empire, 1876–1909*. London: I.B. Tauris, 2011.

Dinçer, Nahid. *Yabancı Özel Okullar: Osmanlı İmparatorluğu'nun Kültür Yoluyla Parçalanması* [Foreign private colleges: The disintegration of the Ottoman Empire by cultural means]. Istanbul: ER-TU Matbaası, 1970.

Dittes, James E. "The Christian Mission and Turkish Islam." *Muslim World* 45, no. 2 (1955): 134–44.

Dodd, Edward Mills. *The Beloved Physician: An Intimate Life of William Schauffler Dodd*. New York: Scribner, 1931.
– *How Far to the Nearest Doctor? Stories of Medical Missions around the World*. New York: Friendship, 1933.
– *Our Medical Task Overseas*. New York: Board of Foreign Missions of the Presbyterian Church, 1934.
– *Why Medical Missions?* New York: Board of Foreign Missions of the Presbyterian Church, 1956.

"Dodd, Edward Mills (1824–65)." In *New American Supplement to the Encyclopedia Britannica*, vol. 26, 431. Ohio: Werner, 1907.

Doğan, Mehmet Ali. "American Board of Commissioners for Foreign Missions (ABCFM) and 'Nominal Christians': Elias Riggs (1810–1901) and American Missionary Activities in the Ottoman Empire." PhD diss., University of Utah, 2013.

Doğan, Mehmet Ali, and Heather J. Sharkey, eds. *American Missionaries and the Middle East: Foundational Encounters*. Salt Lake City: University of Utah Press, 2011.

Draaisma, Douwe. *Metaphors of Memory: A History of Ideas about the Mind*. Cambridge, UK: Cambridge University Press, 2000.

Driessen, Henk. "Mediterranean Port Cities: Cosmopolitanism Reconsidered." *History and Anthropology* 16, no. 1 (2005): 129–41.

Druckman, Daniel. *Doing Research: Methods of Inquiry for Conflict Analysis*. Thousand Oaks, CA: Sage, 2005.

Duguid, Stephen R. "Centralization and Localism: Aspects of Ottoman Policy in Eastern Anatolia, 1878–1908." MA thesis, Simon Fraser University, 1970.

Duncan, Perry M. *The Politics of Terror: The Macedonian Liberation Movements, 1893–1903*. Durham, NC: Duke University Press, 1988.

Dupeyrat, André. *Savage Papua: A Missionary among Cannibals*. New York: Dutton, 1954.

Dwight, Henry Otis. *The Centennial History of the American Bible Society*. New York: Macmillan, 1916.

– *Constantinople and Its Problems: Its Peoples, Customs, Religions and Progress*. New York: Young People's Missionary Movement; Chicago: Fleming H. Revell, 1901.
– *Treaty Rights of the American Missionaries in Turkey*. New York: Foreign Missions Library, 1893.
– *Turkish Life in War Time*. New York: C. Scribner's Sons, 1881.
Dyer, Gwynne. "Turkish 'Falsifiers' and Armenian 'Deceivers': Historiography and the Armenian Massacres." *Middle Eastern Studies* 12, no. 1 (1976): 99–107.
Earle, Edward Mead. "Early American Policy Concerning Ottoman Minorities." *Political Science Quarterly* 42, no. 3 (1927): 337–67.
Edwards, Jonathan. "Sinners in the Hands of an Angry God." 1741. In Harry S. Stout, Nathan O. Hatch, and Kyle P. Farley, eds, *The Works of Jonathan Edwards*, vol. 22, *Sermons and Discourses, 1739–1742*, 400–35. New Haven, CT: Yale University Press, 2003.
Eldem, Edhem. "Ottoman Financial Integration with Europe: Foreign Loans, the Ottoman Bank and the Ottoman Public Debt." *European Review* 13, no. 3 (2005): 431–45.
Eldem, Edhem, Daniel Goffman, and Bruce Masters, eds. *The Ottoman City between East and West: Aleppo, Izmir, and Istanbul*. Cambridge, UK: Cambridge University Press, 1999.
Elder, Earl E. *Vindicating a Vision: The Story of the American Mission in Egypt, 1854–1954*. Philadelphia: Board of Foreign Missions of the United Presbyterian Church of North America, 1958.
Ellington, Barbara Reeves. *Domestic Frontiers: Gender, Reform, and American Interventions in the Ottoman Balkans and the Near East*. Amherst: University of Massachusetts Press, 2013.
Ellington, Barbara Reeves, et al., eds. *Competing Kingdoms: Women, Mission, Nation, and the American Protestant Empire, 1812–1960*. Durham, NC: Duke University Press, 2010.
Enver, İsmail. "Misyoner Tehlikesine Karşı" [Against the missionary threat]. *Sebilürreşad* 15, no. 366 (August 1918): 36–7.
Ergene, Boğaç A. "On Ottoman Justice: Interpretations in Conflict, 1600–1800." *Islamic Law and Society* 8, no. 1 (2001): 52–87.
Ergut, Ferdan. "Policing the Poor in the Late Ottoman Empire." *Middle Eastern Studies* 38, no. 2 (2002): 149–64.
Erhan, Çağrı. "Main Trends in Ottoman-American Relations." In Mustafa Aydın and Çağrı Erhan, eds, *Turkish-American Relations: Past, Present and Future*, 3–25. London and New York: Routledge, 2004.
– "Ottoman Official Attitudes towards American Missionaries." *Turkish Yearbook* 30 (2000): 191–212. Reprinted in Abbas Amanat and

Magnus Thorkell Bernhardsson, eds, *The United States and the Middle East: Cultural Encounters*, 319–32. New Haven, CT: Yale Center for International and Area Studies, 2002.

Ertuğrul, Kürşad. "A Reading of the Turkish Novel: Three Ways of Constituting the 'Turkish Modern.'" *International Journal of Middle East Studies* 41, no. 4 (2009): 635–52.

Esayan, Markar. "Ergenekon: An Illegitimate Form of Government." *Insight Turkey* 15, no. 4 (Fall 2013): 29–40.

European Court of Human Rights. *European Convention on Human Rights*. Strasburg: Council of Europe, 1953.

Evered, Emine. *Empire and Education under the Ottomans: Politics, Reform, and Resistance from the Tanzimat to the Young Turks*. London: I.B. Tauris, 2012.

Fairbank, John K. "Assignment for the '70's." *American Historical Review* 74, no. 3 (1969): 861–79.

Farber, David R. *Taken Hostage: The Iran Hostage Crisis and America's First Encounter with Radical Islam*. Princeton, NJ: Princeton University Press, 2005.

Faroqhi, Suraiya. *Approaching Ottoman History: An Introduction to the Sources*. Cambridge, UK: Cambridge University Press, 1999.

– *The Ottoman Empire and the World around It*. London: I.B. Tauris, 2006.

Fendoğlu, Tahsin. *Modernleşme Bağlamında Osmanlı-Amerika İlişkileri* [Ottoman-American relations in the context of modernity]. Ankara: Beyan Yayınları, 2002.

Field, James A. *America and the Mediterranean World, 1776–1882*. Princeton, NJ: Princeton University Press, 1969.

Findley, Carter V. *Bureaucratic Reform in the Ottoman Empire: The Sublime Porte, 1789–1922*. Princeton, NJ: Princeton University Press, 1980.

– *Ottoman Civil Officialdom: A Social History*. Princeton, NJ: Princeton University Press, 1989.

– *The Turks in World History*. New York: Oxford University Press, 2005.

Finkel, Caroline. *Osman's Dream: The Story of the Ottoman Empire, 1300–1923*. New York: Basic Books, 2006.

Fleischer, Cornell. *Bureaucrat and Intellectual in the Ottoman Empire: The Historian Mustafa Âli, 1541–1600*. Princeton, NJ: Princeton University Press, 1986.

Fortna, Benjamin C. *Imperial Classroom: Islam, the State, and Education in the Late Ottoman Empire*. Oxford: Oxford University Press, 2002.

– *Learning to Read in the Late Ottoman Empire and the Early Turkish Republic*. Basingstoke, UK: Palgrave Macmillan, 2011.

Freely, John. *A History of Robert College: The American College for Girls, and Boğaziçi University*. Istanbul: Yapı Kredi Yayınları, 2000.

Fuhrmann, Malte, and Vangelis Kechriotis. "The Late Ottoman Port-Cities and Their Inhabitants: Subjectivity, Urbanity, and Conflicting Orders." *Mediterranean Historical Review* 24, no. 2 (December 2009): 71–8.

Genç, Mehmet. *Osmanlı İmparatorluğunda Devlet ve Ekonomi* [State and economy in the Ottoman Empire]. Istanbul: Ötüken, 2003.

– "Ottoman Industry." In Donald Quataert, ed., *Ottoman Manufacturing in the Ottoman Empire and Turkey, 1500–1950*, 59–86. Albany, NY: State University of New York Press, 1994.

– "The Principle of Ottoman's Economical World View." *Sosyoloji Dergisi* 3, no. 1 (1988–89): 175–85.

Georgeon, François. *Abdulhamid II: Le Sultan Calife, 1876–1909*. Paris: Librairie Artheme Fayard, 2003.

Gerber, Anna Maria. *Passed Experiences, Present Conditions, Hope for the Future*. Pasadena, CA: Ramsey Burns Printing, 1917.

Göçek, Fatma Müge. "Ethnic Segmentation, Western Education, and Political Outcomes: Nineteenth-Century Ottoman Society." *Poetics Today* 14, no. 3 (Autumn 1993): 507–38.

– *Rise of the Bourgeoisie, Demise of Empire: Ottoman Westernization and Social Change*. New York: Oxford University Press, 1996.

– *The Transformation of Turkey: Redefining State and Society from the Ottoman Empire to the Modern Era*. London: I.B. Tauris, 2011.

Gök, Nejdet. "Introduction of the Berat in Ottoman Diplomatics." *Bulgarian Historical Review*, nos 3–4 (2001): 141–50.

Göknar, Erdağ, Cemal Kafadar, and Cemil Aydın. *Istanbul: A Multi-Perspectival City*. Video, Rethinking Global Cities project, Duke University, North Carolina, Febrary 2015. https://trinity.duke.edu/videos/istanbul-a-multiperspectival-city.

Goodsell, Fred F. *150 Years in the Near East*. New York: United Church Board for World Ministries, 1969.

Gordon, Leland J. *American Relations with Turkey, 1830–1930: An Economic Interpretation*. Philadelphia: University of Pennsylvania Press; London: H. Milford and Oxford University Press, 1966.

– "Turkish-American Treaty Relations." *American Political Science Review* 22, no. 3 (1928): 711–21.

Grabill, Joseph L. *Protestant Diplomacy and the Near East: Missionary Influence on American Policy, 1810–1927*. Minneapolis: University of Minnesota Press, 1971.

Grabowski, John. "Prospects and Challenges: The Study of Early Turkish Immigration to the United States." *Journal of American Ethnic History* 25, no. 1 (2005): 85–100.

Grace Knapp Papers, 1893–1953. LD 7096.6, 1893, Mount Holyoke College Manuscript Collections, Massachusetts.

Grandits, Hannes, Nathalie Clayer, and Robert Pichler, eds. *Conflicting Loyalties in the Balkans: The Great Powers, the Ottoman Empire and Nation-Building*. London: I.B. Tauris, 2011.

Greenwood, Keith M. *Robert College: The American Founders*. Istanbul: Boğaziçi University Press, 2003.

Gresh, Geoffrey F., and Tugrul Keskin, eds. *U.S. Foreign Policy in the Middle East: From American Missionaries to the Islamic State*. London and New York: Routledge, 2018.

Güçtürk, Yavuz. "A Comparative Study of the Press Laws of 1909 and 1931." MA thesis, Middle East Technical University, 2005.

Guide on the General Directorate of State Archives. Ankara: Prime Ministry Printing House, 2001.

Guide to the Microfilm Collection: Papers of the American Board of Commissioners for Foreign Missions. Woodbridge, CT: Research Publications International, 1994.

Gümüş, Hami İ. *American Missionaries in the Ottoman Empire: A Conceptual Metaphor Analysis of Missionary Narrative, 1820–1898*. Bielefeld, Germany: Transcript Verlag, 2017.

Habermas, Jürgen. *Legitimation Crisis*. Trans. from German by Thomas McCarthy. Boston: Beacon, 1975.

Hamdan, Wadad, and Nuha Hitti. "Glimpses into Student Life at the American University of Beirut." *American Journal of Nursing* 49, no. 9 (1949): 605–6.

Hamlin, Cyrus. *Among the Turks*. New York: R. Carter and Brothers, 1878.

– *My Life and Times*. Boston: Congregational Sunday-School and Publishing Society, 1893.

– *The Oriental Churches and Mohammedans*. Boston: ABCFM, 1853.

Hanioğlu, M. Şükrü. *A Brief History of the Late Ottoman Empire*. Princeton, NJ: Princeton University Press, 2008.

– *Osmanlı'dan Cumhuriyet'e Zihniyet, Siyaset ve Tarih* [Mentality, politics, and history from the Ottoman Empire to the republic]. Istanbul: Bağlam, 2006.

– *Young Turks in Opposition*. New York: Oxford University Press, 1995.

Hanssen, Jens. *Fin de Siècle Beirut: The Making of an Ottoman Provincial Capital*. New York: Oxford University Press, 2005.

Harvey, David. *Spaces of Capital: Toward a Critical Geography*. New York: Routledge, 2001.

Haskell, Edward B. "A Plan for Social Work in the Foreign Mission Field." *The Orient* 2, no. 35 (13 December 1911): 2–3.

Haydaroğlu, İlknur Polat. *Osmanlı İmparatorluğu'nda Yabancı Okullar* [Foreign schools in the Ottoman Empire]. Ankara: Kültür Bakanlığı, 1990.

Haynes, Jeffrey. "Politics, Identity and Religious Nationalism in Turkey." *Australian Journal of International Affairs* 64, no. 3 (2010): 312–27.

Hays, Evan. "Henry Jessup and the Presbyterian Mission to Syria under Abdul Hamid II." MA thesis, University of Michigan, 2011.

Heper, Metin. "Center and Periphery in the Ottoman Empire: With Special Reference to the Nineteenth Century." *International Political Science Review* 1, no. 1 (1980): 81–105.

Herrick, George F. "The Power of Islam." *Bibliotheca Sacra* 32, no. 126 (April 1875): 362–75.

Hogan, Patrick Colm. *The Mind and Its Stories: Narrative Universals and Human Emotion*. Cambridge, UK: Cambridge University Press, 2003.

– "Stories, Wars, and Emotions." In Brian Richardson, ed., *Narrative Beginnings: Theories and Practices*, 44–62. Lincoln: University of Nebraska Press, 2008.

The Holy Bible. New York: Viking, 1999.

Hornblow, Arthur. *The Private Life of the Sultan of Turkey*. New York: Appleton, 1901.

Horowitz, Richard S. "International Law and State Transformation in China, Siam, and the Ottoman Empire during the Nineteenth Century." *Journal of World History* 15, no. 4 (December 2004): 445–86.

Hoskins, F.E. "The Press." In Presbyterian Historical Society, *Syria Mission Papers*, RG 115-1-26, Presbyterian Church National Archives, Philadelphia.

Hourihan, William J. "Roosevelt and the Sultans: The United States Navy in the Mediterranean, 1904." PhD diss., University of Massachusetts Amherst, 1975.

Howard, Harry. "The Bicentennial in American-Turkish Relations." *Middle East Journal* 30, no. 3 (1976): 291–310.

Howe, Julia Ward, and Mary H. Graves, eds. *Sketches of Representative Women of New England*. Boston: New England Historical Publications, 1904.

Human Rights Foundation of Turkey. "TİHV Dokümantasyon Merkezi Verilerine Göre 16 Ağustos 2015–18 Mart 2016 Tarihleri Arasında Sokağa Çıkma Yasakları ve Yaşamlarını Yitiren Siviller" [Curfews and civilians who lost their lives between 16 August 2015 and 18 March 2016]. 22 March 2016. https://tihv.org.tr/wp-content/uploads/2016/03/T%C4%B0HV-Soka%C4%9Fa-%C3%87%C4%B1kma-Yasaklar%C4%B1-Bilgi-Notu-18-Mart-2016.pdf.

Hurewitz, J.C. *Middle East Dilemmas: The Background of the United States Policy*. New York: Harper, 1953.

Hutchison, William R. *Errand to the World: American Protestant Thought and Foreign Missions*. Chicago: University of Chicago Press, 1987.

İnalcık, Halil. "Decision Making in the Ottoman State." In Caesar E. Farah, ed., *Decision Making and Change in the Ottoman Empire*, 9–18. Kirksville, MO: Thomas Jefferson University Press, 1993.

– *Essays in Ottoman History*. Istanbul: Eren, 1998.

– "Istanbul: An Islamic City." *Journal of Islamic Studies* 1, no. 1 (1990): 1–23.

– "The Nature of Traditional Society." In Robert E. Ward and Dankwart A. Rustow, eds, *Political Modernization in Japan and Turkey*, 42–63. Princeton, NJ: Princeton University Press, 1964.

– *Osmanlı İmparatorluğu: Toplum ve Ekonomi* [The Ottoman Empire: Society and economy]. Istanbul: Eren, 1996.

– "The Status of the Greek Orthodox Patriarch under the Ottomans." *Turcica* 21–3 (1991): 407–36.

İnalcık, Halil, and Robert Anhegger. *Kanunname-i Sultani Ber Muceb-i Örf-i Osmani* [Sultanic codex by virtue of the Ottoman mores]. Ankara: Türk Tarih Kurumu, 2000.

İnalcık, Halil, and Donald Quataert, eds. *An Economic and Social History of the Ottoman Empire, 1300–1914*. Cambridge, UK: Cambridge University Press, 1994.

İnalcık, Halil, and Mehmet Seyitdanoğlu, eds. *Tanzimat: Değişim Sürecinde Osmanlı İmparatorluğu* [Reforms: The Ottoman Empire in the process of change]. Istanbul: Phoenix, 2006.

İpşirli, Mehmet. "Bâb-ı Âli" [The Sublime Porte]. In *Türkiye Diyanet Vakfı İslam Ansiklopedisi* [Turkiye Diyanet Foundation encyclopedia of Islam], vol. 4, 378–89. Istanbul: Türkiye Diyanet Vakfı, 1991.

İskit, Server R. *Türkiye'de Neşriyat Hareketlerine Bir Bakış* [An inquiry into publishing activities in Turkey]. Istanbul: Devlet Basımevi, 1939.

Isom-Verhaaren, Christine. *Allies with the Infidel: The Ottoman and French Alliance in the Sixteenth Century*. London: I.B. Tauris, 2011.

Issawi, Charles. "British Trade and the Rise of Beirut, 1830–1860." *International Journal of Middle East Studies* 8, no. 1 (January 1977): 91–101.

Jackson, Sherman, ed. *On the Boundaries of Theological Tolerance in Islam*. Oxford: Oxford University Press, 2002.

Jennings, Ronald C. *Studies on Ottoman Social History in the Sixteenth and Seventeenth Centuries: Women, Zimmis and Sharia Courts in Kayseri, Cyprus and Trabzon*. Istanbul: ISIS Press, 1999.
Jessup, Henry Harris. *Fifty-Three Years in Syria*. Vol. 2. New York: Fleming H. Revell, 1873.
– *Kamil: A Moslem Convert*. Philadelphia: Westminster, 1898.
– *The Mohammedan Missionary Problem*. Philadelphia: Presbyterian Board of Publication, 1879.
– *Syrian Home Life*. New York: Dodd and Mead, 1874.
– *The Women of the Arabs*. New York: Dodd and Mead, 1873.
Jongerden, Joost, and Jelle Verheij, eds. *Social Relations in Ottoman Diyarbekir, 1870–1915*. Leiden: Brill, 2012.
Kafadar, Cemal. *Between Two Worlds: The Construction of the Ottoman State*. Berkeley: University of California Press, 1995.
– "The Question of Ottoman Decline." *Harvard Middle Eastern and Islamic Review* 4, nos 1–2 (1997–98): 30–75.
Kansu, Aykut. *The Revolution of 1908 in Turkey*. Leiden: Brill, 1997.
Karabekir, Kazım. *Birinci Cihan Harbine Neden Girdik, Nasıl Girdik, Nasıl İdare Ettik?* [Why and how did we go to the First World War and how did we administer it?] Istanbul: Emre Yayınları, 1994.
Karaman, K. Kıvanç, and Şevket Pamuk. "Ottoman State Finances in European Perspective, 1500–1914." *Journal of Economic History* 70, no. 3 (2010): 593–629.
Karateke, Hakan T. "The Challenge of Periodization: New Patterns in Nineteenth-Century Ottoman Historiography." In H. Erdem Çıpa and Emine Fetvacı, eds, *Writing History at the Ottoman Court: Editing the Past, Fashioning the Future*, 129–54. Bloomington: Indiana University Press, 2013.
Karateke, Hakan T., and Maurus Reinkowski, eds. *Legitimizing the Order: The Ottoman Rhetoric of State Power*. Leiden: Brill, 2005.
Karpat, Kemal H. "The Ottoman Emigration to America, 1860–1914." *International Journal of Middle East Studies* 17, no. 2 (1985): 175–209.
– *Ottoman Population, 1830–1914: Demographic and Social Characteristics*. Madison: University of Wisconsin Press, 1985.
– "Ottoman Population Records and the Census of 1881/82–1893." *International Journal of Middle East Studies* 9, no. 2 (1978): 237–74.
– *The Politicization of Islam: Reconstructing Identity, State, Faith, and Community in the Late Ottoman State*. New York: Oxford University Press, 2001.
– *Studies on Ottoman Social and Political History*. Leiden: Brill, 2002.

– "The Transformation of the Ottoman State." *International Journal of Middle East Studies* 3, no. 3 (1972): 243–81.

Karpat, Kemal H., and Deniz Balgamış, eds. *Turkish Migration to the United States: From Ottoman Times to the Present*. Madison, WI: University of Wisconsin Press, 2008.

Kasaba, Reşat, ed. *Turkey in the Modern World*. Cambridge, UK: Cambridge University Press, 2008.

Katzenstein, Peter J., and Nobuo Okawara. "Japan, Asian-Pacific Security, and the Case for Analytical Eclecticism." *International Security* 26, no. 3 (Winter 2001–02): 153–85.

Kayalı, Hasan. *Arabs and Young Turks: Ottomanism, Arabism, and Islamism in the Ottoman Empire, 1908–1918*. Berkeley, CA: University of California Press, 1997.

Kazıcı, Ziya. "Osmanlı Devletinde Dinî Hoşgörü" [Religious tolerance in the Ottoman state]. *Köprü* 65 (1999): 75–81.

Kidd, Thomas S. *American Christians and Islam: Evangelical Culture and Muslims from the Colonial Period to the Age of Terrorism*. Princeton, NJ: Princeton University Press, 2009.

Kieser, Hans-Lukas. *Iskalanmış Barış: Doğu Vilayetleri'nde Misyonerlik, Etnik Kimlik ve Devlet, 1839–1938* [The missed peace: Mission, ethnicity, and state in the eastern provinces of Turkey, 1839–1938]. Trans. from German. Istanbul: İletişim Yayınları, 2013.

– *Nearest East: American Millennialism and Mission to the Middle East*. Philadelphia: Temple University Press, 2010.

– "U. Makdisi: Artillery of Heaven." Review of Ussama Makdisi, *Artillery of Heaven: American Missionaries and the Failed Conversion of the Middle East*. H-Net, October 2010. http://www.h-net.org/reviews/showrev.php?id=31695.

– ed. *Turkey beyond Nationalism: Towards Post-Nationalist Identities*. London: I.B. Tauris, 2006.

Kılıç, Recep. "Türkçe İnternet Ortamında Misyonerlik Araştırması" [A survey of missionary work on Turkish Internet]. In Asife Ünal, ed., *Dinler Tarihçileri Gözüyle Misyonerlik* [Missionary activity from the perspective of the historians of religion], 103–10. Ankara: Türkiye Dinler Tarihi Derneği Yayınları, 2005.

Kilmeade, Brian, and Don Yaeger. *Thomas Jefferson and the Tripoli Pirates: The Forgotten War That Changed American History*. New York: Sentinel, 2015.

Knapp, Grace. *The Mission at Van in Turkey in War Time*. Privately printed, 1916. https://archive.org/details/bub_gb_Q1K-OsFXqtUC.

– *The Tragedy of Bitlis*. New York: Fleming H. Revell, 1919. https://archive.org/details/tragedyofbitlisooknap.

Kocabaşoğlu, Uygur. *Kendi Belgeleriyle Anadolu'daki Amerika: 19. Yüzyılda Osmanlı İmparatorluğundaki Amerikan Misyoner Okulları* [America in Anatolia based on American sources: American missionary schools in the Ottoman Empire in the nineteenth century]. Istanbul: Arba, 1989.

– "Osmanlı İmparatorluğu'nda XIX. Yüzyılda Amerikan Matbaaları ve Yayımcılığı" [American presses and publishing in the nineteenth-century Ottoman Empire]. In Aydın Aybay and Rona Aybay, eds, *Murat Sarıca Armağanı* [In honour of Murat Sarıca], 267–85. Istanbul: Aybay Yayınları, 1988.

Kohn, Edward P. *Heir to the Empire City: New York and the Making of Theodore Roosevelt*. New York: Basic Books, 2014.

Köksal, Yonca. "Rethinking Nationalism: State Projects and Community Networks in 19th-Century Ottoman Empire." *American Behavioral Scientist* 51, no. 10 (June 2008): 1498–515.

Kolluoğlu, Biray, and Meltem Toksöz. *Cities of the Mediterranean: From the Ottomans to the Present Day*. London: I.B. Tauris, 2010.

Koloğlu, Orhan. "The Penetration and Effects of the Printing Techniques on the Muslim Societies." In Ekmeleddin İhsanoğlu, ed., *Transfer of Modern Science and Technology to the Muslim World*, 239–49. Istanbul: IRCICA, 1992.

Köprülü, Orhan. "Tarihte Türk Amerikan Münasebetleri" [Turkish-American relations in history]. *Belleten* 51, no. 200 (August 1987): 927–47.

Kortepeter, Carl M. "American Liberalism Establishes Bases: Robert College and the American University of Beirut." *Journal of the American Institute for the Study of Middle Eastern Civilization* 1, no. 1 (1980): 22–37.

Küçük, Cevdet. "Osmanlı İmparatorluğu'nda 'Millet Sistemi' ve 'Tanzimat'" [The millet system and the reform age in the Ottoman Empire]. In Halil İnalcık and Mehmet Seyitdanoğlu, eds, *Tanzimat: Değişim Sürecinde Osmanlı İmparatorluğu* [Reforms: The Ottoman Empire in the process of change], 375–86. Istanbul: Phoenix, 2006.

Küçükkalay, Mesud A. "Imports to Smyrna between 1794 and 1802: New Statistics from the Ottoman Sources." *Journal of the Economic and Social History of the Orient* 51, no. 3 (2008): 487–512.

Kuneralp, Sinan. "Ottoman Diplomacy and Controversy over the Interpretation of the Article IV of the Turco-American Treaty of 1830." *Turkish Year Book* 31, no. 2 (2000): 7–20.

Kuran, Aptullah. "A Spatial Study of Three Ottoman Capitals: Bursa, Edirne, and Istanbul." *Muqarnas* 13, no. 1 (1996): 114–31.

Kuran, Ercümend. "Küçük Said Paşa (1840–1914) as a Turkish Modernist." *International Journal of Middle East Studies* 1, no. 2 (1970): 124–32.

Kuran, Timur, and Scott Lustig. "Judicial Biases in Ottoman Istanbul: Islamic Justice and Its Compatibility with Modern Economic Life." *Journal of Law and Economics* 55, no. 3 (August 2012): 631–66.

Kurşun, Zekeriya. "Mehmed Memduh Paşa." In *Türkiye Diyanet Vakfı İslam Ansiklopedisi* [Turkiye Diyanet Foundation encyclopedia of Islam], vol. 28, 495–7. Istanbul: Türkiye Diyanet Vakfı, 2003.

Kut, Turgut. "Matbaa Hurufatı" [Movable type]. In *Türkiye Diyanet Vakfı İslam Ansiklopedisi* [Turkiye Diyanet Foundation encyclopedia of Islam], vol. 28, 111–13. Istanbul: Türkiye Diyanet Vakfı, 2003.

Labaki, Boutros. "The Commercial Network of Beirut in the Last Twenty-Five Years of Ottoman Rule." In Caesar E. Farah, ed., *Decision Making and Change in the Ottoman Empire*, 243–62. Kirksville, MO: Thomas Jefferson University Press, 1993.

Lee, Richard E., ed. *The Longue Durée and World-Systems Analysis*. New York: State University of New York Press, 2012.

Levy, Avigdor. "Military Reform and the Problem of Centralization in the Ottoman Empire in the Eighteenth Century." *Middle Eastern Studies* 18, no. 3 (July 1982): 227–49.

Lévy, Noémi. "La police ottomane au tournant des XIXe et XXe siècles: Les mémoires d'un commissaire d'Izmir." *Revue d'histoire moderne et contemporaine* 54, no. 2 (2007): 140–60.

Lévy, Noémi, and Alexendre Toumarkine, eds. *Osmanlı'da Asayiş, Suç ve Ceza* [Public security, crime, and punishment in the Ottoman Empire]. Istanbul: Tarih Vakfı, 2007.

Lewis, Bernard. *Faith and Power: Religion and Politics in the Middle East*. Oxford: Oxford University Press, 2010.

– *The Middle East: 2000 Years of History from the Rise of Christianity to the Present Day*. London: Phoenix, 2000.

Lewis, Reina, and Nancy Micklewright, eds. *Gender, Modernity, and Liberty: Middle Eastern Women's Writings: A Critical Sourcebook*. London: I.B. Tauris, 2006.

Lowry, Heath W. *The Nature of the Early Ottoman State*. Albany: State University of New York Press, 2003.

Madi-Şişman, Ozlem, and Cengiz Şişman. "From 'Heathen Turks' to 'Cruel Turks': Changing American Perception and Foreign Policy towards the

Middle East." In Geoffrey F. Gresh and Tugrul Keskin, eds, *U.S. Foreign Policy in the Middle East: From American Missionaries to the Islamic State*, 13–28. London and New York: Routledge, 2018.

Mahjoubian, Charles N. *Garbis to America: Fifteen Years in Konya (Holy City of Turkish Islam) and One Year in Greece during the Years of the Armenian Genocide*. Wayne, PA: Charles N. Mahjoubian, 1995.

Makdisi, Ussama S. *Artillery of Heaven: American Missionaries and the Failed Conversion of the Middle East*. Ithaca, NY: Cornell University Press, 2008.

– *Faith Misplaced: The Broken Promise of U.S.-Arab Relations, 1820–2001*. New York: Public Affairs, 2010.

– "Ottoman Orientalism." *American Historical Review* 107, no. 3 (June 2002): 768–96.

Maksudyan, Nazan. "Amerikan Kaynaklarında Merzifon Anadolu Koleji'nin Kısa Tarihçesi ve Boğos Piranyan" [A history of Merzifon Anatolia College based on U.S. sources and Boğos Piranyan]. *Kebikeç* 18, no. 36 (2013): 131–54.

Marden, Etta Doane. *The American School at Gedik Pasha, Constantinople*. Boston: ABCFM, 1933.

– *Gedik Pasha: Its Needs and Opportunities*. Boston: Woman's Board of Missions, n.d.

Mardin, Şerif. *Religion, Society, and Modernity in Turkey*. New York: Syracuse University Press, 2006.

Margolis, Eric S. "Turkey's Violent Storms – Courtesy of Mother Nature, Ergenekon Trial." *Washington Report on Middle East Affairs* 28, no. 8 (November 2009): 30.

Marquis, Albert Nelson, ed. *Who's Who in New England*. Chicago: A.N. Marquis and Company, 1916.

Matuz, J.E. "Transmission of Directives from Center to Periphery in the Ottoman State until the Seventeen Century." In Caesar E. Farah, ed., *Decision Making and Change in the Ottoman Empire*, 19–28. Kirksville, MO: Thomas Jefferson University Press, 1993.

Mayewski, Vladimir Feofilovich. *Les Massacres d'Arménie: D'après les constatations authentiques du général russe Mayewski* [Armenian massacres: According to the original findings of Russian general Mayewski]. Saint Petersburg: Imprimerie Militaire, 1916.

McCarthy, Justin. *Muslims and Minorities: The Population of Ottoman Anatolia and the End of the Empire*. New York: New York University Press, 1983.

– *The Turk in America: The Creation of an Enduring Prejudice*. Salt Lake City: University of Utah Press, 2010.

McGrew, William. *Educating across Cultures: Anatolia College in Turkey and Greece*. Lanham, MD: Rowman and Littlefield, 2015.

McQuillan, Kevin. *Culture, Religion, and Demographic Behavior: Catholics and Lutherans in Alsace, 1750–1870*. Montreal and Kingston: McGill-Queen's University Press, 1999.

Mead, Walter R. *Special Providence: American Foreign Policy and How It Changed the World*. New York and London: Routledge, 2002.

Meisami, Julie, and Paul Starkey. *Encyclopedia of Arabic Literature*. Vol. 2. London and New York: Routledge, 1998.

Memduh, Mehmet. *Mirat-i Şûûnât* [The mirror of affairs]. Izmir: Ahenk, 1911.

Merk, Frederick, and Lois Merk, eds. *Manifest Destiny and Mission in American History: A Reinterpretation*. New York: Knopf, 1963.

Meyer, James H. *Turks across Empires: Marketing Muslim Identity in the Russian-Ottoman Borderlands, 1856–1914*. Oxford: Oxford University Press, 2015.

Miller, Owen. "Sasun 1894: Mountains, Missionaries and Massacres at the End of the Ottoman Empire." PhD diss., Columbia University, 2015.

Moody, Dwight. *To the Work! To the Work! Exhortations to Christians*. Chicago: Fleming H. Revell, 1884.

Morack, Ellinor. *The Dowry of the State? The Politics of Abandoned Property and Population Exchange in Turkey, 1921–45*. Bamberg: University of Bamberg Press, 2017.

Moran, Berna. *Türk Romanına Eleştirel Bir Bakış: Ahmet Mithat'tan A.H. Tanpınar'a* [A critical look at Turkish novels: From Ahmet Mithat to Ahmet Hamdi]. Istanbul: İletişim, 1998.

Muahedat Mecmuası [Collection of treaties]. Vol. 2. Istanbul: Hakikat, 1878.

Murphey, Rhoads. "Continuity and Discontinuity in Ottoman Administrative Theory and Practice during the Late Seventeenth Century." *Poetics Today* 14, no. 2 (1993): 439–43.

Murre-van den Berg, Heleen. "The Middle East: Western Missions and the Eastern Churches, Islam and Judaism." In Sheridan Gilley and Brian Stanley, eds, *The Cambridge History of Christianity*, vol. 8, *World Christianities c. 1815–1914*, 458–72. Cambridge, UK: Cambridge University Press, 2006.

– ed. *New Faith in Ancient Lands: Western Missions in the Middle East in the Nineteenth and Early Twentieth Centuries*. Leiden: Brill, 2006.

Nazım, Hüseyin. *Ermeni Olayları Tarihi* [History of Armenian incidents]. Vol. 1. Ankara: Başbakanlık Basımevi, 1994.

Neumann, Christoph. "Integrity and Integration: Assumptions and Expectations behind Nineteenth-Century Decision Making." In Caesar E. Farah, ed., *Decision Making and Change in the Ottoman Empire*, 39–52. Kirksville, MO: Thomas Jefferson University Press, 1993.

Nizamoğlu, Yüksel. "Yanya Vilayetinin Durumuna Dair Hazırlanan Layihalar ve Sonuçları" [Memoranda on the Ioannina province and their results]. *OTAM* 33 (Spring 2013): 197–228.

Okçabol, Derviş. *Türk Zabıta Tarihi ve Teşkilâtı Tarihçesi* [History of Turkish police and a history of its institutions]. Ankara: Ankara Polis Enstitüsü, 1940.

The Oldest Christian Nation – Shall It Perish? Exclusive Material for Pastors. New York: New East Relief, 1920. World War I Pamphlet Collection, McGill-McLennan Library, Montreal.

Ongley, F. *The Ottoman Land Code*. London: William Clowes and Sons, 1892.

Opal, Jason. *Beyond the Farm: National Ambitions in Rural New England*. Philadelphia: University of Pennsylvania Press, 2008.

Oren, Michael B. *Power, Faith, and Fantasy: America in the Middle East, 1776 to the Present*. New York and London: W.W. Norton, 2007.

Ortaylı, İlber. *Osmanlı Barışı* [Ottoman peace]. Istanbul: Ufuk, 2004.

– *Osmanlı Mirası* [Ottoman legacy]. Istanbul: Timaş, 2010.

– "The Ottoman Millet System and Its Social Dimensions." In Rikard Larrson, ed., *Boundaries of Europe*, 120–6. Stockholm: Forksningsrad-namnden, 1998.

– "Some Observations on American Schools in the Ottoman Empire." *Turkish Public Administration Annual* 8, no. 1 (1981): 93–110.

– "Tanzimat Adamı ve Tanzimat Toplumu" [Man and society in the age of reforms]. In Halil İnalcık and Mehmet Seyitdanoğlu, eds, *Tanzimat: Değişim Sürecinde Osmanlı İmparatorluğu* [Reforms: The Ottoman Empire in the process of change], 188–95. Istanbul: Phoenix, 2006.

– *Tanzimat Devrinde Osmanlı Mahalli İdareleri, 1840–1880* [Ottoman local administrations during the Tanzimat age, 1840–1880]. Ankara: Türk Tarih Kurumu, 1974.

O'Sullivan, John. "Annexation." *United States Magazine and Democratic Review* 17, no. 1 (July-August 1845): 5–10.

Ousterhout, Robert. "Ethnic Identity and Cultural Appropriation in Early Ottoman Architecture." *Muqarnas* 12, no. 1 (1995): 48–62.

Özalp, Reşat, and Aydoğan Ataünal. *Türk Milli Eğitim Sisteminde Düzenleme Teşkilatı* [Regulatory organization in the Turkish national education system]. Istanbul: Milli Eğitim, 1977.

Özbek, Nadir. "Philanthropic Activity, Ottoman Patriotism, and the Hamidian Regime, 1876–1909." *International Journal of Middle East Studies* 37, no. 1 (2005): 59–81.

Özdalga, Elisabeth, ed. *Late Ottoman Society: The Intellectual Legacy*. London and New York: Routledge Curzon, 2005.

Özdemir, Hüseyin. *Osmanlı Devletinde Bürokrasi* [Bureaucracy in the Ottoman state]. Istanbul: Okumuş Adam, 2001.

Pakin, Esra. "American Studies in Turkey during the 'Cultural' Cold War." *Turkish Studies* 9, no. 3 (2008): 507–24.

Pamuk, Şevket. "The Ottoman Empire in 'the Great Depression' of 1873–1896." *Journal of Economic History* 44, no. 1 (1984): 107–18.

Papers Relating to the Foreign Relations of the United States. Washington, DC: Government Printing Office, 1888, 1896, 1903, 1904.

Patterson, George. *Missionary Life among the Cannibals: Being the Life of Rev. John Geddia, D.D., First Missionary to the New Hebrides: With a History of the Nova Scotia Presbyterian Mission on that Group*. Toronto: James Campbell and Son, 1882.

Peirce, Leslie. *Morality Tales: Law and Gender in the Ottoman Court of Aintab*. Berkeley: University of California Press, 2003.

Philip, M., and Ethel Klutznik. *Pilgrims and Travelers to the Holy Land*. Omaha, NE: Creighton University Press, 1996.

Piranyan, Boğos. *Aşçının Kitabı: Merzifon Amerikan Anadolu Koleji Aşçısı, 1914* [The cook's book: The cook of Merzifon American Anatolia College, 1914]. Istanbul: Aras, 2008.

Polk, W.R., and Richard L. Chambers, eds. *Beginnings of Modernization in the Middle East: The Nineteenth Century*. Chicago: University of Chicago Press, 1968.

Prime, Edward D.G. *Forty Years in the Turkish Empire, or Memoirs of Rev. William Goodell*. New York: Robert Carter, 1876.

Provence, Michael. "Ottoman Modernity, Colonialism, and Insurgency in the Interwar Arab East." *International Journal of Middle East Studies* 43, no. 2 (May 2011): 205–25.

Putney, Clifford, and Paul T. Burlin, eds. *The Role of the American Board in the World: Bicentennial Reflections on the Organization's Missionary Work, 1810–2010*. Eugene, OR: Wipf and Stock, 2012.

Quataert, Donald. "The Massacre of Ottoman Armenians and the Writing of Ottoman History." *Journal of Interdisciplinary History* 37, no. 2 (2006): 249–59.

– *The Ottoman Empire, 1700–1922*. Cambridge, UK: Cambridge University Press, 2005.

Rayman, Ronald. "Joseph Lancaster's Monitorial System of Instruction and American Indian Education, 1815–1838." *History of Education Quarterly* 21, no. 4 (1981): 395–409.

Redding, Richard W. "The Pig and the Chicken in the Middle East: Modeling Human Subsistence Behavior in the Archaeological Record Using Historical and Animal Husbandry Data." *Journal of Archaeological Research* 23, no. 4 (2015): 325–68.

Reeves-Ellington, Barbara. *Domestic Frontiers: Gender, Reform, and American Interventions in the Ottoman Balkans and the Near East*. Amherst: University of Massachusetts Press, 2013.

Reidy, David, and Walter Riker, eds. *Coercion and the State*. New York: Springer, 2008.

Report and Catalogue of Anatolia College and Girls' Boarding School. Marsovan: Anatolia College, 1901.

Roberts, Timothy, and Emrah Şahin. "Construction of National Identities in Early Republics: A Comparison of the American and Turkish Cases." *Journal of the Historical Society* 10, no. 4 (2010): 507–31.

Rogan, Eugene L. *Frontiers of the State in the Late Ottoman Empire*. Cambridge, UK: Cambridge University Press, 1999.

Roosevelt, Theodore. *The Winning of the West*. 6 vols. New York: Current Literature Publications, 1905.

Rothenberg, Gadi. *Catalysis, God's Algorithm, and the Green Demon*. Amsterdam: Amsterdam University Press, 2009.

Rowe, George S. *The Life of John Hunt: Missionary to the Cannibals in Fiji*. London: Wesleyan Conference Office, 1874.

Ruiu, Adina. "Conflicting Visions of the Jesuit Missions to the Ottoman Empire, 1609–1628." *Journal of Jesuit Studies* 1, no. 2 (2014): 260–80.

Şafak, Nurdan. *Osmanlı-Amerikan İlişkileri* [Ottoman-American relations]. Istanbul: Osmanlı Araştırmaları Vakfı, 2003.

Şahin, Emrah. "American-Turkish Relations in Retrospective." *International Journal of Turkish Studies* 12, nos 1–2 (Fall 2006): 195–8.

– "Capitulations." In Andrea L. Stanton, ed., *Cultural Sociology of the Middle East, Asia, and Africa: An Encyclopedia*, vol. 1, *The Middle East*, 177–9. Thousand Oaks, CA: Sage, 2012.

– *Errand into the East: A Social History of American Missionaries in Istanbul, 1830–1900*. Köln: Lambert, 2009.

– "Sultan's America: Lessons from Ottoman Encounters with the United States." *Journal of American Studies of Turkey* 39, no. 1 (2014): 55–76.

– ed. *Bir Zamanlar Amerika ve Türkler: Siyasi, Sosyal, Dini ve Ticari Temaslar* [Once upon a time America and the Turks: Political, social, religious, and commercial exchanges]. Istanbul: Libra Books, 2017.

Said, Edward W. *Orientalism*. New York: Vintage Books, 1979.

Salnâme-i Vilayet-i Bitlis [Almanac of the province of Bitlis]. Bitlis: Vilayet Matbaası, 1893.

Salt, Jeremy. *Imperialism, Evangelism, and the Ottoman Armenians, 1878–1896*. London and New York: Routledge, 1993.

– "Trouble Wherever They Went: American Missionaries in Anatolia and Ottoman Syria in the Nineteenth Century." *Muslim World* 92, nos 3–4 (2002): 287–313.

Salzmann, Ariel. *Tocqueville in the Ottoman Empire: Rival Paths to the Modern State*. Boston: Brill, 2004.

Sedra, Paul. "Exposure to the Eyes of God: Monitorial Schools and Evangelicals in Early Nineteenth-Century England." *Paedagogica Historica* 47, no. 3 (June 2011): 263–81.

Şehremaneti İstatistik Şubesi. *1330 Senesi İstanbul Beldesi İhsaiyyat Mecmuası* [The 1911 statistics journal of the Istanbul municipality]. Istanbul: Arşak Garoyan, 1912.

Sertoğlu, Midhat. *Muhteva Bakımından Başvekalet Arşivi* [Prime Ministry archives with regard to their contents]. Ankara: Türk Tarih Kurumu, 1955.

Setrakian, Aida A. "Armenians in the Ottoman Legal System, 16th-18th Centuries." MA thesis, McGill University, 2006.

Sevinç, Necdet. *Ajan Okulları* [Colleges for spies]. Istanbul: Oymak Yayınları, n.d.

Sha'ban, Fuad. *Islam and Arabs in Early American Thought: Roots of Orientalism in America*. Durham, NC: Thomson Gale, 1991.

Shami, Seteney, and Cynthia Millet-Idriss, eds. *Middle East Studies for the New Millennium: Infrastructures of Knowledge*. New York: New York University Press, 2016.

Shaw, Stanford J. "The Central Legislative Councils in the Nineteenth Century Ottoman Reform Movement before 1876." *International Journal of Middle East Studies* 1, no. 1 (1970): 51–84.

– "The Nineteenth-Century Ottoman Tax Reforms and Revenue System." *International Journal of Middle East Studies* 6, no. 4 (October 1975): 421–59.

– "Ottoman Archival Materials for the Nineteenth and Early Twentieth Centuries: The Archives." *International Journal of Middle East Studies* 6, no. 1 (January 1975): 94–114.

– "The Ottoman Archives as a Source for Egyptian History." *Journal of the American Oriental Society* 83, no. 4 (1963): 447–52.

– "The Ottoman Census System and Population." *International Journal of Middle East Studies* 9, no. 3 (1978): 325–38.

Shaw, Stanford J., and Ezel Kural Shaw. *Osmanlı İmparatorluğu ve Modern Türkiye* [History of the Ottoman Empire and modern Turkey]. Vol. 2. Istanbul: E Yayınları, 2000.

Sipahi, Ali. "At Arm's Length: Historical Ethnography of Proximity in Harput." PhD diss., University of Michigan, 2015.

Şişman, Adnan. "Egyptian and Armenian Schools Where the Ottoman Students Studied in Paris." In Colin Imber, Keiko Kiyotaki, and Rhoads Murphey, eds, *Frontiers of Ottoman Studies: State, Province, and the West*, vol. 2, 157–63. London: I.B. Tauris, 2005.

Smyth, Warrington W. *A Year with the Turks, or Sketches of Travel in the European and Asiatic Dominions of the Sultan*. New York: Redfield, 1854.

Somel, Selçuk Akşin. *The Modernization of Public Education in the Ottoman Empire, 1839–1908: Islamization, Autocracy, and Discipline*. Leiden: Brill, 2001.

Spry, W.J.J. *Life on the Bosphorus: Doings in the City of the Sultan, Turkey, Past and Present, Including Chronicles of the Caliphs from Mahomet to Abdulhamid II*. London: H.S. Nichols, 1895.

Stevens, Georgiana, ed. *The United States and the Middle East*. New Jersey: Prentice-Hall, 1964.

Strauss, Johann. "'Kütüp ve Resail-i Mevkute' [Books and periodicals]: Printing and Publishing in a Multi-Ethnic Society." In Elisabeth Özdalga, ed., *Late Ottoman Society: The Intellectual Legacy*, 225–53. London and New York: Routledge Curzon, 2005.

– "Les livres et l'imprimerie à Istanbul, 1800–1908" [Books and printing in Istanbul, 1800–1908]. In Paul Dumont, ed., *Turquie: Livres d'hier, livres d'aujourd'hui*, 5–24. Istanbul: Édition Isis, 1992.

– "Zum Istanbuler Buchwesen in der zweiten Hiilfte des 19. Jahrhunderts" [Istanbul publishing houses in the second half of the nineteenth century]. *Osmanlı Araştırmaları* 12 (1992): 307–38.

Strohmeier, Martin. "Muslim Education in the Vilayet of Beirut, 1880–1918." In Caesar E. Farah, ed., *Decision Making and Change in the Ottoman Empire*, 215–42. Kirksville, MO: Thomas Jefferson University Press, 1993.

Stuart, Clément. *A History of Arabic Literature*. New York: D. Appleton and Co., 1903.

Suny, Ronald Grigor, Fatma Müge Göçek, and Norman M. Naimark, eds. *A Question of Genocide: Armenians and Turks at the End of the Ottoman Empire*. Oxford: Oxford University Press, 2011.

Swanson, Glen W. "The Ottoman Police." *Journal of Contemporary History* 7, nos 1–2 (1972): 243–60.

Tanör, Bülent. *Osmanlı-Türk Anayasal Gelişmeleri* [Ottoman-Turkish constitutional developments]. Istanbul: Yapı Kredi Yayınları, 1999.

Taş, Hakkı. "Turkey's Ergenekon Imbroglio and Academia's Apathy." *Insight Turkey* 16, no. 1 (2014): 163–79.

Tezcan, Baki. *The Second Ottoman Empire: Political and Social Transformation in the Early Modern World*. New York: Cambridge University Press, 2010.

Thayer, Lucius E. "The Capitulations of the Ottoman Empire and the Question of Their Abrogation as It Affects the United States." *American Journal of International Law* 17, no. 2 (1923): 207–33.

Timberg, Thomas A. "Cannibals and Missionaries." *Economic and Political Weekly* 19, no. 37 (1984): 1611.

Tokgöz, Ahmed İhsan. *Matbuat Hatıralarım 1888–1923* [Memoirs of my life and printing]. Vol. 1. Istanbul: Ahmet İhsan Matbaası, 1931.

Tracy, Charles C. *A Cry to Heaven from a Housetop*. Boston: ABCFM, 1893.

– *Silkenbraid, or A Story of Mission Life in Turkey*. Boston: ABCFM, 1893.

Treaties, Conventions, International Acts, Protocols, and Agreements between the United States of America and Other Powers. Vol. 2. Washington, DC: Government Printing Office, 1910–38.

Turgay, Üner A. "Ottoman-American Trade during the Nineteenth Century." *Journal of Ottoman Studies* 3 (1982): 189–246.

Türkiye Diyanet Vakfı İslam Ansiklopedisi [Turkiye Diyanet Foundation encyclopedia of Islam]. 44 vols. Istanbul: Türkiye Diyanet Vakfı, 1988–2013.

Üçel-Aybet, Gülgûn. *Avrupalı Seyyahların Gözünden Osmanlı Dünyası ve İnsanları, 1530–1699* [The Ottoman world and peoples as observed by European travellers]. Istanbul: *İ*letişim, 2003.

Uyar, Mesut, and Edward Erickson. *A Military History of the Ottomans: From Osman to Atatürk*. Santa Barbara, CA: Praeger, 2009.

Uzer, Umut. *Identity and Foreign Policy: The Kemalist Influence in Cyprus and Caucasus*. London: I.B. Tauris, 2011.

Verheij, Jelle. "Diyarbekir and the Armenian Crisis of 1895." In Joost Jongerden and Jelle Verheij, eds., *Social Relations in Ottoman Diyarbekir, 1870–1915*, 85–145. Leiden: Brill, 2012.

Walsh, R. *A Residence at Constantinople*. 2 vols. London: Bentley, 1836.

Walton, Douglas. "Plausible Deniability and Evasion of Burden of Proof." *Argumentation* 10, no. 1 (1996): 47–58.

Washburn, George. *Fifty Years in Constantinople and Recollections of Robert College*. Boston: Houghton Mifflin, 1909.

Webster, Diana. "Cannibals and Kava." *Hudson Review* 52, no. 2 (1999): 182, 184–9.

Weiker, Walter F. "The Ottoman Bureaucracy: Modernization and Reform." *Administrative Science Quarterly* 13, no. 3 (1968): 451–70.

Weiss, Roslyn. *Virtue in the Cave: Moral Inquiry in Plato's Meno*. New York: Oxford University Press, 2001.

Wheatcroft, Andrew. *The Ottomans*. London: Viking, 1993.

White, George E. *Adventuring with Anatolia College*. Grinnell, IA: Herald-Register Publishing Company, March 1940. http://www.oswego.edu/~baloglou/anatolia/college.html.

– *Charles Chapin Tracy: Missionary, Philanthropist, Educator*. Boston and Chicago: Pilgrim, 1928.

Wilson, Ann Marie. "In the Name of God, Civilization, and Humanity: The United States and the Armenian Massacres of the 1890s." *Le mouvement social* 227, no. 2 (2009): 27–44.

Womack, Deanna F., and Christine B. Lindner. "'Pick Up the Pearls of Knowledge and Adorn Ourselves with the Jewelry of Literature': An Analysis of Three Arab Women Writers in al-Nashra al-Usbu'iyya." In Mary Grey, Duncan Macpherson, Anthony O'Mahony, and Colin South, eds, *Christianity Engages with Islam: Contexts, Creativity, and Tensions*, 125–57. Hertfordshire, UK: Melisende, 2014.

World Evangelical Alliance. "I Simply Cried: An Interview with Thomas Schirrmacher, President of Martin Bucher Seminary and Director of the International Institute for Religious Freedom." 28 April 2007. http://www.worldea.org/news/1056/I-Simply-Cried.

– "Martin Bucer Seminary Says Good Bye to Student Necati Aydin." 28 April 2007. http://www.worldea.org/news/1058/Martin-Bucer-Seminary-says-Good-Bye-to-Student-Necati-Aydin.

Worringer, Renée. "'Sick Man of Europe' or 'Japan of the Near East'?: Constructing Ottoman Modernity in the Hamidian and Young Turk Eras." *International Journal of Middle East Studies* 36, no. 2 (May 2004): 207–30.

Yalçınkaya, M. Alper. *Learned Patriots: Debating Science, State, and Society in the Nineteenth-Century Ottoman Empire*. Chicago: University of Chicago Press, 2015.

Yalman, Ahmet Emin. *Turkey in My Time*. Norman: University of Oklahoma Press, 1956.

Yanmış, Mehmet. *Resurgence of the Kurdish Conflict in Turkey: How Kurds View It*. Washington, DC: Rethink Institute, 2016.

Yanow, Dvora, and Peregrine Schwartz-Shea, eds. *Interpretation and Method: Empirical Research Methods and the Interpretive Turn*. Armonk, NY: M.E. Sharp, 2014.

Yeğen, Mesut, Uğraş Ulaş Tol, and Mehmet Ali Çalışkan. *Kürtler Ne İstiyor? Kürdistan'da Etnik Kimlik, Dindarlık, Sınıf ve Seçimler* [What do the Kurds want? Ethnic identity, piety, class, and elections in Kurdistan]. Istanbul: İletişim, 2016.

Yerasimos, Stephane. *Les voyageurs dans l'Empire Ottoman, XIVe-XVIe siècles*. Ankara: Imprimerie de la société turque d'histoire, 1991.

Yıldırım, Uğur. "Tarihten Bugüne Türkiye'de Misyonerlik" [Missionary work from the past to the present]. *Jeopolitik* 16 (May 2005): 73–83.

Yılmaz, Şuhnaz. *Turkish-American Relations, 1800–1952: Between the Stars, Stripes and the Crescent*. New York: Routledge, 2015.

Yurdusev, A. Nuri. *Ottoman Diplomacy: Conventional or Unconventional?* Basingstoke, UK: Palgrave Macmillan, 2004.

Zirve Davası ve Gerçekler [Zirve trial and hidden facts]. http://www.zirvedavasivegercekler.com/tutanaklar.

Zürcher, Erik Jan. *The Unionist Factor: The Role of the Committee of Union and Progress in the Turkish National Movement, 1905–1926*. Leiden: Brill, 1984.

Zürcher, Erik Jan. "Young Turk Memoirs as a Historical Source: Kazim Karabekir's 'Istiklal Harbimiz.'" *Middle Eastern Studies* 22, no. 4 (1986): 562–70.

Index